Get Out of Jail Free:

Breaking Out of Legalism!

By

Bruce Guckelberg, Ph.D.

To My Devoted Wife Carol

Table of Contents

Forward

Faith. Forgiveness. Freedom. For Christians who have been forgiven by faith in Jesus Christ's love for them expressed in his self-sacrificing atonement for them paid at the cross, the result is a refreshing, wildly exuberant sense of freedom. "My sins have been paid for, I'm forgiven, I'm *free!*"

Unfortunately, this feeling of freedom and joy sometimes fades and is gradually replaced by a nagging worry that "Maybe I'm not doing enough. Maybe God is disappointed in me. Maybe if I do 'just a little more' God will be more pleased with me and love me more (than I feel he does now)." The various forms of these vague uneasy feelings of if-I-do-this God-will-do-that can be grouped under the broad category of "legalism."

Legalism is a tendency in human religious behavior that has a long history. From time immemorial, humans have believed they can (and must) "buy off" God with various self-chosen propitiatory offerings. In addition, God himself has revealed high standards that he expects of his children. So, from the time of Moses down through Jesus' time and that of the earliest apostles of the Christian church, earnest believers and followers of the God of Israel, of Jesus, have wrestled with issues of "How can I be sure God loves me? If I do more for him, will he love me more? If I *don't* do what he says I should do, does that nullify my relationship with him?"

Dr. Guckelberg takes on these pressing issues with care and precision. He shows how the Bible itself presents the problem; for example, in Jesus' controversies with the religious legal experts of his time. He takes us through the earliest church's painstaking analyses of questions about how the believer in Jesus, graciously forgiven and set free by the atonement paid at Calvary, is to relate to the Law of God delivered through Moses. Individuals like Peter and Paul and Jesus' brother James wrestled with understanding how the new life of freedom, cast against a backdrop of strict Biblical law-keeping, was to be lived, as we do still today.

It is that contemporary context that compels keen interest in this topic Guckelberg is addressing. More than a historical study of the earliest church's resolutions of the questions of legalism and Christ-bought freedom, this book recognizes frankly that many Christians today are not only troubled by weak consciences, but often burdened and shackled by legalistic and overbearing church cultures that discourage and threaten them, rather than encourage and support their daily Christian life. In addition, the enemy of God and of our souls, the Devil, actually fosters and contributes to the dominance of legalism as the prevailing ethos in many bodies of Christian believers, impoverishing their experience and their testimony to the world.

Dr. Guckelberg methodically takes apart the pieces of this complex issue and examines the pertinent elements one by one, chapter by chapter, balancing biblical examples with easy-to-recognize contemporary patterns and illustrations of legalism. The reader may wince with pain as he or she recognizes familiar patterns of actual spiritual abuse that occur in our churches today. But they will be relieved to read, also, that there is a solution to the ubiquitous problem of legalism: joyous recognition of the blood-bought freedom which Jesus offers those who come to him for "rest; for my yoke is not burdensome, but light."

Gene R. Smillie, Ph.D.
Adjunct Professor, Trinity International University
Pastor, missionary, educator in the Christian & Missionary Alliance

Author's Preface

When Christians are conversing with one another it isn't uncommon to hear the term "legalism" or "legalistic." In fact, it's one of those terms that are in the Christian-ese dialect. I often hear people say things such as: "those people are extremely legalistic!" "Pastor so-and-so's teaching is very legalistic." "We had to leave our previous church because they are so legalistic we couldn't take it any more." Strangely enough there are some people who leave their church to attend one that is more legalistic because they find comfort in being in that type of environment.

Legalism exists everywhere Christians gather in varying degrees. Having traveled extensively in the Dominican Republic I've come to see that legalism is pervasive in that country. It is one of the biggest hurdles to jump over in building healthy churches and leading believers to maturity in Christ. With the encouragement of my friend Don Schulz, who also serves as the Director of Meeting God in Baseball, I've undertaken this writing project for the purpose of better understanding the dynamics of legalism, so that people can find freedom from man-made rules that the Lord Jesus died to give them.

Some churches are legalistic toxic environments that can traumatize people and sap the life out of them. If you attend a church like that your walk with the Lord may not be a joyful experience—it is probably more of a burden than anything else. Legalism is a spiritual disease—it is like a flesh eating bacteria that can make your spiritual experience one of drudgery. The remedy for this spiritual disease is a healthy dose of teaching on sanctification and liberty. These two topics will help one who is in the quagmire of legalism find freedom and joy in their walk with the Lord. The fallacy of legalism is that God's love has to be earned by working harder, sacrificing more, and keeping every rule in the book. This understanding can be crippling to a disciple of Christ.

I want to thank Dr. Gene Smillie for interacting with me throughout the writing of this book. His insights were invaluable to me in working through some of the more complex issues I faced. He is a gifted scholar, professor, preacher, author, pastor, and former missionary. He is a blessing to the body of Christ and a dear friend.

I also want to thank the many people that have shared their personal experiences with me regarding their trek in legalism. All the stories I'm sharing are totally truthful, but I've changed the names of the people to protect their identity, unless they have specifically given me permission to mention them by name. In writing this book I've had to jog my memory of three decades worth of stories of people that have struggled with legalism. Some legalistic people I've known do not consider themselves to be legalists at all. Some people know they are legalistic, but can't seem to find freedom from the battery of man-made rules and regulations that have been imposed on them. It is almost like being in jail.

Most importantly I want to thank my wife Carol for giving me the encouragement to write this book and do what the Lord has laid on my heart. I also want to thank the many pastors, friends, and colleagues that I've bounced ideas off of, which provided me with more insights about legalism. Everyone I talked to about this topic was in some way, shape, or form affected by legalistic influences in their life—it touches everybody.

The parameters I set forth in writing this book were to have solid exegesis of Biblical texts combined with many practical stories from real life settings. As I've written this book I've done a great deal of reflecting on my own walk with the Lord, and have gained a greater level of appreciation of the liberty that I have as a believer in Christ. I hope reading "Get Out of Jail Free" will help you discover a greater level of freedom and joy in your walk with the Lord Jesus.

Bruce Guckelberg, Ph.D.
Director of Theological Education in Latin America
Meeting God in Baseball

Part I - The Harmful Effects of Legalism

Introduction

It was 1918 and WWI was winding down with peace finally appearing on the horizon. The world's most lethal war was at an end, but a new enemy appeared. This enemy didn't wear a uniform, was totally indiscriminate in that he went after everybody. Regardless of one's ethnicity, national allegiance, culture, or language this enemy was an indiscriminate killer. He was far more lethal than all the weapons utilized in the Great War. This killer put to death more people than were claimed in the entire war. The antagonist was the influenza pandemic. It appeared during the final stages of the war, and soldiers brought the disease back to the states. It spread around the globe and claimed millions of lives.

No one knows exactly how many people died during the 1918-1919 influenza pandemic. During the 1920s, researchers estimated that 21.5 million people died as a result of the pandemic. More recent studies have estimated global mortality from the 1918-1919 pandemic at anywhere between 30 and 50 million. An estimated 675,000 Americans were among the casualties. (http://www.flu.gov/pandemic/history/1918/the_pandemic/legacypen demic, retrieved 3.16.16)

There is a spiritual pandemic that circles the globe and wreaks havoc among believers in Christ. This spiritual virus is known as legalism. Anywhere believers gather, legalism will be found in varying degrees. This is nothing new. Jesus battled the legalism of the Pharisees and scribes, the apostle Paul did battle with the Judaizers, and on one occasion even Peter fell prey to this spiritual virus.

What are the symptoms of the dreaded disease of legalism? On the extreme end of the spectrum legalism can block the way of salvation and keep people out of heaven. On the milder side of legalism there may be attitudes and practices that people have picked up that aren't rooted in Scripture. They are the product of questionable teaching, and people's opinions rather than the word of God. Some examples of this include: don't listen to secular music, you can't watch TV on Sunday, Christians shouldn't go dancing, women have to wear dresses to church, and things of this nature.

The primary symptom of legalism is that it robs people of their freedom in Christ and places them in a degree of bondage—from mild to severe. Some people live in a spiritual prison because of the legalism they are under. They need to be freed from this dreaded disease and get out of jail, which is what this book is all about. For this reason I've decided to title this writing project "Get Out of Jail Free!" Jesus offers everybody freedom so they can walk out of the spiritual prison cell they may be in and find liberty and joy as a disciple of Christ.

What exactly is legalism? There are many definitions of the term. One common understanding of legalism is an obsession with keeping the rules. Another definition of the term is obsessing on the letter of the law at the expense of grace. Some people understand legalism as an attempt to gain God's approval by following certain rules. In other words, the presence or absence of certain behaviors in one's life makes him more worthy in God's sight. There is some truth in each of these definitions, but the heart of the matter is captured in a definition offered by Don Kistler:

> Legalism is behavior motivated by the false notion that sinners can earn favor with God, either before or after salvation, through legal means—obedience, ritual, self-denial, or whatever. (Kistler, *Law & Liberty: A Biblical Look at Legalism*, Kindle file.)

This definition has much merit. A person can manifest certain behaviors in his life, and conform to an outward code while having no relationship with God whatsoever. Legalism is about outward behavior that neglects the heart. The Pharisees were great at conformity to rules and regulations, but Jesus found their righteousness lacking (Mat 5:20), and their hearts were far away from God (Mat 15:8). Outward conformity to rules and regulations, especially when they are man-made, will not bring us closer to God and gain his favor.

One of the characteristics of the gospel is that it brings liberty to those who believe in Jesus Christ for the forgiveness of their sins. Becoming a believer in Christ has a freeing effect on the sinner in that he becomes liberated from the power of sin, along with the penalty of sin because Jesus bore the punishment for our transgressions when he died on the cross. Additionally, the believer is freed from all man-made rules, regulations, and religious systems that supplant the word of God in favor of their traditions (Mark 7:1-13; Gal 4:9; 5:1). Becoming a Christian should be like walking out of jail and becoming free.

Believers in Christ are people who are truly free! *Legalism is a frontal assault on the believer's liberty.* When the disciple's liberty is removed the result will be like stepping into a spiritual prison cell where there is bondage and spiritual oppression. When a believer comes under legalistic influences, it can be like having a ball and chain attached to his ankle, the effects of which are never good. In light of the above I define legalism in the following way:

> Legalism is an attempt to replace the liberty inherent in the gospel with conformity to rules and regulations to earn God's favor. Whether for salvation or sanctification, one's adherence to a code is the means by which he gains God's approval.

Legalism is a spiritual pandemic that raises its ugly head wherever Christians gather. There are a variety of ways that legalism manifests itself which this book will cover. One deadly strain of legalism is the belief that in addition to believing in Christ to be saved, one must add good works to his faith to be accepted by God. Paul battled those who advocated that one is saved by faith in Christ plus adherence to certain aspects of the Law of Moses. He made it crystal clear that adding any kind of works to the gospel is a false gospel, to be avoided like the plague. This false belief will obscure the way of salvation to those who seek God and keep people out of heaven.

Another strain of legalism is more common, and exists in every church in varying degrees. In this form of legalism a person's spirituality is judged by whether they do or don't do certain things that often have no Scriptural basis. For instance, one is thought to be a mature Christian if she doesn't smoke, drink alcohol, go dancing, and so forth. If a believer doesn't display these behaviors they are considered a godly individual. On the other hand, the believer that goes dancing, drinks a glass of wine with his dinner, and goes to the movies is considered to be lacking in his growth in godliness. He is considered to be an immature believer who needs to tighten things up regarding his sanctification. In some extreme cases he may even be considered to be a nonbeliever by legalistic people in his church.

The third strain of legalism deals with one's personal preferences. Everybody is entitled to their own opinion about what they prefer in their worship experience. We all have different tastes and preferences because the body of Christ is diverse. For example, some people feel very comfortable worshiping in a liturgical format, others prefer contemporary worship, and so on. Some people like expository preaching while others prefer a narrative story-telling sermon. There is nothing wrong with having personal preferences in worshiping God. Legalism appears when someone tries to project their personal preferences on other worshipers, making their preferences normative for all believers. The way they like it done should be law for everybody else. In this type of legalism, there is no room for tolerance of other views. Pastors can do much harm to their congregation when they impose their personal preferences on their flock and make it law to be followed by everybody. If someone objects to the pastor's views or practices, they may be considered rebellious and less than spiritual. In some extreme cases they may be ostracized and accused of not even being a Christian if they don't line up.

The fourth strain of legalism is the erroneous belief that once saved, to keep one's salvation the believer has to produce good works. This believer understands that he was saved by God's grace, having nothing to do with his own works. But now that he's saved, in order to keep his salvation, he must generate good works. His assurance of salvation isn't based on his relationship with Christ; it's based on his ability to manufacture good deeds. This can be a crippling burden for

14

a believer to live under, but many well-intentioned worshipers of Christ live in that space.

A cursory reading of the gospels reveals that Jesus and the Pharisees didn't get along very well. He confronted them head on about their traditions superseding the word of God, their hypocritical righteousness, their ineffective shepherding, and the crushing legalism they placed people under. This book will examine several confrontations that Jesus had with the religious establishment regarding their legalistic practices, while exposing the freedom that Jesus offered those who worship him. In a sense, Jesus offers people a "Get Out of Jail Free Card" (like in playing Monopoly).

The apostle Paul was also a combatant in the battle against legalism. False teachers appeared in many of his churches, which placed Paul in the front line of combat, trying to protect his congregations from a false gospel that advocated a combination of faith in Christ plus adherence to the Mosaic Law. Paul would have none of that, so he protected the integrity of the true gospel by exposing the error of the false teachers. This book will explore some of Paul's teaching to see how he spoke against legalism, and championed Christian liberty.

Paul went through a unique transformation because at one time he was a hyper-legalist. One couldn't be more zealous in following the traditions of his ancestors, and living by the letter of the law than Paul. He was extremely zealous, albeit misguided, for his traditions that he persecuted Christians to their death because he perceived them as a threat to the traditions that he held so close to his heart. When Paul became a believer in Christ he went through a radical transformation, such that he became completely emancipated from Pharisee-ism and cherished the newfound liberty he had in Christ. He went from being a hyper-legalist to being a hyper-liberated believer. His life before and after Christ appears to be polar opposites. This book will delve into Paul's unique transformation and uncover his teaching on liberty. It is almost as if Paul's transformation was like getting out of jail and finding the joy of being free from spiritual oppression.

Peter also went through a transformation, which enabled him to reach out to Cornelius and bring the Gentiles into the church of Christ. He needed divine assistance to go through his liberation from the ancestral traditions that Jews followed, and appears to have been completely emancipated from all the aspects of the law that Christ fulfilled. However, when he was in Antioch he had a fall from grace and slipped right back into the legalism that he appeared to be liberated from. It was like Peter deliberately walked back into the prison cell of legalism that Christ freed him from. The apostle Paul confronted him on his backward steps and corrected him regarding his error.

This book will also examine the use of one's liberty in disputable matters that Christians may not all agree on. For example, some believers have strong convictions that drinking any alcohol is sinful and to be avoided. Other believers may have no problem whatsoever drinking a beer while watching the game on TV. When believers have differing opinions on matters of this sort, how can they peacefully coexist with one another? This book will provide answers to these questions by examining the Biblical teaching on liberty.

Legalism establishes a false set of criteria to measure spiritual maturity. One of the solutions to overcoming legalism is a proper understanding of the sanctification process that all believers go through. An examination of the criteria that the Bible sets forth as markers of spiritual maturity reveals how drastically off base the legalists are in their understanding of what constitutes a mature Christian.

Each church has its own culture. Some churches may be more legalistic than others. Some pastors may place their congregation under a burden that is unnecessary and harmful. This book will bring to light some of the signs that point to legalism and will encourage pastors and the governing bodies of churches to take a look at themselves, and assess whether or not they have legalistic practices that need to be repented of and discarded.

My intent in writing this book, "Get Out of Jail Free" is to help every believer walk out of the prison cell of legalism, they may be in, and discover the freedom and joy that Christ died to give him. Being a

Christian shouldn't be an oppressive experience! God calls us to be free.

Christ has truly made us free: then keep your free condition and let no man put a yoke on you again.

Galatians 5:1 (BBE)

Chapter 1 ~ Rules Were Made to Be Broken

Throughout history there have been two extreme ways of handling rules. One is adding more rules to the list, which is what legalists do. The list of rules gets more detailed, longer, and more difficult to keep. The mentality is more is better! The other approach is to get rid of rules and simplify things. Christians often proclaim "we're under grace not law" and may use that phrase to justify doing away with commands in Scripture, even to the point of justifying their engagement in sinful activity. Both of these extremes are to be avoided by believers' in Christ.

The more rules that are presented to a religious community the more likely someone will break those rules. In fact, one approach to excessive rules is to do away with them altogether, or reduce them to just a few. This position has been referred to as the antinomian view. *Anti* meaning against, and the Greek word *nomos*, means law. Therefore, the *antinomian* is one who is opposed to law and may take excessive strides in his personal liberty. His mantra may be "we are under grace not law!" Some people may label a person of this sort a *libertarian* in addition to being *antinomian*.

Secular society has presented challenges to many of Christianity's foundational truths. There are philosophies that have been introduced that attack the idea of absolute truth. Post modernism is a philosophy and worldview that is pervasive in many Western cultures. It is very difficult to define as a movement, so describing its tenets gives the reader the best insight into what it is. It developed in the late 20th Century and is characterized by skepticism, relativism, suspicion of reason, and rejection of ideology in asserting and maintaining political and economic power. This worldview deeply values the following: spirituality, pluralism, the experiential, relativity, altruism, community, creativity, the arts, environmentalism, globalism, holism, and authenticity.

One of the basic principles of Christianity is that God's word is truth. It is objective truth that is knowable and to be obeyed. God's truth is absolute truth. Postmodernism rejects this belief. Rather than claiming truth is absolute they advocate that truth is relative to the individual. Truth is what the individual thinks it is. To know an author's intent is a highly subjective matter, thus one can't know what the Biblical author's intent was in penning Scripture. The notion of knowing authorial intent is rejected, which makes the interpretation of a Biblical text totally subjective.

One can see how Christianity and this particular aspect of postmodernism don't get along very well. They stand at odds with each other. Once God's word is rejected as objective absolute truth, it can mean whatever the individual wants it to mean. This belief is totally incompatible with the Christian faith and opens the door to a morality that is based on the individual's view of what is right and wrong. The new moral / ethical mantra of the day becomes: "It may be wrong for you, but it's right for me." One's view of God, reality, and morality can be whatever he interprets it to be.

The antinomian position and this aspect of postmodernism are very compatible. Many believers are influenced by postmodern thinking, which is being championed in secular colleges and universities across the country. What this view does is muddy the waters of God's moral standards and justifies disobedience to God's commands. Many people who are regular church attendees throughout their high school years go off to college and are inundated with postmodern views that challenge their presuppositions about Christianity. Many of these students experience spiritual trauma when they are exposed to these views, and go into a crisis of faith.

In addition to postmodernism, Joseph Fletcher released a best seller in 1966 titled "Situational Ethics." His position is that decision-making should be based upon an individual's specific circumstances, not upon established Law. The only absolute, according to Fletcher, is Love. Love should be the driving motive behind every decision one makes. As long as Love is the intention in decision-making, the end justifies the means. Justice is displayed in the way love is demonstrated, not in the letter of the law. Fletcher, who was an Episcopalian priest, founded his model upon a statement found in 1 John 4:8: "God is love."

Situational ethics has become another troublesome influence that creeps into Christian thought. According to this view God's commands can be broken as long as the outcome is displaying love. This fits right into the antinomian position, such that situational ethics and antinomians are good friends. This is a dangerous philosophy of life to embrace and stands at odds with Christianity's absolute moral standards.

This new morality is pervasive in our generation. Unlike post-modernism, which says there are no absolutes, situational ethicists claim the only absolute is love and everything else is a variable. Under this view one can defend ungodly behavior by claiming "it doesn't hurt anybody." "If it feels good do it." "Nobody gets hurt." "Everybody else is doing it." According to this view premarital sex is justifiable, viewing pornography, breaking your word, taking recreational drugs, casually dissolving a marriage, adultery for fun, and just about anything can be justified under this rubric. As long as it's done in love it's OK. For example, when two consenting adults have premarital sex because they love each other that is perfectly acceptable in situational ethics. However, it isn't acceptable to God for it is contrary to his word.

There is a serious problem with this view. Love isn't to be used as an excuse to sin. When a believer walks in God's love he will want to obey his commands, and sin will take on a repulsive posture. One way that we show our love for God is by obeying him, and having the desire to please him. Situational ethics isn't based on God's sacrificial, unrelenting love, it is selfishly based love that enhances and satisfies one's sinful appetite. Additionally, justifying sinful behavior that is supposedly done in love will hurt the people involved. Those who engage in premarital sex, adultery for fun, and so on, are doing things that will hurt them, and their actions aren't driven by the type of love advocated by the Bible.

In fairness to Fletcher, I don't think he intended to develop an ethical system that was designed to enable each individual to satisfy his sinful appetite. He was dealing with some complex ethical issues. It appears that many people misuse Fletcher's view for their own selfish ends.

Jesus said some insightful things about how he views love and obedience in John 14:21-24:

He who has My commandments and keeps them is the one who loves Me; and he who loves Me will be loved by My Father, and I will love him and will disclose Myself to him." ²²Judas (not Iscariot) said to Him, "Lord, what then has happened that You are going to disclose Yourself to us and not to the world?" ²³Jesus answered and said to him, "If anyone loves Me, he will keep My word; and My Father will love him, and We will come to him and make Our abode with him. ²⁴He who does not love Me does not keep My words; and the word which you hear is not Mine, but the Father's who sent Me.

The believer's love for Christ will be demonstrated by obeying his word. The one who doesn't love Jesus will not obey his word. As believers obey God out of their love for him, God will disclose himself to those disciples. As the believer grows in love and obedience to God's word, he will experience more of God's love disclosed to him. Jesus and God—the Father—will make their abode with him. The way to have more intimacy with God and experience more of his love in our life is to obey his word. Obedience is the pathway to experiencing more of God's love in our daily experience.

Another insightful passage is Matthew 22:34-40:

But when the Pharisees heard that Jesus had silenced the Sadducees, they gathered themselves together. ³⁵One of them, a lawyer, asked Him *a question*, testing Him, ³⁶"Teacher, which is the great commandment in the Law?" ³⁷And He said to him, "'YOU SHALL LOVE THE LORD YOUR GOD WITH ALL YOUR HEART, AND WITH ALL YOUR SOUL, AND WITH ALL YOUR MIND.' ³⁸This is the great and foremost commandment. ³⁹The second is like it, 'YOU SHALL LOVE YOUR NEIGHBOR AS YOURSELF.' ⁴⁰On these two commandments depend the whole Law and the Prophets."

One who practices situational ethics, as a means of self-gratification doesn't love God and his neighbor as himself. Those who lie, steal, and so on, aren't demonstrating love to their fellow man. In reality, situational ethics isn't an ethic of love; it is an ethic that lends itself to justify self-gratification and endorses disobedience to God's word. Jesus also said:

In everything, therefore, treat people the same way you want them to treat you, for this is the Law and the Prophets. (Matthew 7:12)

This statement of Jesus causes the believer to think of how he would want to be treated in a given situation, which then becomes the way he will treat the person in question. Situational ethics aren't compatible with Christianity. Jesus stands at odds with situational ethics and the rejection of God's word being absolute truth, which postmodern philosophy advocates. The First Century world was very similar to what exists today. The characteristics of the First Century and Postmodernism are very similar regarding: pluralism, tolerance, relativism, rejection of absolute truth, multiple religions, and so on.

Law and Grace

There is a subtle form of antinomianism displayed among some believers today who maintain a radical contrast between law and grace. The mantra "we're not under law but grace" is a popular phrase thrown around by Christians today from Romans 6:14. It's almost as if some believers look at the commands in Scripture in a negative way. The Law has been fulfilled in Christ (Mat 5:17). This means that the ceremonial law involving the sacrifices, festivals, and dietary regulations don't need to be practiced today because Christ has fulfilled those aspects of the law. The civil law, which were the laws pertaining to the way Israel was governed as a theocracy, have also been fulfilled by Christ. The law exists today as Christ has fulfilled it. He brought it to its intended goal.

The moral aspect of the law regarding the Ten Commandments and other moral imperatives are still binding upon the believer. To say that New Testament believers have no rules to follow can't be supported by Scripture. Some believers may claim the only responsibility Christians have is to walk in the Spirit and they will never violate the intent of the law. Therefore the only thing the believer needs to do is live a Spirit-filled life, and he will be living on the high moral ground that Jesus calls the believer to walk on. While I agree that one who is walking in the Spirit will not be living a lifestyle characterized by sinful behavior, that doesn't do away with the commands in God's word. Certainly, there are commands given to the New Testament believer that are to be obeyed. They have never been done away with because we live under grace not law.

It would be incorrect to say that there was no concept of grace in the Old Testament—as if grace never existed prior to the New Testament. Grace was evident in God's dealings with man all throughout the Bible. Rather than seeing a radical distinction between law and grace as if they are totally incompatible, standing as polar opposites, it is better to view them as complementary. The moral imperatives (law) are to be obeyed, and God extends grace to believers to keep them (Titus 2:11-12). In this view, law and grace are totally compatible and complementary. Walking in the Spirit enables the believer to keep the commandments in Scripture.

The Free Grace Position

There is a position known as *free grace,* which is another form of antinomianism. This position states that for salvation the sinner needs to place his faith in Jesus as Savior, without the need to repent. Later in the new believer's life he needs to accept Jesus as Lord and begin his life of discipleship. When someone accepts Jesus as Savior there is no commitment required, no repentance necessary, no demands placed upon the believer whatsoever. The person is saved but has no responsibility to live an obedient life that glorifies God. The only time the Lordship of Christ should be taught is to those who are already believers, but the only thing that needs to be taught to nonbelievers is the Saviorhood of Jesus. The free grace position is essentially a two-tier classification of believers: those who know Jesus as Savior, and those who know Jesus as Savior and Lord. There are some very high profile scholars and preachers that maintain this view.

The contrasting view is known as "Lordship Salvation" which states that when a sinner accepts Jesus by faith he accepts him as both Savior and Lord at the same time. In this framework faith and repentance go hand-in-hand. The sinner turns to Christ in faith, but turns away from sin in repentance. Once the person is saved he immediately is called to live a life of discipleship, and begin his journey of sanctification. John MacArthur wrote a book titled "The Gospel of Jesus" and argued convincingly for this position. Faith and repentance are essential to the gospel, thus one must receive Jesus as both Savior and Lord.

I have known people who were advocates of the free grace position, and claimed that they are saved and going to heaven, but they have no desire to be in fellowship with other believers, read God's word, grow as a disciple, or practice the Christian life in any way, shape, or form. But they are convinced they are saved and going to heaven. Something is wrong with this picture!

How Did People Regard Jesus?

His opponents considered Jesus an antinomian because he rejected their multitude of oral traditions. Of course, Jesus wasn't antinomian, he upheld the law and prophets and always held the Scripture in high regard (Mat 5:17). He saw God's word as completely authoritative, binding, and never disobeyed Scripture. Jesus wasn't a legalist either. How should Jesus be viewed in the spectrum between antinomianism and legalism? *Jesus was free!* He wasn't bound by man-made regulations set forth by the religious leaders of his day; rather he was free to obey God's word. He wasn't captive to any religious system, rules or regulations that conflicted with Scripture. Jesus walked in liberty and because of that was able to demonstrate what a life of freedom looks like, and never broke the law.

His desire for today's believer is to be completely free from man-made rules and religious systems that restrain the believer from obeying his word, or place him under a crushing burden. When the believer discovers his freedom in Christ he finds the liberty to serve and do so in a loving manner (Gal 5:13-15). His freedom isn't to be used as an opportunity to indulge in a sinful lifestyle and be an antinomian.

Conclusion

In this chapter the term *antinomianism* was introduced, which refers to those who are against law. One of the characteristics of today's post-modern worldview is the claim that there is no absolute truth. This view stands in stark contrast to the Christian worldview, which says that God's truth is absolute and knowable. In the postmodern worldview truth is relative to each individual. *Situational ethics* is another term that was introduced in this chapter and is complementary to post-modernism. The situational ethicist justifies any behavior as long as it is done in love. Both these views are at odds with the Bible because they do violence to the absolute truthfulness of God's word.

The view known as *Free Grace* was also introduced, which claims that one can accept Jesus as Savior without any need for repentance, or for living a life of discipleship as the Bible advocates.   After accepting Jesus as Savior, this view avers, the believer must accept Jesus as Lord and begin his journey of sanctification and discipleship. This view is popular in some circles of Christianity. The opposing view is known as *Lordship Salvation*, which advocates the view that when one accepts Jesus in his heart he accepts him as both Savior and Lord. Faith and repentance are essential to becoming a believer so beginning the journey of discipleship and sanctification should begin immediately with one's conversion.

Rather than viewing law and grace as polar opposites, I've suggested that they should be viewed as complementary. The Bible is filled with moral imperatives that are binding on believers, and God supplies us with the grace necessary to be obedient and live a lifestyle that pleases him. In the next chapter we will examine the other extreme regarding rules, which is to make up more rules—something legalists excel at.

Chapter 2 ~ We Need More Rules

The other approach to keeping rules is to add to the body of rules and regulations, which is precisely what the religious leaders of Jesus' day did. They added their oral traditions to the Scriptures, which placed the people under a crushing load that they couldn't bear. Trying to obey all the oral traditions of the Pharisees and scribes was oppressive and actually served as a roadblock to knowing God. In Matthew 23 Jesus pronounced seven woes upon the Pharisees and scribes: the hyper-legalists of the day. The first two of those woes will be discussed in this chapter. Reading through the woes reveals how damaging legalism can be to converts who desire to know God. Following is the first woe Jesus directed at the religious leaders:

But woe to you, scribes and Pharisees, hypocrites, because you shut off the kingdom of heaven from people; for you do not enter in yourselves, nor do you allow those who are entering to go in. (Matthew 23:13)

When Jesus pronounces a "woe" this is serious business. He is casting judgment upon the religious leaders of the day for their ineffective shepherding. He singles out the scribes and Pharisees, identifying them as hypocrites because as the spiritual leaders of the nation they should be making the pathway to heaven clear and unmistakable to those who seek God. However, through their catalogue of rules and regulations they are closing the door to the Kingdom of heaven to those who seek it. Thus, they make themselves out to be hypocrites.

They don't enter the Kingdom of heaven themselves, and through their crushing legalism those who are trying to enter are blocked from going in. When someone tried to enter the Kingdom of heaven by establishing a faith relationship with God, the Pharisees' practices actually served as a roadblock to him or her. Paying attention to all their rules and regulations deemphasized a personal relationship with God through faith, and presented God as approachable through their minutia of rules and regulations. Their presentation of God to the people was that he was virtually impossible to please. They rejected Jesus as the Messiah and taught others to do the same, thus slamming the door to the Kingdom of heaven in their faces.

The irony is striking! Those entrusted with the spiritual care of Israel are not entering the Kingdom of heaven, they are not believers, and they are preventing people who want to know God from entering the Kingdom of heaven as well. It doesn't get any worse than that.

Verse four of Matthew 23 sheds more light on the negligent activity of the Pharisees.

They tie up heavy burdens and lay them on men's shoulders, but they themselves are unwilling to move them with *so much as* a finger. (Matthew 23:4)

The "heavy burdens" the leaders lay on people's shoulders are all their rules and oral traditions. Jesus sees their traditions as "heavy burdens" that weigh people down and cause spiritual oppression. The leaders are portrayed as unwilling to help those who were being crushed by the sheer difficulty of keeping the traditions. The religious authorities were living in their ivory towers and were somewhat disconnected from the people regarding giving them practical advice on how to keep all the rules. They weren't able to offer the people much help in developing a relationship with the heavenly Father. The teaching of the leaders was doing more harm than good, which further adds to the irony of the situation.

Jesus presented himself as the opposite of the Pharisees in Matthew 11:28-30:

"Come to Me, all who are weary and heavy-laden, and I will give you rest. [29]Take My yoke upon you and learn from Me, for I am gentle and humble in heart, and YOU WILL FIND REST FOR YOUR SOULS. [30]For My yoke is easy and My burden is light."

When contrasting the effects of knowing Jesus, with that of being under the teaching of the religious leaders, one can see how liberating it is to know Jesus. All those who are "weary and heavy-laden" are those who are under the plethora of oppressive rules of the Pharisees. Knowing Jesus sets people free from all those man-made regulations and gives the convert rest. Jesus' description of himself has to be seen in contrast to the Pharisees. Note the following contrasts:

- Jesus gives rest – The Pharisees demand constant striving in keeping rules

- Jesus is gentle – The Pharisees are harsh and demanding

- Jesus' teaching opens the door to heaven – The Pharisees' teaching closes the door to heaven

- Jesus' teaching liberates – The Pharisees' teaching oppresses

- Jesus is humble – The Pharisees are proud and love recognition from men

- Jesus' yoke is easy – The Pharisees' yoke is heavy

- Jesus' burden is light – The Pharisees' burden is crushing

One can see how worshiping Jesus gives people freedom and joy, whereas being under the Pharisees' teaching is sheer oppression and burdensome.

Jesus pronounces another woe on the leaders, which further indicts them for their ineffective shepherding:

Woe to you, scribes and Pharisees, hypocrites, because you travel around on sea and land to make one proselyte; and when he becomes one, you make him twice as much a son of hell as yourselves. (Matthew 23:15)

The First Century up to the fall of Jerusalem in 70 A.D. was actually a time of great missionary zeal in Judaism. In becoming a convert to Judaism there were two steps: the first was to understand monotheism, the belief in one God as opposed to many gods. The

28

second was to get circumcised. This goes back to Moses and was the sign of being incorporated into the covenant community. It appears that the Jews restricted their missionary efforts to "God-fearers," who were Gentiles that were loosely affiliated with Jewish customs. They wouldn't mix with unclean Gentiles, so their missionary zeal was directed at the God-fearers.

In their travels they would go to various Jewish cities and try to persuade God-fearers to complete the final act of circumcision and become a full convert to Judaism. Jesus didn't criticize them for their missionary zeal, which was very real indeed. However, the effect on the new covert was disastrous: "when he becomes one, you make him twice as much a son of hell as yourselves." Perhaps, the attraction of the God-fearers to Judaism was keeping all the rules, but the Jews were supposed to point the convert to God. Unfortunately, their religious system bypassed true faith and deemphasized a relationship with God. Hypocrites appear to be attracting more hypocrites. Their converts became more Pharisaical than the Pharisees, which wasn't good because Jesus said that their converts become "twice as much a son of hell as yourselves."

Their converts followed in the footsteps of their teachers. They were hypocrites and their converts were more hypocritical. They were converted to a place Jesus referred to as being a "son of hell," because the theological grid advocated by the Pharisees eliminated Jesus from the framework, leaving no possibility of entering the Kingdom of heaven. They tragically became "sons of hell" in becoming one of their converts.

Conclusion

This chapter demonstrates how harmful it can be to come under the influence of legalists who want more rules, more regulations and codes to follow. They feel that the pathway to being a righteous individual is though adherence to more rules and codes. The Pharisees' converts became "sons of hell" which is no laughing matter. Any system of religion, or theology that eliminates faith in Jesus from the picture, slams the door to the Kingdom of heaven and welds it shut. This is precisely what the Pharisees had done to those who were seeking God. By adding all their rules and regulations they placed people under a burden they couldn't possible keep.

The Pharisees and the scribes were studious people, who knew the word of God like the back of their hands! They worked hard at observing the Torah and all their ancestral traditions so they would be righteous. However, Jesus had a serious problem with the righteousness they demonstrated. In fact, he didn't see them as being righteous at all—he saw them as impious hypocrites. How did this happen? How did it get to the point where Jesus describes them as being "sons of hell" and making their converts twice the "sons of hell" as they were? The next chapter will provide information regarding how this happened.

Chapter 3 ~ The Righteousness of the Scribes and Pharisees

For I say to you that unless your righteousness surpasses *that* of the scribes and Pharisees, you will not enter the kingdom of heaven. (Matthew 5:20)

If ever there was a group of people that was concerned about displaying righteous behavior it was the scribes and Pharisees. They took it seriously, and make no mistake about it they were good at it! These were Jews who kept every minute detail of the law (Old Testament) with exactitude and precision. In today's vernacular they would be considered hyper-legalists. Jesus, quite often, mentions both these groups in the same breath. Even a superficial reading of the gospels reveals that Jesus butted heads with the scribes and Pharisees, and they didn't like him. When Jesus began his ministry it became obvious that he was on a collision course with these people.

Who were these Jewish groups, and why were they so antagonistic toward Jesus? Why did Jesus find their righteousness to be lacking, especially when they expended so much effort at being righteous people? To answer these questions it is necessary to explain some things about their history, and the state of Judaism in Jesus' day.

After the return from Babylonian exile the Jews wanted to put a fence around the law, because they feared it would be lost. They set out to preserve Jewish customs and religion from the influence of the Gentiles. They guarded the oral traditions that were developed over the generations that offered a layer of interpretation to the Law of Moses. For example, the Law prohibits work on the Sabbath, but what was to be considered work? The oral traditions answered these kinds of questions by providing commentary on what constituted work on the Sabbath. There were 39 different activities that were identified as work, and were therefore to be avoided on the Sabbath.

Another example of the oral tradition was providing commentary on "an eye for an eye" (Ex 21:24). Did this passage mean that if somebody accidentally blinded another person that he should be blinded as well? Taken literally, that seems to be what the passage calls for. The oral tradition provided guidelines that called for monetary compensation, so the value of an eye is what must be compensated for. With 613 commandments in the Torah it makes sense that there needed to be some type of commentary to assist Jews in knowing how to apply them. Without additional commentary on the Torah it was thought that the law was insufficient for Jewish life.

During the Bar-Kokhba rebellion one million Jews were killed, many of whom were rabbinic scholars and students. With this devastating loss Rabbi Judah began to write down the oral tradition in 200 C.E. because he feared it might be lost. This document became known as the Mishnah. This was a decisive step in Judaism because it had always been thought that the best way to preserve the oral traditions was by memory. Students maintained a close relationship with their teachers and learned the oral traditions through them, because it was believed that teachers could do a better job imparting knowledge than books. But with the dispersal of Jews after the Bar-Kokhba revolt, one was never sure to have a competent teacher nearby, so Rabbi Judah wrote down the laws in a systematized fashion so that all the traditions regarding the Sabbath, marriage and divorce, laws of sacrifice, the festivals, and so on, were compiled topically. This was considered a guide and central component to Jewish life.

For generations the Mishnah was studied rigorously, then around the year 400 A.D. rabbis' wrote a commentary on the Mishnah known as the Palestinian Talmud. About 100 years later the Babylonian Jewish scholars wrote another Talmud that was more comprehensive than its Palestinian counterpart. When Jews speak of the Talmud today they are usually referring to the Babylonian Talmud.

Although the writing down of the oral traditions began 200 years after Jesus' day, it demonstrates how crucial they were to Jewish living. It was these oral traditions that developed over the generations that caused a problem between Jesus and the Pharisees before they were written down. Their oral traditions, in many cases, superseded the word of God placing the people under a crushing burden of rules and regulations. Jesus stood at odds with the scribes and Pharisees over their traditions, which they resented and viewed him as a threat to Judaism. This is also why they viewed him as being antinomian.

The scribes were considered to be the scholars of the day. These were people of great learning who were considered to be legal experts, or lawyers that would be called upon in court settings to provide council in legal matters and help settle disputes about the law. Many Pharisees studied under scribes, and like the Pharisees the scribes were zealous for maintaining the oral traditions that were handed down from one generation to another.

In the passage cited above: "For I say to you that unless your righteousness surpasses *that* of the scribes and Pharisees, you will not enter the kingdom of heaven" (Mat 5:20), Jesus found their righteousness to be less than what it should be to enter the Kingdom of Heaven. This is a shocking statement because these were the spiritual leaders of Israel. These were the shepherds and teachers of the people, yet Jesus said the type of righteousness they displayed would not grant them access to heaven, and those who emulated their example of righteousness wouldn't enter the kingdom of heaven either.

What Did Jesus Mean by Righteousness?

Jesus was referring to the behavior of the Pharisees when he criticized their righteousness. If one obeys the Bible in their daily experience they will be viewed as living righteously. The Pharisees and scribes kept the law and oral traditions of their ancestors with precision, but they were merely conforming to a code. Their righteousness was defective in that they conformed scrupulously to rules and regulations, but their behavior bypassed the heart. They felt they were righteous if they kept the rules, and they were good at that, but Jesus didn't see it that way. True righteousness comes from a heart that loves God and desires to do his will. When a sinner becomes a believer in Christ and experiences a transformed life, righteous behavior should naturally follow and be a characteristic of the person's life. A believer obeys the Scripture out of love for God.

The righteousness the Pharisees and scribes displayed was merely outward conformity to a code, but Jesus detected that they were lacking in heartfelt love for God. This is why Jesus condemned their righteousness. Nonbelievers can conform to rules and regulations and appear to be righteous, but God looks into the heart. The commands in Scripture should not be kept just for the sake of keeping them. They are obeyed because the believer loves God and desires to do what is pleasing to him. Obedience to God's word should always result in the believer coming closer to God, and deepening his relationship with Christ. Outward conformity to rules without a corresponding heartfelt love for God becomes self-righteousness. One thinks of himself as good / righteous because he keeps the commands, which is what the Pharisees exceled at, but their hearts were barren of faith and love for God.

In the Sermon on the Mount Jesus overturned the false interpretations the religious establishment set forth regarding murder, adultery, divorce, oaths, retaliation, and treatment of enemies (Mat 5:21-47). He was offering correctives to the malicious views held by the Pharisees regarding these issues. The type of righteousness Jesus called for went beyond the outward behavior a person would display, to the inner recesses of the heart.

For example, one isn't considered righteous if he doesn't commit murder. He's considered righteous if he isn't angry with his brother. Anger at another person is murder in seed form. One isn't considered righteous if he doesn't commit adultery, he's considered righteous if he doesn't have lustful thoughts when he looks at a woman. Lust is considered adultery in seed form. One isn't considered righteous if he marries, he is considered righteous if he keeps his marriage commitments. One isn't considered righteous if he makes vows, he's considered righteous if he keeps his word and means what he says. One isn't considered righteous if he seeks retaliation according to the law, he's considered righteous if he gives up his rights and doesn't seek to get even. Finally, one isn't considered righteous if he hates his enemies, he is considered righteous if he loves his enemies and prays for them.

In each of the above correctives Jesus is bypassing the outward behavior and pointing to the inner condition of the heart. He has raised the bar on righteousness, focusing true righteousness where it should be—flowing from the heart. One can externally keep all the rules, but in his heart can break every one of them at the same time. Such was the case with the righteousness of the Pharisees and scribes.

Transformational Righteousness vs. Self-Righteousness

When one keeps the commandments externally and thinks that enables him to merit a good standing with God he is deceived. External behavior devoid of corresponding love for God becomes the epitome of *self-righteousness*, which is reprehensible to God. The Pharisees exceled at self-righteousness but lacked the inner transformation of the heart.

The righteousness Jesus advocated comes from a transformed life that occurs when a sinner invites him into his heart by faith. Because of the inner transformation of the heart, outward behavior that pleases God will naturally follow. This type of righteousness is *transformational righteousness* that occurs through a relationship with Christ.

Fake Righteousness

Jesus also criticized and exposed the shallowness of the Pharisees righteousness in Matthew 6:1-18. In that passage Jesus mentioned three things that were commonly practiced by Jews: giving, praying, and fasting, which were considered the pillars of Judaism. He issued a word of caution to his audience (Mat 6:1):

> Be careful that you don't do your charitable giving before men, to be seen by them, or else you have no reward from your Father who is in heaven.

Jesus was addressing the motives behind the Pharisees' behavior. Were they doing things out of love for God, or was this just for show so that they could gain praise from the people? Their righteousness was for show to get pats on the back by impressing the crowds. Maybe the people who watched the Pharisees and scribes thought they were spiritual giants, but Jesus did not. He saw through their improper motives and declared that their superficial righteousness would earn them no rewards from God. The people may hold them in high regard, but God does not.

Jesus called them hypocrites. The word in the original language meant someone who wore a mask, like an actor who was playing a character. The idea of the word is that one appears to be something that he isn't. The Pharisees appeared to be righteous but, in point of fact, they were playacting by presenting themselves as something that they were not. They looked good on the outside, but on the inside Jesus found their heart motivation to be lacking.

Conclusion

Legalistic people will often be overly concerned about impressing other people and keeping the status quo. Such was the case with the scribes and Pharisees. They appear to be righteous because they excel at keeping all the rules, but often their hearts' motivation is suspect. Outward appearances can be deceiving. Those who appear to be righteous individuals because they do the right things can have a corrupted heart. Their righteousness is merely self-righteousness, which is repulsive to God. It is ironic that the scribes and Pharisees expended so much energy at trying to be righteous, but were found to be suspect by the Lord Jesus. In fact, Jesus condemned their righteousness making it clear that their righteousness would not gain them access to the Kingdom of heaven. They could externally keep the rules, but in their hearts break every one of them.

In the next chapter we will take a look at the controversies that developed between Jesus and the religious establishment, which will enable us to gain some insights into the depth of legalism they advocated, and how Jesus was opposed to the heavy burdens they placed on worshipers.

Chapter 4 ~ Jesus' Conflict With the Religious Authorities

It didn't take long for Jesus to stir things up. Mark's gospel is an action-packed drama of Jesus that hits the ground running. By the end of chapter one Jesus had healed many people, amazed the crowds by his teaching, and had displayed his power over the archenemy of God—Satan—by casting out demons and setting people free. Jesus had totally outclassed the demonic realm on the field of battle for they were no match for him. After healing a leper Jesus told him not to tell anybody about it, but go to the priest and offer the appropriate sacrifice. The healed leper couldn't keep his mouth shut and spread the news about Jesus so that his popularity had skyrocketed to the point where he couldn't openly enter a town (Mark 1:40-45). The people were coming to Jesus from everywhere, for they recognized something special about him; specifically, they saw his authority.

A new enemy would appear to Jesus that was just as dangerous as the demons, if not more so. As Jesus conducted his ministry the religious establishment resisted him and wanted to put him out of business. They were threatened by his ever-expanding popularity, his teaching ruffled their feathers, and he wasn't in compliance with their ancestral traditions. For these reasons tension escalated between Jesus and the Pharisees and scribes throughout his ministry. The religious establishment didn't recognize the authority that the people clearly saw in Jesus. This is what they questioned about him throughout his ministry, and this rises to the surface in chapter two of Mark's gospel.

There are five conflict narratives between Jesus and the religious leaders that Mark records for us in 2:1 – 3:6. As the episodes unfold the tension escalates with the religious leaders plotting Jesus' death in the last confrontation (3:6). In this chapter we will examine the first conflict episode, which is recorded in Mark 2:1-12.

When he entered again into Capernaum after some days, it was heard that he was in the house. ²Immediately many were gathered together, so that there was no more room, not even around the door; and he spoke the word to them. ³Four people came, carrying a paralytic to him. ⁴When they could not come near to him for the crowd, they removed the roof where he was. When they had broken it up, they let down the mat that the paralytic was lying on. ⁵Jesus, seeing their faith, said to the paralytic, "Son, your sins are forgiven you."   ⁶But there were some of the scribes sitting there, and reasoning in their hearts, ⁷"Why does this man speak blasphemies like that? Who can forgive sins but God alone?" ⁸Immediately Jesus, perceiving in his spirit that they so reasoned within themselves, said to them, "Why do you reason these things in your hearts? ⁹Which is easier, to tell the paralytic, 'Your sins are forgiven;' or to say, 'Arise, and take up your bed, and walk?' ¹⁰But that you may know that the Son of Man has authority on earth to forgive sins"—he said to the paralytic—¹¹"I tell you, arise, take up your mat, and go to your house." ¹²He arose, and immediately took up the mat, and went out in front of them all; so that they were all amazed, and glorified God, saying, "We never saw anything like this!" (Mark 2:1-12)

Jesus is inside a house in Capernaum that is packed to capacity such that people were even crowded outside of the place to hear his electrifying teaching. In desperation some men brought a paralytic to Jesus so he could heal him, but there was no way to get the man to Jesus because of the crowd that had assembled. People were glued to Jesus as they listened to his teaching.   These four men had determination mixed with ingenuity and wouldn't be denied access to Jesus, so they got on the roof and began to dig it up.   Roofs in Palestine were flat, covered with a layer of packed clay, along with tar, mortar, and branches across the wooden beams. The parallel passage in Luke informs us that the roof had tiles that they pried apart (5:19). Often salt was placed on the roof to make it somewhat waterproof and hardened. The houses had stairways that led up to the roof, so the men carried their bed-ridden friend up to the roof and begin to dig it up, then using ropes they lower the man down in front of Jesus.

His sermon is interrupted as debris from the roof falls to the floor, and all the commotion of the event turns the attention of the crowd toward the man being lowered in front of Jesus. Some preachers might have been upset that their sermon came to a screeching halt because of the intrusion, but not Jesus.

Mark records that Jesus "saw their faith" and says to the paralyzed man "Son, your sins are forgiven you" (v. 5). It appears that the faith Jesus saw was in the four people who brought their paralytic friend and lowered him through the roof. Their determination to present their friend to Jesus impressed him. Jesus' statement seems to be odd because one would think that Jesus would say "be healed" and the story ends right there. Jesus didn't address his physical condition initially because the man's deeper need was for forgiveness of sins that only Jesus can offer.

What good would it have done to heal the man, but not address his deeper need to be forgiven? Why was the man in this condition? We don't know because the text gives us no clues. All sickness found in the human condition can be attributed to sin and usually the Devil has his hand in there somewhere as well. When Jesus offered the man forgiveness he wasn't implying that he was sick because God was punishing him because of specific sins that he had committed. It was thought by Jews, during that time, that when someone is sick it is because of sin that brought God's judgment on him. Sometimes people are born with defects, develop medical conditions, and suffer physical maladies in their life. This is one of the consequences of life in a fallen world. Therefore, to make the conclusion that the man was a paralytic because of sin(s) he had committed wouldn't be a correct conclusion to draw. Nor would it be accurate to say that God was punishing the man for something he had done.

Jesus offered the man what he needed most: the forgiveness of his sins. Now Jesus would address his physical condition, but first the antagonists are introduced.

But there were some of the scribes sitting there, and reasoning in their hearts, 7"Why does this man speak blasphemies like that? Who can forgive sins but God alone?" 8Immediately Jesus, perceiving in his spirit that they so reasoned within themselves, said to them, "Why do you reason these things in your hearts? 9Which is easier, to tell

the paralytic, 'Your sins are forgiven;' or to say, 'Arise, and take up your bed, and walk?' ¹⁰But that you may know that the Son of Man has authority on earth to forgive sins"—he said to the paralytic—¹¹"I tell you, arise, take up your mat, and go to your house." ¹²He arose, and immediately took up the mat, and went out in front of them all; so that they were all amazed, and glorified God, saying, "We never saw anything like this!" (Mark 2:6-12)

The scribes were the legal experts, lawyers, and teachers of the law. They were the ivory tower theologians of the day, who were very influential in their time. Often they would be called upon to settle legal disputes in a court setting. These were men of great learning who were held in high regard by the people and were practically venerated by their culture.

When Jesus pronounced the man's sins forgiven, this caused great disturbance in the minds of the scribes because they reasoned that only God can forgiven sins. It was considered blasphemy to claim to be God, or do something that only God could do. Additionally, blasphemy was so serious that according to the Law of Moses it was punishable by death (Lev 24:16). The scribes were correct in stating that only God can forgiven sins. Jesus was asserting his divine prerogatives by forgiving the man's sins, however the scribes didn't recognize Jesus' divine status and corresponding authority. They just saw him as a blasphemer. Later it would be the charge of blasphemy that finally condemned Jesus (Mark 14:64).

We gain another insight into Jesus' divine power: Immediately Jesus, perceiving in his spirit that they so reasoned within themselves, said to them, "Why do you reason these things in your hearts?" (v. 8). He was able to peer into their hearts and perceive their thoughts. Thus, Mark records for us another attribute of Jesus' deity. In his omniscience, he knew exactly what they were thinking and provided an answer to their questions.

Which is easier, to tell the paralytic, 'Your sins are forgiven;' or to say, 'Arise, and take up your bed, and walk?' ¹⁰But that you may know that the Son of Man has authority on earth to forgive sins"—he

said to the paralytic—[11]"I tell you, arise, take up your mat, and go to your house." (Mark 2:9-11)

There were many prophets that preceded Jesus who were able to perform miracles, so when Jesus says "which is easier, to tell the paralytic," it is easier to pronounce healing because other human beings have been used by God to bring healing to people, thus healing wasn't unique to Jesus. Anybody can say a man's sins are forgiven, but how do you prove it? Jesus healed the man, which provided testimony to his divine authority to forgiven sins. In other words, Jesus backed up his pronouncement of the man's forgiveness by performing a miracle of healing. This should have been proof to the scribes that the Son of Man has authority to forgive sins.

Jesus identified himself as the Son of Man, which is an allusion to Daniel 7:13, to identify himself as the Messiah. This was Jesus' most frequent way of identifying himself. He commanded the man: "to arise, take up your mat, and go to your house" (v. 11). The results are recorded in the next verse.

He arose, and immediately took up the mat, and went out in front of them all; so that they were all amazed, and glorified God, saying, "We never saw anything like this!" (Mark 2:12)

The healing occurred instantaneously. The paralytic rose, gathered up his mat and walked out of the house. The people had just witnessed a miracle and they were amazed, filled with awe, and glorified God. They had never seen anything like this before. The people were awestruck, but what was the reaction of the scribes? We are left wondering because Mark doesn't record anything about them after the healing. The people plainly recognized Jesus' authority, but the scribes questioned Jesus' source of authority. The common people were all amazed at Jesus' authority, but the scribes, who were the top-level scholars of the day, didn't seem to get it. We are left wondering how the scribes reacted to the healing. Perhaps they were also filled with awe, but in their antagonism toward Jesus were skeptical! The reader will notice that the tension begins to increase between Jesus and the religious leaders in subsequent episodes. They view him as a blasphemer because of his declaration of the man's forgiveness, which is a most serious charge!

Conclusion

This dramatic scene has brought to the foreground Jesus' authority to forgive sins, his divine omniscience in looking into the hearts of the scribes and knowing their thoughts, and, of course, his power to heal the paralytic. Early in his ministry Jesus identified himself as the Son of Man—a Messianic title. Clearly, Jesus has God-given authority to forgive sin and heal the sick, which the scribes didn't recognize, but the common people did. The scribes saw Jesus as a blasphemer, which is a serious matter to them. It appears that the common folk have better discernment regarding Jesus than the ivory tower theologians. It should have been the other way around. One senses the Pharisees and scribes have the root of bitterness and resentment toward Jesus beginning to grow in their hearts.

Chapter 5 ~ The People Jesus Associated With

People are often judged by the company they keep, which was the case with Jesus. He regularly befriended sinners and tax collectors, which was considered unacceptable behavior by the religious establishment. In the second conflict episode that Mark presents his readers, Jesus reaches out to Levi who works as a tax collector. This didn't go over very well with the disciples or with the scribes and Pharisees. The tension between Jesus and the religious authorities continues to escalate because of the people Jesus associated with.

He went out again by the seaside. All the multitude came to him, and he taught them. [14]As he passed by, he saw Levi, the son of Alphaeus, sitting at the tax office, and he said to him, "Follow me." And he arose and followed him. [15]He was reclining at the table in his house, and many tax collectors and sinners sat down with Jesus and his disciples, for there were many, and they followed him. [16]The scribes and the Pharisees, when they saw that he was eating with the sinners and tax collectors, said to his disciples, "Why is it that he eats and drinks with tax collectors and sinners?" [17]When Jesus heard it, he said to them, "Those who are healthy have no need for a physician, but those who are sick. I came not to call the righteous, but sinners to repentance." (Mark 2:13-17)

Jesus was teaching the multitude along the seaside as they came to him. From among the multitude Jesus was teaching, Mark focuses our attention on one man that Jesus encounters—a tax collector named Levi. He issued an invitation to Levi to be his disciple by saying, "Follow me." Levi instantly left the tax collector's booth and followed Jesus. Why did Levi respond with such immediacy to Jesus' invitation? One would assume that Levi had heard of Jesus previously, or actually heard him teach on earlier occasions. After all, Jesus' popularity was ever expanding and he seemed to be the talk of every town in Capernaum.

I can just imagine Jesus looking eye-to-eye with Levi. Something struck a chord in Levi when Jesus said, "Follow me" which caused him to respond with great rapidity to Jesus' invitation. Tax collectors were the most hated people in Jewish society because they were working for the Romans collecting taxes for them. They made a commission on the taxes they collected and were known to be notoriously dishonest. They lined their pockets with dishonest money and Rome turned their back on their practices; so as long as they got their money they were happy.

Tax collectors were excommunicated from the synagogue, and were shamed by their culture. The shame they bore extended to their families. They were in effect the scum of Jewish society, and were considered to be the worst kind of traitor. The tax collectors lived much better than the majority of people, which only made the public resent them all the more. Although tax collectors made a lot of money and lived much better than the majority of people, the shame they bore was extreme. When tax collectors walked about they would get a cold shoulder from everybody and would feel rejection on a grand scale. The only solace they would find would be among each other.

Perhaps, it was this sense of shame Levi bore that caused him to immediately follow Jesus. It may have been that Levi saw in Jesus a way of redeeming himself from the life he chose. It may have been that the shame that he bore wasn't worth it any more and he wanted a second chance in life by aligning himself with Jesus.

Why would Jesus invite a tax collector to follow him? Who would want to have a tax collector as one of the twelve disciples? Who would want anything to do with a hated tax collector—a traitor to the Jews? One would think that Jesus' choice of Levi would rock the boat and the other disciples would reject him, but Jesus knew what he was doing. He had Simon the Zealot on his team and a tax collector. One would think they would be at each other's throats, but it all worked out.

He was reclining at the table in his house, and many tax collectors and sinners sat down with Jesus and his disciples, for there were many, and they followed him. (Mark 2:15)

Levi must be excited about his new friendship with Jesus because he's going to throw a party for Jesus at his house. He invites his friends who are also tax collectors and sinners; after all with whom do tax collectors hang out with? Other tax collectors and sinners, no doubt! That shouldn't be surprising to anybody. Imagine the scene, Levi throws a party and spares no expenses. He's got this one catered with the finest food and wine money can buy. The parallel passage in Luke informs us that Levi threw a "great feast" and there were "great crowds" of tax collectors and sinners at his house (Luke 5:29). He spreads the word to his friends and tells them he's having Jesus over as the guest of honor. You've got to meet him; he's a great teacher so you've got to hear him speak.

Jesus seems to be right at home with this motley crew of people for Mark tells us that there were many that followed Jesus. This is a beautiful picture of how to do outreach. Levi is excited about his relationship with Jesus, so he calls all his friends and has them over to his house to introduce them to him. Jesus brings his disciples along for the ride, which I believe was a teaching experience for them. Jesus is tapping into Levi's network of people so that he can love them and offer them a life of forgiveness and discipleship.

The scribes and the Pharisees, when they saw that he was eating with the sinners and tax collectors, said to his disciples, "Why is it that he eats and drinks with tax collectors and sinners?" (Mark 2:16)

The scribes and Pharisees didn't approve of the company that Jesus kept. When they saw Jesus with the tax collectors and sinners they asked Jesus' disciples why he eats and drinks with people of this sort. Their reaction toward Jesus was what just about anybody would have thought in that day. To be under the same roof and share a meal with tax collectors was a taboo in Jewish culture, especially for a learned rabbi. Perhaps, the scribes and Pharisees were standing at the doorway, and didn't actually come into the house. The disciples might

46

have been in close proximity to the door when they were asked why Jesus associates with these types of people.

I'll bet the disciples may have been asking themselves the same question. They may have thought Jesus should avoid people like this because it could damage his reputation and hurt his ministry. They may have thought they should try to protect Jesus' reputation by staying away from this crew, because people might get the wrong idea about him.

The question they ask the disciples may seem like a no-brainer to the contemporary reader. Jesus wanted to extend his offer of forgiveness and new life to them. The scribes and Pharisees didn't get that. All they could see was Jesus associating with sinners—the scum of the earth. It was considered out of character for a rabbi to associate with sinners, especially to eat with them. The Pharisees thought God's grace was only extended to those who kept the Law of Moses. In their eyes the thought of God accepting sinners who didn't keep the law was a pill they couldn't swallow. Jesus accepted people right where they were at—the good, the bad, and the ugly.

When Jesus heard it, he said to them, "Those who are healthy have no need for a physician, but those who are sick. I came not to call the righteous, but sinners to repentance." (Mark 2:17)

Jesus overheard the conversation and provided an answer to their question. Perhaps the disciples didn't know how to answer the question so Jesus chimed in. Jesus' answer reveals something about the religious leaders that is noteworthy. Those who are healthy are the religious leaders who don't see their need for a spiritual physician. The sick people, who are the sinners and tax collectors, realize their need for a spiritual doctor. Jesus calls those people to repentance. He didn't come to call the righteous, the scribes and Pharisees, but sinners.

One of the things about legalistic people is that they don't see their spiritual need. They view themselves as healthy because they keep the rules. But Jesus sees their righteousness as self-righteousness, which is abhorrent to him. It is extremely hard to reach self-righteous people because they don't see their spiritual need. They are deluded into thinking that because they keep the rules that their culture approves of, that they are in good standing with God.

Conclusion

It is not possible to come to Jesus if one doesn't see his need to be forgiven. If one doesn't view himself as a sinner, how can he repent and express his need for Jesus? The scribes and Pharisees didn't see themselves as having a spiritual need because they kept the law and saw themselves as righteous because of that, but Jesus saw it otherwise. It is almost impossible to convince legalistic people that they have a spiritual need in their life; because they believe they are in good standing with God because they keep the rules. On the other hand, the sinners and tax collectors know they don't keep the rules, and know they aren't in good standing with their Maker, so their spiritual sickness and need is very evident to them. Jesus reaches out to people like this—who see their need for forgiveness and embrace it.

Thus far Levi has made the greatest sacrifice in following Jesus. Once he left his life as a tax collector he couldn't go back. He just burned his bridges behind him with the Romans, and the Jews would have nothing to do with him because of his profession, so it was Jesus or nothing. He had nowhere else to go. He is an example of one who forsook everything to follow Jesus (Mark 8:34).

No doubt, Jesus associating with tax collectors and sinners was disgraceful to the scribes and Pharisees, and deeply offended them. Jesus was breaking cultural taboos by eating with people of this sort, so one can sense the tension growing between the religious leaders and Jesus. In the next chapter we will see how tension continues to escalate as Jesus is questioned about fasting.

Chapter 6 ~ Questions About Fasting

The third conflict episode focuses on fasting, which was a common practice in Judaism. The only mandatory fast was on the Day of Atonement (Lev 16:29), which all Jews had to participate in. Pharisees fasted twice per week, Monday and Thursday, as a sign of piety, while the disciples' of John the Baptist also fasted regularly. They felt it was odd that Jesus' disciples didn't fast in like fashion. It was assumed that the disciples would be like their teacher, who was responsible for their actions. John the Baptist was already in prison and it appears that his disciples were siding with the Pharisees on this issue. To satisfy their curiosity they asked Jesus why his disciples don't fast.

John's disciples and the Pharisees were fasting, and they came and asked him, "Why do John's disciples and the disciples of the Pharisees fast, but your disciples don't fast?" [19]Jesus said to them, "Can the groomsmen fast while the bridegroom is with them? As long as they have the bridegroom with them, they can't fast. [20]But the days will come when the bridegroom will be taken away from them, and then will they fast in that day. [21]No one sews a piece of unshrunk cloth on an old garment, or else the patch shrinks and the new tears away from the old, and a worse hole is made. [22]No one puts new wine into old wineskins, or else the new wine will burst the skins, and the wine pours out, and the skins will be destroyed; but they put new wine into fresh wineskins." (Mark 2:18-22)

Jesus answers their question by pointing to a wedding feast. In Jewish culture a wedding was a time of great celebration with the festival lasting up to seven days. Jesus refers to his disciples as the groomsmen and himself as the bridegroom. At a wedding nobody fasts because all are celebrating the festive occasion. As long as Jesus is with them it is a time for great celebration because the Messiah has appeared. Jesus isn't condemning fasting for he also fasted, but this is the time when people should be celebrating because of his presence. This is the reason his disciples weren't fasting.

Jesus will not be with the disciples for long. He is referring to his death in v. 20, at which time the disciples will mourn and then fasting would be appropriate (John 16:20). The disciples were filled with grief when Jesus was crucified, but their grief eventually turned to joy when they saw the Savior raised from the grave.

No one sews a piece of unshrunk cloth on an old garment, or else the patch shrinks and the new tears away from the old, and a worse hole is made. (Mark 2:21)

Jesus offers an illustration to explain that with his appearance there is something new that will happen on the religious stage of Judaism. He refers to someone who is sewing up a hole in a garment by putting on a patch of unshrunk cloth. Since the garment is old it won't shrink when washed, but the new patch will, resulting in a bigger tear. The point Jesus is making is that he came to do something entirely new. He inaugurated the coming of the Kingdom, and the New Covenant. He came to fulfill the law and bring it to its intended goal. Jesus ushered in a new age for God's people that fulfilled the present practices of Judaism.

The newness that Jesus brought to the stage was incompatible with the present state of Judaism. It was as incompatible as sewing an unshrunk cloth to patch an old garment because it just creates a tear that is worse than the one being fixed. Jesus didn't come to patch up Judaism he came to fulfill it and start something brand new. Putting Jesus into the old form (garment) of Judaism won't work. Jesus was transforming Judaism into an entirely new garment.

No one puts new wine into old wineskins, or else the new wine will burst the skins, and the wine pours out, and the skins will be destroyed; but they put new wine into fresh wineskins."
(Mark 2:22)

Jesus offers another illustration to make the same point he did in v. 21. New wine has to be put in new wine skins because during the fermenting process the skins stretch. If new wine is put into old wineskins they will burst open and the wine is lost. New wine must be put into new wineskins. Jesus is the new wine that is completely incompatible with the old wineskins of Judaism. The new wine Jesus offers must be put into an entirely new form, meaning the old practices of Judaism are fulfilled with his appearance bringing about a new age. Old wineskins can't contain what Jesus has to offer.

The Pharisees and scribes were the guardians of the traditions of Judaism—the old garment, and old wineskins. To accept Jesus meant they had to be willing to part with their legalistic traditions, Temple sacrifices, food regulations, and all the other practices that were engrained in their culture. In order to accept Jesus one needed to be willing to be flexible and forego many traditions they held close to their hearts. Many of the Pharisees and scribes couldn't do that. They held the old garment and old wineskins of Judaism too close to their hearts to part with them and accept Jesus. The religious establishment was in a sense glued to the Law of Moses, which we today call the Old Covenant.

With Jesus a new way of life would emerge that had to destroy the old form of things. It is likely that the banquet at Levi's house, with tax collectors and sinners, was an example of this new manner of life that Jesus was introducing. Ben Witherington III suggests:

> It's also possible that the wedding metaphor that Jesus uses was meant to conjure up the notion that a new covenant was being initiated with new rules about what behavior was and wasn't appropriate. (Witherington, p. 127)

If this is correct, with Jesus' appearance and the initiation of the new Messianic era this is all the more reason to celebrate. The Old Covenant that goes all the way back to Moses is on the way out, to be replaced by something new and far better. From a salvation historical context this is a time for great celebration! Messiah has appeared, is fulfilling the Law and prophets, and ushering in the New Covenant, which is vastly superior to the Old Covenant. This time is what all the prophets were looking ahead to, so it is a time for celebrating, not mourning and fasting. The Pharisees and scribes didn't recognize what was happening in the grand scheme of things regarding the time they were living in. Rather than embracing Jesus, and recognizing how privileged they were to be alive at this time in their history, their adherence to their way of life, ancestral traditions, and strict Torah observance prevented many of them from coming to Jesus and celebrating this epochal moment in history. They couldn't let go of the old to embrace the newness Jesus offered.

This is why many people opposed Jesus with such passion. He threatened their cultural and religious practices that they had been doing for hundreds of years. This was no small matter to over-zealous Pharisees and scribes; that's why they perceived Jesus as a threat to their way of life.

Conclusion

It is important to note that the Jews held on to their ancestral traditions for hundreds of years. They were both religious and cultural. There were cultural norms that weren't compatible with the newness Jesus was introducing. Culturally conditioned behavior that prevents one from experiencing the newness Jesus offers must be overcome. However, this is no small matter to accomplish for people who have been indoctrinated with traditions and practices beginning in their childhood. Jesus is calling for an eradication of the old form of Judaism, so that people can step into the new Messianic era and experience something vastly superior (the new wine and new garment) to that which they were currently experiencing.

Some people may have been indoctrinated with legalistic practices from their infancy. They may have been raised in legalistic families, attended a legalistic church, and been conditioned since childhood to have legalistic attitudes and practices. It isn't easy for them to break free from their culturally conditioned behavior. Like the Pharisees and scribes, it is incredibly difficult for the contemporary believer to cast aside all the legalistic influences exerted on him since childhood. Those of us who don't have any history with legalism may not be able to appreciate how difficult it is for someone to break away from the rules that were imposed in his spiritual upbringing. As we turn our attention back to Mark's gospel, the tension is continuing to mount between Jesus and the religious leaders. In the next episode the controversy extends to the Sabbath and things really get tense.

Chapter 7 ~ Sabbath Controversy

Keeping the Sabbath was of paramount importance to Jewish life. In fact, keeping the Sabbath was one of the major litmus tests of one's piety for the Pharisees. Scripture commanded that no work was to be done on the Sabbath—it was a day of rest, but the question to be answered was: what was considered work? Over the generations the oral tradition was created that defined 39 different types of work that were to be avoided on the Sabbath. If one worked on the Sabbath he was considered to have broken the Sabbath, which was no small matter to the Pharisees (Exo 31:15). One of the things that was considered unlawful to do on the Sabbath was to harvest. This brings us to the fourth controversy that Jesus had with the religious establishment. The reader should note that the resentment and hostility they have toward Jesus is escalating.

He was going on the Sabbath day through the grain fields, and his disciples began, as they went, to pluck the ears of grain. ²⁴The Pharisees said to him, "Behold, why do they do that which is not lawful on the Sabbath day?" ²⁵He said to them, "Did you never read what David did, when he had need, and was hungry—he, and those who were with him? ²⁶How he entered into God's house when Abiathar was high priest, and ate the show bread, which is not lawful to eat except for the priests, and gave also to those who were with him?" ²⁷He said to them, "The Sabbath was made for man, not man for the Sabbath. ²⁸Therefore the Son of Man is lord even of the Sabbath." (Mark 2:23-28)

In this passage, Jesus was taking a stroll with his disciples through a farmer's grain field on a Sabbath. While they were walking they plucked the ears of grain and rubbed them in their hands, then had a snack. To the Pharisees this constituted work because the disciples were harvesting, so they considered this unacceptable behavior—they broke the Sabbath. The Pharisees called Jesus on this, because the teacher is considered responsible for the behavior of his disciples, and asked why they were doing what was unlawful on the Sabbath.

To the modern reader this may seem ridiculous that the Pharisees considered this work, but that's how oppressive the rules and traditions handed down from the ancestors had become. With all the Sabbath regulations they had instituted, the day of rest had become burdensome to the people. Keeping the Sabbath wasn't easy. All the regulations put in place by the religious establishment infringed on the intent of the Sabbath, which was to have a day of rest. It almost required more work to keep the Sabbath than to enjoy it.

Technically speaking, Jesus and his disciples weren't breaking the Sabbath by doing any work. Farming wasn't their day job, and they weren't harvesting for profit. The Law of Moses allowed for what the disciples were doing (Deu 23:25), so God's word wasn't violated, but the Pharisees' rules were. Throughout Jesus' ministry he had many clashes with the Jewish authorities because he didn't observe their rules regarding the Sabbath, but he was always in compliance with God's word.

He said to them, "Did you never read what David did, when he had need, and was hungry—he, and those who were with him? [26]How he entered into God's house when Abiathar was high priest, and ate the show bread, which is not lawful to eat except for the priests, and gave also to those who were with him?" (Mark 2:25-26)

The incident Jesus is referring to is recorded in 1 Samuel 21:1-6. King David was on the run from Saul and paid a visit to Abiathar the high priest. In the Samuel passage Ahimelech is mentioned as the high priest, but Abiathar was his son and successor. David and his men were hungry, so he asked the priest for loaves of bread. The only bread available at the moment was the Bread of the Presence. Twelve loaves of bread were consecrated to the Lord, representing the twelve tribes of Israel, and were placed on a table in the Tabernacle, which David calls God's house. After its use only the priests could eat this bread. Fresh bread had been placed on the table, so Abiathar gave the old bread to David.

God didn't punish David for doing what was unlawful, nor did he punish Abiathar the priest for giving David the bread. Technically speaking they broke the law, but there is a greater principle that Jesus brings to the surface. Human need supersedes various aspects of the ceremonial law. Was harm done, or was good accomplished by giving David the bread? Jesus answered the Pharisees by saying, "Did you never read what David did?" implying that they should know this. Certainly, they had read the story many times and had complete familiarity with it, but they missed its meaning. They were unable to grasp the significance of the event, or grasp its application for their own day. This should have been elementary teaching to the Pharisees, but it was over their heads!

Abiathar apparently saw that the need of David, and his men was greater than the need to keep the technicalities of the law. At times compassion for people in their suffering has to take precedence over keeping the rigid details of the law. In essence, Jesus was saying if you accuse me of being guilty, you also have to charge David of being guilty. The Pharisees and scribes were lacking in compassion, which is something that Jesus indicted them for in Matthew 23:23. They focused on all the details of the law, but did so in a matter that was uncaring toward the people.

He said to them, "The Sabbath was made for man, not man for the Sabbath. ²⁸Therefore the Son of Man is lord even of the Sabbath." (Mark 2:27-28)

Jesus now states the divine intent of the Sabbath, which the Pharisees had lost sight of. The Sabbath was instituted to benefit mankind by providing a day of rest. The normal grind of the workweek comes to a screeching halt on the Sabbath so one is able to recharge his battery. A day of rest is a good thing. However, the Jews in their obsession to define what constituted work, came up with things that made the Sabbath a burden and overthrew God's intent for the day.

Jesus' point is the Sabbath was made to serve man by giving him a break from the daily routine of life. He was freed up to worship God, relax, spend time with family, and have an enjoyable day. The Pharisees had it the other way around: they thought the Sabbath was

56

created so that man could serve it. With all the Sabbath regulations they imposed, keeping the Sabbath was like being put in a legalistic straightjacket. The freedom that the day was designed to offer people was taken away so that the Sabbath was like going to jail for the day. They had inadvertently made themselves lord's of the Sabbath through the imposition of their regulations.

What Jesus said next, no doubt, ruffled their feathers: "Therefore the Son of Man is Lord even of the Sabbath" (v. 28). Jesus has every right to assert his Lordship over the Sabbath because he created it. As the Son of Man, Messiah, and God's only begotten Son, who was given authority by God, he is Lord over the Sabbath.

By making this declaration he is claiming the right to overrule the Sabbath regulations imposed by the Pharisees and bring the day back to its original intent. Jesus captured the spirit of the law and applied it to everyday life with compassion and mercy. The Pharisees were wrapped up in the minutia of every detail of the letter of the law, and applied it without compassion and mercy toward the people.

Jesus had the right to overturn all the Sabbath regulations of the Pharisees, which was unacceptable to them and considered heresy. Mark doesn't record their reaction to Jesus' words, but it can be safely concluded that they weren't very happy about what Jesus said. He directly challenged their Sabbath practices and claimed authority to negate their Sabbath rules. The hostility between Jesus and the Pharisees continues to escalate.

Conclusion

The Sabbath was a gift that God gave to the people so they could have a day of rest. However, what God creates for the benefit of man is often improperly utilized and becomes burdensome. The religious leaders viewed the Sabbath through the lens of a microscope, such that they added more-and-more rules and restrictions. This almost served the purpose of making the Sabbath a day of work, rather than a day of rest. In Jewish life observing the Sabbath was a vital test of one's piety and devotion to God. The Pharisees and scribes would not tolerate anybody challenging or defying their Sabbath practices. The fact that Jesus did just that was intolerable to them, as the next episode points out.

Chapter 8 ~ Things Have Gone Too Far

This episode is the fifth, and final, in a series of conflict encounters that Jesus had with the Pharisees and scribes. The conflict controversies reach their zenith with the Pharisees and Herodians plotting Jesus' death. He had posed such a threat to them that things went over the top with his adversaries determining he had to go. Breaking their Sabbath regulations was too much for them to bear, and appears to be the straw that broke the camel's back.

He entered again into the synagogue, and there was a man there who had his hand withered. ²They watched him, whether he would heal him on the Sabbath day, that they might accuse him. ³He said to the man who had his hand withered, "Stand up." ⁴He said to them, "Is it lawful on the Sabbath day to do good, or to do harm? To save a life, or to kill?" But they were silent. ⁵When he had looked around at them with anger, being grieved at the hardening of their hearts, he said to the man, "Stretch out your hand." He stretched it out, and his hand was restored as healthy as the other. ⁶The Pharisees went out, and immediately conspired with the Herodians against him, how they might destroy him. (Mark 3:1-6)

Every Sabbath Jesus went to a synagogue; most likely in this story he is in Capernaum. There was a man with a withered hand in attendance. Whether he was born that way, or if his hand was injured, is not known; but his right hand (Luke 6:6) was out of commission. This appears to be a setup. The Pharisees may have manipulated the situation so that they brought him in the synagogue to see if Jesus would heal him. They were looking for a way to accuse Jesus of being a Sabbath-breaker, so they may have baited Jesus to do what they considered unlawful. They wanted to discredit Jesus publically and bring him down. Evidently Jesus saw through their plotting and ordered the man with the withered hand to stand so all could see what he would do.

No work was to be done on the Sabbath according to Scripture. If a man's life was at stake then the Jews Sabbath regulations allowed for doctors to practice their profession and work on the Sabbath. However, if the man's life wasn't in danger, then healing was to be suspended until the next day. The man with the withered hand wasn't in a life-threatening situation, so Jesus could have met him the following day and healed him at that time. It is important to note that the Pharisees didn't question Jesus' ability to heal, for they knew he had the power to do that. They had seen him in action before. The issue is whether he would heal on the Sabbath and break their regulations, and whether his power-source was Satan (Mark 3:22).

Jesus' question is directed to the Pharisees, but brings to the surface something about the divine intent of the Sabbath.

He said to them, "Is it lawful on the Sabbath day to do good, or to do harm? To save a life, or to kill?" But they were silent. (Mark 3:4)

The Pharisees were silent as Jesus waited for them to answer. They wouldn't debate Jesus. The answer to Jesus' question is obvious. The Sabbath was intended for the benefit of man so to heal the man is considered a good thing. Imparting life on the Sabbath and setting the man free from his handicap was all good. The parallel passage in Matthew brings out another point that Jesus made:

> He said to them, "What man is there among you, who has one sheep, and if this one falls into a pit on the Sabbath day, won't he grab on to it, and lift it out? [12]Of how much more value then is a man than a sheep! Therefore it is lawful to do good on the Sabbath day." (Mat 12:11-12)

If a man can rescue a lamb on the Sabbath, how much more can Jesus heal a man on the Sabbath, for people are far more important than animals.

When he had looked around at them with anger, being grieved at the hardening of their hearts, he said to the man, "Stretch out your hand." He stretched it out, and his hand was restored as healthy as

the other. ⁶The Pharisees went out, and immediately conspired with the Herodians against him, how they might destroy him. (Mark 3:5-6)

It is rare to find places in the Scripture where Jesus is recorded as having righteous anger (John 2:14-16). He was deeply grieved at the hardness of their hearts. Grieved is the Greek word *sullupeo,* which is written as a present participle denoting continuous action. The significance of this is that Jesus was grieved at the Pharisees' hard-heartedness, not for a brief moment, but it was a continuous grief. Jesus had anger over their obtuse hearts, but felt compassion for his adversaries as well.

Righteous anger over the things that hurt people is necessary, as any pastor should know, but that anger must be tempered with compassion or it will lead to animosity. Compassion without righteous anger will lead to tolerance of the very things that plague the human condition. Jesus had both these qualities in the right proportion.

The Lord ordered him to stretch out his hand, and it was as good as new—just as healthy as his other hand. The healing seems to be instantaneous. Strictly speaking Jesus didn't do any work, he just told the man to stretch out his hand. The Jews didn't object to Jesus speaking. One can only imagine how the man felt. His shame and embarrassment has been taken away, his handicap is gone, and he can live a normal life now. This is cause for celebration in that life has been enhanced and restored on the Sabbath.

One might think that the Pharisees would have rejoiced with the man who just had his hand healed, but they didn't. They displayed no compassion for the man whatsoever for they had withered hearts that needed to be healed. In their way of thinking Jesus had crossed a serious line with them and he had to be stopped, so they plotted with the Herodians how they might kill him. The Herodians were a political sect that supported the Herods and were pro-Roman. They actually had very little in common with the Pharisees until Jesus appeared and then they united against him as their common enemy. Jesus' talk of a Kingdom threatened the Herodians' position with the Romans, and Jesus' lack of regard for their traditions posed a threat to the Pharisees that they couldn't ignore. For these reasons they conspired together about how to do away with Jesus.

This episode reveals that the Pharisees were Sabbath breakers. It was they who had evil thoughts in their hearts and did what was unlawful on the Sabbath—not Jesus. The Messiah wanted to restore a man's hand while the Pharisees were plotting to trap Jesus and then how to kill him. Who did the will of God on the Sabbath, Jesus or the Pharisees?

This episode is filled with irony. Jesus heals, thereby imparting life to man, but in so doing puts his own life at risk. Jesus does good on the Sabbath and is rewarded by being plotted against by the religious leaders of the day, who should have been the guiding light of morality for the nation. The response of the Pharisees reveals that their hearts are as withered as the man's hand before Jesus healed him.

Application and Insights

I've been a pastor for over 30 years and prayed for people during services; in fact, I've had healing services where people were anointed with oil in the name of the Lord and prayed for. If a long time member of the congregation who had a withered hand stood up during a Sunday morning worship service, and was prayed for, then healed instantly by the Lord, everybody would be praising God. I'm sure there may be a few skeptics present, but the overwhelming majority would rejoice about the healing.

To see a miracle take place right before their eyes and display no emotion whatsoever reveals the depth of their hardness of heart toward Jesus. They showed no regard for the man in that they used him as an object to be manipulated to trap Jesus. They attributed his power to Satan and couldn't tolerate his disregard for their Sabbath regulations. The hostilities escalated throughout these five episodes ending with people plotting Jesus' death. It was the Sabbath controversy where things went over the top.

It would be interesting for Christians to consider what activities they think are inappropriate to do on Sundays and why. Do they view Sunday in a similar way to the Sabbath as a day of rest? Do they view Sunday as completely disconnected from the Old Testament rules regarding the Sabbath? Each person needs to probe deep into his heart and ask why he feels certain activities must be refrained from on Sunday. Where do these views come from: Scripture, culture, one's upbringing, or church culture?

Why Such Hostility Toward Jesus?

Jesus was considered to be a counter-cultural person who went against the grain of Jewish society. The status quo didn't work for Jesus. Jewish cultural mores that had been in existence for generations had to go with the newness that Jesus offers. Jesus' new wine couldn't be put into the religious cultural wine skins that contained the old wine of Judaism. To embrace Jesus the old had to go, which is precisely why many people had such a hard time with him. One has to place himself in the shoes of each group of people to understand how threatened they were by Jesus. Ben Witherington III makes a comment that is apropos to this discussion:

> There is a sense in which he (Jesus) asked each group in Israelite society to give up what was most dear to them in order to embrace him. To the disciples the challenge meant giving up family and job, to the Pharisees it meant giving up their position of chief religious figures of their age, to the scribes it meant giving up being the providers of the correct interpretation of the oral and written Torah, for Sadducees and priests it was to mean giving up a certain kind of temple-centered approach to Judaism, for ordinary Jews it meant giving up certain attitudes about the moral outcasts and the diseased in society. The wonder is not that Jesus was eventually rejected by all these groups, but that he was not rejected and killed sooner. (Witherington, p. 134)

What Jesus required these groups to give up was more than many could part with. If they accepted Jesus it would turn their life upside down, bring persecution, economic privation, loss of social standing, and more. There was a lot at stake in becoming a follower of Jesus.

The deeper people go into legalism the more violent their reaction will be to those who challenge their practices, and oppose them. The legalistic practices were so dear to the hearts of the Pharisees that they plotted Jesus' death with the Herodians.

Conclusion

The deeper people go into legalistic behavior the harder it is for them to break free of the things that keep them bound and cause them spiritual harm. When people try to help them break free from legalism their response will often be harsh and violent. In fact, they may not even consider themselves to be legalistic, and don't see that they are in any type of spiritual bondage or oppression. They may think they are Bible-believing Christians who are living obediently for God. I don't think the Pharisees and scribes saw themselves as legalists.

Some people find comfort in being inside a legalistic box. By keeping the rules they derive a sense of security that they are pleasing God. If someone challenges these rules, or tries to inform them that they are unnecessary to follow, do not be surprised if their reaction is harsh. When someone tries to inform a legalist that their practices are not based on Scripture, they will be threatened because you are challenging what gives them a sense of security and comfort.

In the next chapter, another passage in Mark's gospel will be examined that depicts how the oral traditions of the religious leaders actually supplanted the word of God. Of course, the tension continues to escalate as Jesus calls them on their hypocrisy and disregard for God's word.

Chapter 9 ~ The Traditions of Men

The passage below (Mark 7:1-13) reveals how Jesus is investigated by a delegation of leaders that comes from Jerusalem, which is the hub of Jewish life. The Temple is located there, the sacrifices are made there, and it is the place where God's presence is manifested in the Most Holy Place, where the Ark of the Covenant resided, until it disappeared in 586 BC when the Babylonians sacked Jerusalem. The Sanhedrin, which is the ruling body of Israel, convenes there and is presided over by the High Priest. Jews from all over travel to Jerusalem for the Passover celebration. Jerusalem is the center, where all the ancestral traditions thrive, where famous rabbis and scribes study and teach their students. Jerusalem is the epicenter of Jewish life.

When the delegation arrives they see his disciples eating with unwashed hands thereby violating the traditions of the elders. What Jesus brings to the surface is that the truth of God's word has to take precedence over the traditions of the elders. Additionally, this passage provides the reader with insights into how the Jews regarded cleanness, or holiness. Is a person to be regarded as holy because of the inner state of the heart that loves God and desires to do his will? Or is a person considered holy (clean) because he conforms to an outward code of behavior that has nothing to do with the inner condition of the heart?

Jesus focused on the truth of God's word and advocated holiness that stemmed from the heart, while the Pharisees and scribes focused on their traditions and advocated holiness that was rooted in conformity to an outward code. This delegation may have been sanctioned by the Sanhedrin to go on a fact-finding mission regarding Jesus.

The Pharisees and some of the scribes gathered around Him when they had come from Jerusalem, ²and had seen that some of His disciples were eating their bread with impure hands, that is,

unwashed. ³(For the Pharisees and all the Jews do not eat unless they carefully wash their hands, *thus* observing the traditions of the elders; ⁴and *when they come* from the market place, they do not eat unless they cleanse themselves; and there are many other things which they have received in order to observe, such as the washing of cups and pitchers and copper pots.) ⁵The Pharisees and the scribes asked Him, "Why do Your disciples not walk according to the tradition of the elders, but eat their bread with impure hands?" ⁶And He said to them, "Rightly did Isaiah prophesy of you hypocrites, as it is written:

'THIS PEOPLE HONORS ME WITH THEIR LIPS, BUT THEIR HEART IS FAR AWAY FROM ME. ⁷'BUT IN VAIN DO THEY WORSHIP ME, TEACHING AS DOCTRINES THE PRECEPTS OF MEN.'

⁸Neglecting the commandment of God, you hold to the tradition of men." ⁹He was also saying to them, "You are experts at setting aside the commandment of God in order to keep your tradition. ¹⁰For Moses said, 'HONOR YOUR FATHER AND YOUR MOTHER'; and, 'HE WHO SPEAKS EVIL OF FATHER OR MOTHER, IS TO BE PUT TO DEATH'; ¹¹but you say, 'If a man says to *his* father or *his* mother, whatever I have that would help you is Corban (that is to say, given *to God*),' ¹²you no longer permit him to do anything for *his* father or *his* mother; ¹³*thus* invalidating the word of God by your tradition which you have handed down; and you do many things such as that." (Mark 7:1-13)

In Jewish life the teacher was held responsible for the actions of his disciples, so they questioned Jesus about why his disciples eat bread with unwashed hands, which was alarming to the delegation. Their concern had nothing to do with practicing good hygiene; this was about washing so that one would be considered ceremonially clean according to their traditions (vv. 1-2).

(For the Pharisees and all the Jews do not eat unless they carefully wash their hands, *thus* observing the traditions of the elders; ⁴and *when they come* from the market place, they do not eat unless they cleanse themselves; and there are many other things which they have received in order to observe, such as the washing of cups and pitchers and copper pots.) (Mark 7:3-4)

In vv. 3-4 Mark is providing a commentary for his Roman audience that was unfamiliar with Jewish customs about practices regarding washing, and ceremonial cleanness and uncleanness. Before eating Jews would carefully wash their hands, because if they contacted anything unclean they themselves would be unclean. If they went to the marketplace, they might touch a Gentile, a sinner, or a Jew who was not Torah observing. There were many ways in which a Jew might become unclean in everyday life, so it was of paramount importance to practice this washing ritual and be found in a state of ritual purity. When a Jew would return from the marketplace, or before eating dinner, she would go through a hand-washing ritual to make herself ceremonially clean. The origin of this practice may go back to the laver in the tabernacle where the priests would wash their hands and feet before they would perform their duties (Ex 30:17-21). Their oral tradition extended this practice to all Jews to be done before eating and committing formal prayers to God.

Mark adds that there are many other things to be observed such as washing cups, pitchers, and copper pots. Before these items could be used they had to be washed on the outside. If touched by a sinner, without it being washed, when the user touched the item they would be considered unclean. These laws were exhaustive and tried to control every aspect of one's life. The detail was extreme and virtually impossible to be followed perfectly.

The problem is that these are called "traditions of the elders." These stipulations were not the word of God; rather, they were man-made additions to the word of God that were considered to be just as important and binding as the Scripture. The word translated "tradition" is the Greek word *parádosis*, which is a compound word consisting of *pará* (close or beside) and *dídōmi* (give over). Therefore, the idea of this word is to give over from close beside. In the context of the passage at hand it refers to the elder's traditions being "handed over from close beside" one generation to the next.

Mark is referring to the oral interpretation of the law, which goes back to the Jews' return from exile in Babylon. The Jews felt a need to put a fence around the law because they feared the influence of the Gentiles might dilute the word of God, so they generated oral traditions that provided commentary on the law that were written down around 200 A.D. in the Mishnah. Wherever the law was vague about a specific practice the oral tradition would provide precise instructions about how it should be practiced. These traditions governed every aspect of daily life and were considered by the rabbis to be as binding as the Scripture. The Pharisees and the scribes prided themselves as being the guardians of these traditions. It is these oral traditions that Jesus and the establishment butted heads over.

The Pharisees and the scribes asked Him, "Why do Your disciples not walk according to the tradition of the elders, but eat their bread with impure hands?" ⁶And He said to them, "Rightly did Isaiah prophesy of you hypocrites, as it is written: 'THIS PEOPLE HONORS ME WITH THEIR LIPS, BUT THEIR HEART IS FAR AWAY FROM ME. ⁷'BUT IN VAIN DO THEY WORSHIP ME, TEACHING AS DOCTRINES THE PRECEPTS OF MEN.' (Mark 7:5-7)

The religious leaders question Jesus about his disciples. They wanted to know why Jesus didn't instruct his men in their ancestral traditions, so that they were in compliance with their regulations. Jesus doesn't answer the question directly, he gets right to the heart of the issue with brutal honesty and bluntness by calling out their hypocrisy by quoting Isaiah 29:13.

Jesus called the religious leaders hypocrites many times. Hypocrites have double standards, and present themselves as something they are not. By quoting from Isaiah Jesus is implying that the present religious establishment is just as hypocritical as the leaders were back in Isaiah's day. The condition of their hearts was similar to the spirituality displayed in Isaiah's time. This is a serious indictment of the leaders' defective spirituality.

The Isaiah quote reveals that like the leaders back in Isaiah's day the present religious leaders were just paying God lip service. They could talk it up for God and sound really spiritual, but when it comes to their hearts they were far away from God. Their speech sounded really good, but the condition of their hearts is less than what it should be. This is serious, especially when considering that the Jews recited the Shema twice a day:

"Hear, O Israel! The Lord is our God, the Lord is one! [5]You shall love the Lord your God with all your heart and with all your soul and with all your might. (Deu 6:4-5)

They recited this but their hearts weren't filled with love for God, they were distant from God— void of love for him. When they recited this it was meaningless repetition to God. Their worship was in "vain," which translates the Greek word *mátēn,* which has a range of meaning including: aimless, pointless, without ground, no real purpose, or no real fruitfulness. The worship experience of the religious leaders of Jesus' day *was lacking any real purpose* because they "were teaching as doctrines the precepts of men." Rather than making the focus of their teaching the word of God, they set forth the "doctrines and precepts of men," which is a reference to the volumes of oral traditions that Jesus strenuously objected to.

Any time the teaching of men takes precedence over the teaching of God's word it becomes pointless, lacking any real purpose that will please God, or edify the people. Their worship of God was without foundation of the word so it was fruitless. This is a sad commentary on the spiritual leaders of Jesus' day. The Lord is now going to indict them by providing a specific example of how their traditions, doctrines, and precepts have invalidated a critical part of God's word.

Neglecting the commandment of God, you hold to the tradition of men." [9]He was also saying to them, "You are experts at setting aside the commandment of God in order to keep your tradition. [10]For Moses said, 'HONOR YOUR FATHER AND YOUR MOTHER'; and, 'HE WHO SPEAKS EVIL OF FATHER OR MOTHER, IS TO BE PUT TO DEATH'; [11]but you say, 'If a man says to *his* father or *his* mother, whatever I have that would help you is Corban (that is to say, given *to God*),' [12]you no longer permit him to do anything for *his* father or *his* mother; [13]*thus invalidating the word of God by your tradition which you have handed down; and you do many things such as that. (Mark 7:8-13)

Jesus establishes a contrast between the "command of God" and their "traditions." They have "neglected the command of God and hold to the tradition of men." The word "neglecting" is a translation of the

Greek word *aphiémi*, which has the following range of meaning: send away, release, remit, forgive, and permit. They have "sent away" the word of God but "hold to" the tradition of men. It should be the other way around—they have it backwards. They "sent away" is written in the aorist tense denoting action occurring in the past, but they "hold to" is in the present tense indicating an ongoing practice of keeping their traditions.

Their expertise lies in "setting aside" the commandment of God so that they can "keep" their traditions. The Greek word *atheteō* is translated "setting aside." The word carries with it the idea of rejecting something that has been laid down, to disregard and to make void. God laid down his word to be obeyed and was to be the foundation of their lives, but they "set aside" the commandments so that their traditions took precedence over the Scripture.

The specific example that Jesus cites to prove his point refers to one of the Ten Commandments:

For Moses said, 'HONOR YOUR FATHER AND YOUR MOTHER'; and, 'HE WHO SPEAKS EVIL OF FATHER OR MOTHER, IS TO BE PUT TO DEATH' (Mark 7:10)

Jesus quotes Moses most likely because the religious leaders claimed their traditions went back to him. Honor your father and your mother (Ex 20:12; Deu 5:16) was the expectation placed upon children to treat their parents respectfully and provide care for them when needed. Parents were always to be honored and held in high regard. To get an idea of how serious this commandment was in Jewish life it is stated negatively in Exodus 21:17: "He who speaks evil of Father or Mother, is to be put to death." This command is serious business! One must treat his parents with dignity and respect or it could cost them their life.

but you say, 'If a man says to *his* father or *his* mother, whatever I have that would help you is Corban (that is to say, given *to God*),' ¹²you no longer permit him to do anything for *his* father or *his* mother; ¹³*thus* invalidating the word of God by your tradition which you have handed down; and you do many things such as that. (Mark 7:11-13)

In contrast to what Moses says, "but you say" shows their disregard for Moses' command. Declaring something Corban (literally meaning offering) is devoting something exclusively to God for sacred use. In other words, money that could have been used to care for one's dependent parents was declared Corban, but wasn't given to the Temple. When taking the vow of Corban the person retains control of his money, and can use it any way he wants, but he could use the Corban vow as an excuse not to give any money to his needy parents. The Corban vow was irrevocable so once it was made that was it. The Corban vow became a religiously acceptable way of neglecting one's parents under the guise of spirituality. One might be considered very pious to devote his money to Corban, but it was a sham, it was a way to circumvent caring for his parents, yet retaining control of his funds.

Because the vow was binding the Pharisees wouldn't allow someone to change his mind so that he could offer assistance to his parents, thus Jesus says: "you no longer permit him to do anything for his father or his mother." Their traditions were selfishly based and if someone did want to help his parents after making the Corban vow, the Pharisees wouldn't permit it.

The conclusion Jesus makes is: "*thus* invalidating the word of God by your tradition which you have handed down; and you do many things such as that" (v. 13). To invalidate the word of God is a serious thing. To exempt oneself from keeping one of the commands by taking the Corban vow was just one example of how the Pharisees had invalidated, or made God's word void. This tradition was taught and handed down from one generation to the next, which was just one of many traditions that supplanted the word of God, for Jesus said: "you do many things such as that." There was a long list of their practices that Jesus could have specifically cited that overturned God's commandments. The Corban vow was just one example.

Insights and Application

The Pharisees pose a great irony to me as well as many others. In their attempt to protect God's word their traditions actually nullified it. The original intent of their oral traditions was lost and they had become, in their minds, just as authoritative as God's word. If one didn't accept and practice their traditions they were considered to be out of compliance with God's word.

This episode shows how the leaders were destroying the very laws they were trying to preserve. The intent of developing an oral tradition when they first started may have been noble, but somewhere down the line they completely lost their perspective on the role their traditions played in Jewish life. They meticulously studied the Scripture, and were zealous for God, but they came to a place where they elevated their traditions above God's word because they felt that holiness was achieved by adherence to an outward code.

Ben Witherington III makes a noteworthy observation:

> One might say that the Jesus movement and the Pharisaic movement were both holiness movements, but they disagreed on the proper approach to creating a holy people of God. (Witherington, p. 227)

To miss how holiness ties into the oral tradition would be to miss a critical part of the argument. The Jews thought holiness (being clean vs. unclean) could be attained by keeping their rules and regulations. In other words, holiness was attained through their legalistic practices. Jesus, on the other hand, saw holiness stemming from one's heart that was transformed through God's love. Holiness resulted from a transformed heart on the inside. Once a sinner is transformed by their relationship with Christ, behavior that is pleasing to God will naturally follow. Thus, there are two issues to keep in focus: one is that the Pharisees supplanted the word of God for their traditions, and the other is in their perspective of holiness. On both issues Jesus disagreed with them.

Legalism and Traditions

What was true of the religious leaders of Jesus' day is very true of legalistic people today. What makes one holy is keeping a set of rules: don't drink, don't smoke, don't dance, don't chew tobacco, etc. If one doesn't do these things he is considered by many Christians to be a righteousness person. On the other hand, if a believer does any of these things he is considered by some to be an immature Christian, or may even be labeled a "carnal Christian" who needs to tighten things up regarding his sanctification.

People have a way of placing too high a value on traditions. If utilized properly traditions can greatly enhance worship and facilitate one's experience with God. For example, regarding music we have 2,000 years of different music that was played in worshiping God. Familiarizing oneself with the rich diversity of ways that people worshiped God over the millennia can be an enriching experience. But when traditions begin to supplant the word of God it has gone too far. When believers in Christ elevate their traditions to a place where the measure of one's holiness becomes adherence to those traditions, it goes too far. For some believers, the type of music one employs to worship is a measure of their holiness: hymns, contemporary music, liturgical, free flowing, etc. For some believers holiness is measured by a dress code: women wearing hats, men wearing suits and ties, etc.

It would be interesting for every believer to probe deep into his heart and ask himself where some of the things that he regularly practices come from. Is it the word of God? Is it their church culture? Is it his upbringing? Is it an influential person in his life?

The deeper people go into traditions the more difficult it is for them to let go of. They don't see themselves as being in bondage, but they are. Not only that, but the deeper people go into holding on to their traditions the more violent their reaction will be to people who disagree with them. They may react in a way that is hostile and antagonistic toward people who question some of their practices. The religious leaders reacted so vehemently against Jesus that they plotted his death, and succeeded.

Legalistic people usually derive their assurance of salvation by focusing on their behavior. They keep all the rules and may display pridefulness like the Pharisees about their obedience. Their legalistic practices give them a sense of security with God, such that they feel they are in good standing with him. This too is misguided.

The hypocrisy of the Pharisees was in that they felt righteousness was a matter of outward behavior. They presented themselves as something they were not. They looked great on the outside, but inwardly, where it really matters, they were far away from God. Hence, they were hypocrites. They were intolerant of Jesus, because he opposed their legalistic traditions. They were very inflexible and unwilling to accept other people's point of view regarding their traditions. In my experience, this is a characteristic of legalistic people today. Try to change their mind on some of their practices and you will find them to be inflexible and unbending to change, or often times, reason as well.

Conclusion

In the previous chapters we have stepped into the world of the First Century and examined some of the conflicts that Jesus had with the religious authorities over their legalistic traditions. Both sides in the conflict narratives reacted strongly to the other. The conflicts were serious matters that weren't taken lightly by Jesus or the authorities. However, Jesus had compassion for his opponents and hoped that they would see the light, but they didn't. The religious leaders became allies in plotting to do away with Jesus altogether. Their traditions, and teaching as doctrines the precepts of men, took precedence over the word of God. Any time that happens the results will be disastrous, for legalism always puts people under an unnecessary degree of spiritual trauma and oppression.

In the next chapter, we will examine the essentials of the gospel to see how far off course people are who advocate a combination of faith plus good works to be accepted and forgiven by God.

Chapter 10 ~ Legalism Can Block the Way of Salvation

This chapter will focus on a variety of legalism that adds good works as a requirement for man's salvation, along with believing in Christ. There is nothing new or novel about this, for it has existed throughout the millennia. Scripture portrays a sinner's salvation as a free gift from God, having nothing to do with any goodness in the sinner whatsoever (Rom 3:23-24). In other words, a sinner's good deeds will never secure her a right standing with God. This is what Paul meant when he said "by the works of the law no one will be justified" (Rom 3:20; Gal 3:16-17). The foundation of a sinner's salvation is Jesus' death on the cross. The sinner's response to the gospel call is faith and repentance. In this chapter we will look at the essentials of the gospel and see how the false gospel of legalism completely undermines God's plan for the salvation of sinners, and can block the pathway to heaven for those who seek to know God.

The Importance of Jesus' Death

What exactly happened when Jesus died on the cross? Christians like to throw around the phase: Jesus died for you! The death of Jesus is the heart of the gospel, along with the resurrection (Rom 4:25), but it's crucial for everyone to understand why Jesus died and how that contributes to their salvation.

The human race was guilty of sin and deserving of God's punishment (Rom 1:18-20). God took the initiative and sent his Son to do what we couldn't do for ourselves regarding our sin problem (Rom 5:8). If Jesus hadn't come to earth we would still be making animal sacrifices, if the Temple were in existence, living under the Old Covenant. Blood had to be shed for the forgiveness of sins, which gives us a clue as to how costly atoning for sin can be (Heb 9:22; 1 Pet 18-19). The author of Hebrews made it clear that the sacrifices that were made at the

Temple could never make worshipers of God perfect, which is why sacrifices were continually repeated year-after-year (Heb 10:1-4). All the sacrifices pointed ahead to Jesus, as the Lamb of God (John 1:29; 1 Pet 1:19), who would fulfill the sacrificial system and make it obsolete. By Jesus' one sacrifice there is no need to ever make another animal sacrifice to God (Heb 9:26-28; 10:10; 14).

Substitutionary Atonement

Jesus is both fully human and fully divine. He is the only person in world history that bears that distinction, which qualified him alone to atone for the sins of mankind. Unlike the rest of humanity Jesus didn't have a sin nature. He lived a perfectly sinless life before God, which qualified him to atone for humanity's sins (2 Cor 5:21). If Jesus had sinned one time his death would have been meaningless, and he wouldn't have been able to be the propitiation for the sin's of man.

Jesus identified with the human condition by becoming one of us as Hebrews 2:17 points out:

> Therefore, He had to be made like His brethren in all things, so that He might become a merciful and faithful high priest in things pertaining to God, to make propitiation for the sins of the people.

Jesus is known as our substitute because as a fully human being he died in the place of humanity. He represented the entire human race when he died on the cross, thus he was the substitute of humans. In that sense when people say: "Jesus died for you" that's exactly what he did. He died in your place and bore the punishment for your sins that you deserved to bear.

In the above passage, Jesus made *propitiation* for the sins of the people, which translates the Greek word *hiláskomai*. The meaning of the word is: to appease an offended party, satisfy God's wrath toward sin, or atone. When Jesus died God the Father was propitiated, in the sense that his wrath toward sin was poured out on his Son, and sin was atoned for. God's wrath toward sin was appeased. Punishing

76

Jesus in our place had satisfied God's justice, such that there is no further punishment for sin that is required.

Imputing Our Sin to Jesus

Scripture speaks about imputing in three different ways. The first is that Adam's original sin had been imputed to the rest of mankind such that we are all sinners, with Adam as the head of the human race (Rom 5:12). The second way imputation is described is the sin of the world past, present, and future was imputed to Jesus when he was on the cross (2 Cor 5:21). God punished Jesus for the sins of mankind in our place. The third way imputation is mentioned in Scripture is when the sinner becomes a believer in Christ, Jesus' righteousness is imputed to him, such that God considers Christ's righteousness belonging to the new believer (Rom 4:22-25). This is considered a gift to the new convert (Rom 5:17).

When Jesus was dying on the cross God imputed the sin of mankind to him. In other words, God considered the guilt of man's sin belonging to Jesus, even though he was totally innocent and righteousness. Matthew records in his gospel the precise moment when that happened.

> About the ninth hour Jesus cried out with a loud voice, saying, "ELI, ELI, LAMA SABACHTHANI?" that is, "MY GOD, MY GOD, WHY HAVE YOU FORSAKEN ME?" (Matthew 27:46)

During all the horrific pain and suffering Jesus endured at the hands of his tormentors he was always silent (Isa 53:7). However, Matthew records Jesus as having "cried out with a loud voice...My God, my God, why have you forsaken me?" It was at that point that God imputed the sin of mankind to his Son. The guilt of mans' sin belonged to Jesus, God punished him in our place, and he experienced God's unmitigated wrath poured out on him for the sins' of mankind. That's why he cried out, "Why have you forsaken me?" In his humanity he felt separation from God that sin brings as he was punished for our transgressions.

God demonstrated his love for us by sending his son (Rom 5:8). God's justice has been satisfied (Rom 3:25-26) in that sin has been punished for all time through Christ's one sacrifice and is totally effective in saving sinners. God's desire is that all people repent and believe so they can be reconciled to him (John 14:6; Acts 17:30). Since sin has been atoned for and God has been propitiated, the Father doesn't desire to punish anyone for their sins, because Jesus has already been punished in their place (2 Pet 3:9). For a person to reap the benefits of Jesus' death he must place his trust in Jesus and repent of his sins (John 1:12-13; 3:16; Acts 2:28; 17:30).

Jesus' Death Was Entirely Efficacious

Scripture makes it clear that Jesus death was totally efficacious to atone for the sin of the world, meaning that there is nothing else that God had to do for our salvation. Jesus' death was all that was needed to pay the penalty for our sins, so the entire sacrificial system of the Old Testament is now obsolete, for it has been fulfilled in Christ (Heb 10:1-14). All the sacrifices pointed ahead to the Lamb of God (John 1:29) who would fulfill the Temple sacrifices and bring us into the age of the New Covenant, which is superior to the Old Covenant that Jesus fulfilled (Heb 8).

Everything has been done! God doesn't want to punish sinners because he already punished Jesus in their place so they can be forgiven. All the work has been done, so the only thing the sinner needs to do is respond to the gospel invitation with faith and repentance.

Those who advocate the position that one needs to place his trust in Christ for salvation, but add good works of some type to be accepted by God are making a grave error. Did Jesus' death atone for our sins or not? Was God the Father propitiated or wasn't he? Was his death only partially efficacious? Was it 90% powerful and each person needs to add 10% worth of good works to be accepted by God? Or was it a 70% efficacious work of God, but man needs to add 30% of good works?

Hypothetically speaking, if it's true that in addition to belief in Christ that some good works are needed to be forgiven by God, what could a person possibly contribute to his salvation? What good work could he do that God would find so pleasing that he would accept him? Scripture makes it clear there is nothing inherently good in the human condition, and our good works don't merit God's favor. In fact, our good deeds are considered filthy rags to God, and will never earn his favor (Isa 64:6; Ro 3:9-18).

Taking the position that faith in Christ along with some works is required for salvation is a pure insult to Jesus' work on the cross. The divine Son of God, fully human in every way, lived a perfectly sinless life then bore the wrath of God to bear our penalty for sin. Wasn't that enough for our salvation? Was his death in some way lacking? What else could God do that he hasn't already done? The answer is nothing. All the requirements for man's salvation are completed in Jesus Christ's death and resurrection (Rom 4:25; 1 Cor 15).

Salvation is by Grace

Scripture makes it clear that our salvation is purely an act of God's grace—his gift to mankind (Rom 3:24; Eph 2:8-9). If faith in Christ plus human works are necessary for one's salvation then that negates the role of grace. Salvation is no longer a free gift of God, for it becomes contingent upon the works of man.

Paul's opponents were advocating that salvation was based on one's faith in Christ, plus adherence to the Law of Moses. Theirs was a gospel that combined faith in Christ plus works of men to be saved. One had to be circumcised, or become Jewish, along with exercising faith in Christ. False teachers appeared in Galatia and were duping the Christians into believing their corrupted gospel. Paul pulled no punches and dropped the hammer by letting them know that by believing in their false gospel they were in grave spiritual danger (Gal 1:6-9). Those who taught the above view were not Christians, and those who sat under their teaching and believed their gospel were not Christians either.

Justification by Faith Alone

One of the hallmark doctrines of Christianity is Justification by faith (Rom 4:1-5:21). This is a crucial doctrine because it defines how a sinner is accepted and forgiven by God. That being the case, Christianity stands or falls on a correct understanding of this doctrine.

Theologian Wayne Grudem defines justification as follows:

> Justification is an instantaneous legal act of God in which he (1) thinks of our sins as forgiven and Christ's righteousness as belonging to us, and (2) declares us to be righteous in his sight. (Grudem, p. 723)

Regarding the legal aspect of justification he says:

> It is important to emphasize that this legal declaration in itself does not change our internal nature or character at all. In this sense of "justify" God issues a legal declaration about us. This is why theologians have also said that justification is forensic, where the word forensic means "having to do with legal proceedings." (Grudem, p. 724)

Justification by faith is like a courtroom drama where God presides as judge and the sinner has his day in court. God justifies the sinner, or acquits the sinner of the charges against him because Jesus has paid the penalty for his sins. No longer is the sinner under the sentence of condemnation (Rom 5:18). In our criminal justice system one is presumed innocent until proven guilty. In other words, to be convicted of a crime a case must be made where it is proved beyond any reasonable shadow of doubt that the accused is guilty. If there is reasonable shadow of doubt the accused will probably go free. In God's justice system all are guilty of sin because of their affiliation with Adam, and are born under the sentence of condemnation (Rom 5:12-21). There is no presumption of innocence because all are born guilty.

Because Jesus was punished for our sins God's sense of justice has been satisfied—sin has been atoned for, and God has been propitiated. The sinner receives the benefit of being justified when he places his faith in Christ, and God—the Judge—declares him not guilty or acquitted. The sinner is now in a right standing with God.

Millard Erickson in his volume "Christian Theology" says:

> In the New testament, justification is the declarative act of God by which, *on the basis of the sufficiency of Christ's atoning death,* he pronounces believers to have fulfilled all of the requirements of the law which pertain to them. Justification is a forensic act imputing the righteousness of Christ to the believer; it is not an actual infusing of holiness into the individual. It is a matter of declaring the person righteous, as a judge does in acquitting the accused. It is not a matter of making the person righteous or altering his or her actual spiritual condition. (Erickson, p. 956)

Once God justifies the sinner, thereby placing him in a right standing, the righteousness of Christ is imputed to him. Therefore the believer isn't in a morally neutral position. Christ's righteousness is imputed to him, such that he is in a position of perfect righteousness before God. It is a gift given to the acquitted sinner (Ro 5:17). Sin will still exist in the believer's life, but God views him as righteous in Christ.

Wayne Grudem offers some comments on imputation:

> Therefore the second aspect of justification is that God must declare us not to be merely neutral in his sight but actually to be righteous in his sight. In fact, he must declare us to have the merits of perfect righteousness before him...
>
> When we say that God imputes Christ's righteousness to us it means that God thinks of Christ's righteousness as belonging to us, or regards it as belonging to us. He "reckons" it to our account...Now

in the doctrine of justification we see imputation for the third time. Christ's righteousness is imputed to us, and therefore God thinks of it as belonging to us. It is not our own righteousness but Christ's righteousness that is freely given to us. So Paul can say that God made Christ to be "our wisdom, our righteousness and sanctification and redemption" (1 Cor 1:30). And Paul says that his goal is to be found in Christ, "not having a righteousness of my own, based on law, but that which is through faith in Christ, the righteousness from God that depends on faith" (Phil 3:9). (Grudem, p. 726)

In conclusion, when God justifies the sinner he makes a legal declaration of his acquittal. The sinner is now in a right standing with his Maker. All his sins are forgiven: past, present, and future. He will never come under condemnation from God (Rom 8:1). The second aspect to justification is that the perfect righteousness of Christ is given to the new believer such that God sees Jesus' righteousness as belonging to him. Thus, the new believer isn't in a morally neutral position before God, he is perfectly righteous because Jesus' righteousness becomes his. Therefore, justification by faith is like flip sides of a coin: on one side is God's legal declaration of the sinner's acquittal, placing him in a right standing before him. On the other side of the coin is the imputation of Christ's righteousness. Both sides together make up the doctrine of justification by faith in Christ.

Once a sinner is justified by faith in Christ that doesn't mean he will automatically display righteous behavior, because sin still exists in his life. He now begins his journey with the Lord and starts the process of sanctification—his growth as a disciple of Christ. Justification is considered to be God's grace, and has nothing to do with the sinner's good works. It is entirely a matter of God's work, his grace, in the life of a sinner. It is appropriate to call the doctrine "justification by faith *alone*." Adding any kind of works to justification makes it a false gospel.

Much Freedom Comes From This Doctrine

Comprehending the doctrine of Justification by faith has a freeing effect on people. The one who seeks to know God doesn't have to worry about being good enough to be accepted by him. It is impossible for anybody to be good enough to merit God's favor. Seeking to earn God's favor through good works is like running on a treadmill and getting nowhere. Paul said "by the works of the law no flesh shall be justified" (Rom 3:20; 28; Gal 2:16). This is where grace comes into the picture. Being declared righteous by God, accepted and forgiven is totally his grace applied to the sinner when he places his trust in Jesus for salvation. Our salvation is a free gift from God, having nothing to do with our individual works. God's gift is received through faith and repentance (Acts 17:30; Eph 2:8-9).

Those who are taught that faith and repentance aren't enough for salvation, but good works must be added to gain God's favor are hearing a false gospel. You will never be good enough to merit God's favor, so stop trying. Believe in Jesus and God will accept you just as you are.

Many times over the years, I've heard people say, "I can't become a Christian right now because there are some things that I need to clean up in my life first." It may have been an inappropriate relationship, a drinking problem, some type of addiction, and so forth. The misunderstanding is that God won't accept me while I have this problem in my life, so before I can become a believer in Christ I need to clean up my act. This is not how it works. It is incorrect to think that God will only accept you when you get rid of those bad habits, whatever they are, and clean up your life.

This is not how the gospel works. You can try to clean yourself up but you will never be good enough for God to accept in your own humanity, so give it up and stop trying to do the impossible. You will never have God smile on you and accept you through your own personal goodness. You can marshal all the self-discipline you can, and make improvements in your behavior, but it will never be enough to please God, so give it up.

A sinner presents himself to Jesus just as he is and places his trust in him for salvation, understanding that he has nothing to offer Jesus by way of personal goodness. When that happens God accepts you on the basis of your faith in Jesus, not your good works. Because you place your trust in Jesus, God forgives you, and declares you righteous in his sight. Understanding this has a freeing effect on those who are seeking a relationship with God. Righteousness is a gift to you from God, so you don't have to endlessly strive to be righteous so that God accepts you.

Conclusion

In this chapter we have seen that God's plan for the salvation of man revolved around Jesus Christ. When Jesus died on the cross he was punished for the sin of mankind, such that there is nothing else that needs to be done to pay the penalty of man's sin—it has been paid in full. Jesus was the substitute for mankind who died in our place, and bore the punishment that each of us deserved. God offers salvation and forgiveness as a free gift to those who place their faith in Jesus and repent of their sins.

To add human works to the gospel as a requirement for being forgiven is a corruption of the gospel, and an insult to the work of Jesus dying on the cross. His death was totally efficacious in atoning for sin—not just partially. If human works are necessary for the salvation of man than the gospel is no longer a message of grace.

We also looked at the importance of the doctrine of justification by faith *alone* to establish that one is placed in a right standing with God by faith in Christ, and nothing more. Understanding this crucial doctrine has a freeing effect because you don't have to strive and work to be accepted by God, you just accept his free gift that he offers you through your faith in Jesus. The false gospel of legalism blocks the way of salvation and closes the door to heaven. It is to be avoided like the plague! Sadly, there are many that propagate this false gospel.

Chapter 11 ~ Legalism Puts People in Jail

The second variety of legalism, which will be discussed in this chapter, is the most pervasive form of legalism. It addresses the issue of what characteristics define a mature Christian. In other words, what are the markers of spiritual maturity that legalists identify? More importantly, do these markers line up with what Scripture identifies as the characteristics of spiritual maturity?

Legalism establishes a false set of criteria to measure spiritual maturity that has little, or nothing, to do with Scripture. Most of the markers of spiritual maturity that legalists identify are man-made and may be rooted in their church culture, secular culture, or family upbringing, but not the Bible. This type of legalism is found everywhere in varying degrees. Some churches may be on the extreme end of the spectrum regarding legalistic practices, while others may only express a slight degree of legalistic tendencies. Anywhere Christians gather there will be those who display some form of legalistic behavior and attitudes.

In this chapter I'm going to list some of the false criteria that legalists use to measure spiritual maturity. During the 30 years that I've been a pastor, I've met many people who were extremely legalistic. Some were struggling to break free from their legalistic tendencies, while others have been able to find freedom in their walk with the Lord, and enjoy the liberty they have as a disciple of Christ. I'll be sharing many of the things I've learned from them about their trek in legalism.

I begin with a recent teaching trip I took to the Dominican Republic, where I interviewed a number of people about legalism in their churches. It is quite pervasive in that country as well as many other Latin American countries. In fact, one woman I interviewed made the comment: "Going to church is like going to jail." She described going to church as being oppressive, controlling, and found very little that was edifying about being in church.

Going to Church is Like Going to Jail!

I have never had someone describe going to church being like going to jail. That comment peaked my curiosity so I asked her to explain what she meant by that and she offered me several examples.

One pastor told the women in his church that going to a beauty salon to have your hair done is a worldly practice to be avoided. True Christians don't do that. He told the women in the church, "If you're ugly for your husband you're beautiful for the Lord." Women who go to a beauty salon will be reprimanded by their pastor, and harshly criticized for being worldly. In this particular church, and many others, for a woman to look attractive for her husband by going to a hair stylist is considered behavior unbecoming for a Christian woman.

Another example she shared with me is during a worship service the pastor noticed that there were two women who wore skirts that were slightly above their knees. The pastor had the two women stand up and publically ostracized them by saying they are dressed like prostitutes. Then she had two other women with floor-length skirts stand and proclaimed, "This is how godly women dress. This is how true Christians dress." Showing your knees is a sign of carnality and ungodliness. This type of dress is totally unacceptable in their church and not fitting for professing Christians.

Another example is if you go dancing at a disco or nightclub and it comes back to the pastor you can be disciplined for that. This is also considered worldly behavior that true Christians aren't to engage in. If you drink any type of alcohol you can come under church discipline for that activity. The pastor may not allow you to serve in various places in the church because of that supposedly ungodly behavior, and you may be shunned.

Another example she shared with me is that when someone becomes a believer they are told they must break off all relationships with nonbelievers. If they don't they will be reprimanded for not complying with that rule. They are told that it is sinful to have relationships with nonbelievers. True Christians don't associate with nonbelievers.

Additionally, some pastors will tell their congregation that they are to stay away from Christians who attend churches affiliated with other denominations. So believers that are in another denomination are the enemy that must be avoided. Unfortunately, here in America some pastors do the same thing.

Baseball is Bad

In the Dominican Republic baseball is big! It is the aspiration of just about every young man to play in the majors. Professional baseball teams scout heavily in the Dominican and many players in the majors are Dominicans. One would think that with the popularity of baseball that local churches would run baseball ministries out of their fellowships. It could be a phenomenal outreach that could impact people for Christ.

However, there is a disconnect between pastors and baseball. It is considered inappropriate for a pastor to wear a baseball hat, and it is taboo for a pastor to go to the baseball field and interact with the players. This is supposedly because bad things may happen to baseball players. For these reasons trying to connect baseball to a local church doesn't work in the Dominican Republic. The irony of this is overwhelming in that in a country where baseball is so popular it is completely shunned by pastors and disconnected from churches.

Don't Go to the Park

Every city in the world has parks where people go and play, run their dogs, have picnics, play basketball, go for walks, etc. It is also considered wrong for Christians to hang out at the local park because supposedly bad things happen to people who go to the park. Christians are to avoid being in places like that because drug deals take place there and other bad things.

One Pastor's View of Church Health

My friend Don was talking to a Dominican pastor and asked him what he believes constitutes a healthy church. The pastor stood up and said my church is healthy because people dress like this, as he pointed to his snazzy looking suit. He said people in my church don't dress like you. Don was wearing a pair of shorts, a T-shirt, tennis shoes, and a baseball hat. One criterion this pastor advocated for church health was what people look like. Many pastors in the Dominican Republic hold this view.

When Can Someone Be Baptized?

In the Dominican Republic when someone becomes a Christian and wants to be baptized, most pastors will not consent to do that until he has had time to examine his life. This process of evaluation may go on for a couple of years or more. If the pastor is convinced that their life reflects godliness he will then baptize them. Baptism has nothing to do with a believer setting forth his testimony; it becomes based on the approval of the pastor. The criteria that the pastor uses to evaluate one's spiritual life are often not disclosed. This practice is far removed from the Biblical teaching of baptism. When a sinner becomes a believer in Jesus he should be baptized, just as they were in Scripture (Mat 28:19; Acts 2:41; 8:36-38). Withholding baptism from someone is Biblically untenable.

During my most recent trip to the Dominican Republic I was teaching a seminar on sanctification and a woman, who happened to be single, told me her previous pastor wouldn't baptize her because she wasn't married. Immediately after her comment someone else chimed in and said the he had the same experience in his previous church. Where does the Bible say one of the requirements for baptism is being married? This is nothing more than a man-made rule without Biblical foundation that places people in spiritual prison.

Pastor Felix

One pastor I met was ten months into founding a new church and was being blessed by the Lord. He had about 50 people in attendance, many of which were new converts to Christianity. I asked him what some of the challenges were that he was facing in his work. He replied, "The biggest problem facing churches in the Dominican Republic is the religiosity and legalism that exists in this culture." The legalistic beliefs that have been mentioned above are terribly difficult to overcome. The people need sound Biblical teaching to help them get past these false beliefs, and set them free so they can enjoy a relationship with Christ.

I know people in the Dominican Republic that have experienced freedom from these legalistic restrictions. The woman who made the comment, "Going to church is like going to Jail," is one person who has been set free from these man-made oppressive rules. Through much Biblical study and teaching she came to see that what many churches are teaching is not founded in Scripture. She no longer placed herself under the legalistic burdens advocated by her church, and experienced joy in her relationship with Christ. I've met several people who had the same experience as she did, and they all have discovered that knowing Jesus is a joyful experience, it is no longer a burden. Jesus once said: "If you know the truth the truth shall set you free" (John 8:32). People who are under the oppressive burden of legalism need to be set free from these false beliefs by studying what the Scripture says, and find a church that promotes grace.

These are just a few of the examples that she and others have shared with me about church-life in the Dominican Republic. I can see why she described being in church like being in jail.

Pastor Tim

Here in America legalism also raises its ugly head as well. Pastor Tim was meeting in an elementary school founding a new church. He had a congregation of about 70 people and was doing well. One day he was shocked when a group of people in the church came to him expressing their desire to have the members of the church sign a covenant, which was like a code of conduct. Appearing on the list were such things as: I won't drink alcohol, smoke, watch R rated movies, dress inappropriately, won't go dancing, go into bars, and things of that nature. Their logic was that the church needs to be distinct from the world so one way to accomplish that is to have the members of the church commit to following a detailed code of conduct. They referred to it as a membership covenant.

Pastor Tim adamantly objected to this practice on the basis that it is legalistic and wouldn't agree to the covenant they suggested. He claimed that the things that they listed were false markers of spiritual maturity. His position was that the things mentioned in their proposed membership covenant should be left up to the individual and his conscience before God. Matters that aren't black and white, like what is appropriate dress, what movies one watches, etc., are better left up to each individual and God about what is right and wrong. There were several people that left the church over Tim's refusal to meet their demands. They felt that pastor Tim was advocating worldly behavior by not having a membership covenant.

Many years ago I was talking with an older gentleman who told me he loved going to his church, specifically his Sunday school class because it was taught by one of the professors at a nearby Bible seminary. He said the teaching was profound and life-impacting for him such that he looked forward to being there every Sunday. He wanted to join the church, but he smoked cigarettes, and the church had a membership covenant that all members had to sign and comply with. One of the items on the list was: if I become a member of this church I will not smoke. For that reason he didn't become a member of the church, even though he wanted to. Why should he be disqualified from being a member of the church because he smokes?

Sports Are Not of God

I have always been big into sports. I played football in high school then studied Kenpo Karate and eventually opened my own school making my living teaching martial arts. It always amazed me how many times mothers have approached me and said they would never allow their sons to play contact sports because they are so violent. They didn't feel it was the type of thing that Christians should do. Being in contact sports like martial arts, boxing, Judo, wrestling, football, and so forth, are things that Christians shouldn't be involved in because it goes against the love ethic that Jesus taught.

There are many high school, college, and professional athletes that are Christians and are highly competitive people. Being in the spotlight they have an opportunity to set forth their testimony to the world and lift up Jesus' name. I remember Randal Cunningham, who played quarterback for the Philadelphia Eagles, then had a spectacular year with the Minnesota Vikings as a comeback player. They were a field goal away from going to the Super Bowl, but the kicker, who hadn't missed a field goal all year, missed the game winning kick and they suffered a heartbreaking defeat. When Randal was interviewed after the game he said something to the effect of: "whether in victory or defeat I praise my Savior Jesus Christ." What a great testimony to the world that was. Today Randal pastors a church in Las Vegas and has a vibrant ministry there.

I was recently watching the Olympics and two divers were interviewed that metaled. They said their identity isn't in diving; it is in who they are in Christ. They had just won gold on the biggest stage in the world—the Olympics—and they gave glory to Jesus for all to hear. Some people take the position that Christians shouldn't play sports because it's too worldly, competitive, and, in some cases too violent, but where does it say that in the Bible?

Dancing at the Wedding Reception

A young couple that attended our church got married and had their wedding reception in the church's social hall. They had a Disc Jockey playing music so the people were dancing. The wedding coordinator, who was a long-time church member, told me that when they started dancing it was like Satan showed up. She complained to me about how scantly clad some of the girls were, that attended our church, and asked me what was going to be done about that. I got the impression that she expected me to punish them, or enact church discipline on them. In her mind dancing was of the Devil and should be forbidden in church, and there should be some type of dress code established because the women were wearing clothes that she thought were way too revealing.

A good friend of mine told me in one of the churches in his area they have a written policy that states they don't allow dancing in their church because it is considered an inappropriate activity for Christians. They don't allow the teenagers in church to do any dancing. Most wedding receptions have dancing of some sort—polkas, slow dancing, modern, swing dancing, etc. How is it that this is considered ungodly or sinful activity?

A Pretty Girl on the Worship Team

My associate pastor got a call from a woman in the church who had a complaint. There is a woman who sings on the worship team who is about 23 years old, and happens to be very attractive. The complaint this woman had, that she directed at the associate pastor, was that this woman shouldn't be allowed to sing on the worship team because of the way she looks. She is attractive and it isn't fitting to have a woman like that on the stage, the men will have a problem with a beautiful woman like that.

She wanted her to be banned from being on the stage because she was an attractive woman. She questioned the pastor as to whether or not there was a written dress code that members of the band needed to comply with. The only thing the members of the worship team are required to do is dress in a manner that is respectful and modest. That means women shouldn't wear clothes that are revealing, men should look neat and well groomed, that's it. That's the only dress requirement we had for people on the worship team.

The pastor told the disgruntled woman that the singer in question was dressed modestly and appropriately. He explained that there is no basis for prohibiting her from being on the stage. What am I supposed to tell her: "Sally, you need to get ugly if you want to continue being on the stage. You're to attractive so you can't sing on the worship team any more." When my associate pastor told me this I was shocked at how somebody can come up a complaint like this. She wanted to punish the girl for being beautiful by preventing her from serving the Lord with her excellent singing voice. Unbelievable!

Going Swimming in Blue Jean Cutoffs

When I was in grade school I would often go swimming at my friend Tom Schubert's house. They had an above ground swimming pool where a lot of us would hang out during the summer months. I had gone swimming over there more times than I could count. I remember one Sunday afternoon I got a call from Tom inviting me to come over to the house for a swim. I proceeded to put on my blue jean cutoff shorts that I wore every time I went swimming at his place.

When my mother saw me about to leave the house, she strenuously objected to me wearing the cutoffs I wore all the time. She started ranting and raving about how this is Sunday—it's the Lord's day and you can't go out of the house looking like that. You need to show some respect for God and put on the nice swimming suit we bought for you. Well, the nice swimming suit she got me was too small, it was ugly, and made me feel uncomfortable wearing it. My efforts to convince her to let me wear my cutoffs were in vain, so I lost the argument.

Really, God will be happier with me because I'm wearing an ugly swimming suit instead of the blue jean cutoffs that I always wear? This will put me in a more favorable position with God than if I wear the cutoffs I always wear? Where did this idea come from? How does wearing an ugly swimsuit make me more acceptable and respectful to God? Am I a better Christian because I'm wearing a swimsuit? I just thought it was ridiculous.

The Wine-Drinking Missionary

On one occasion I was on the ordination committee that was interviewing a former missionary to France, who was transitioning to ministry in a local church in America. The committee asks various questions of each candidate based on the paper they write regarding their doctrinal positions, and matters of lifestyle. One of the standard questions that is asked of each candidate is what their position is on social drinking. This candidate explained to the committee that he had no problem drinking socially, to which some of the committee members strenuously objected. He explained that France is a place where everybody drinks wine. It's a culturally acceptable practice to drink wine with your meals. Many places in Europe do that as well. If you don't drink wine you are frowned upon. Drinking wine with meals is a socially acceptable practice that everybody does in that culture, whether you're a Christian or not.

His answer was unacceptable to some of the committee members and they grilled him on that issue. He was encouraged to completely abstain from any alcoholic beverages altogether. It's strange that people object to drinking wine, when Jesus didn't seem to have a problem with it. He turned the water into wine at the wedding feast of Cana, and apparently it was really good stuff, with a little bite to it (John 2:9-10).

Many years ago I was attending a mega church that had a huge sanctuary with a seating capacity of about 1,500. I was sitting in the balcony right in the center of the facility, so the pulpit was directly in front of me. I had a bird's eye view of the entire auditorium. During the pastor's sermon he mentioned that he likes to drink a glass of wine with his dinner. When he said that I could see heads turning all over the sanctuary and hear people whispering into the ears of the person sitting next to them. Judging from the reaction of the people that pastor caused quite a stir when he said that. But is it a sin to drink a glass of wine with your dinner? Of course not!

True Christians Wear a Suit and Tie!

Many years ago I knew an older gentleman who was really having a problem with the way many younger people were showing up in church casually dressed. Some of the people were showing up for church wearing shorts, T-shirts, and running shoes, which was totally unacceptable for him. Of course, he was always wearing a good-looking suit and tie. On one occasion he started complaining to me about the way people were dressing these days, and he made the comment that true Christians wear a suit and tie to church. In his way of thinking an indicator that one has a relationship with Christ is that he wears a suit and tie to church. If you don't dress in this manner you aren't a true believer. Where does this belief come from?

When I was in Bible Seminary, one of my professors was talking about worship during his lecture. He made the comment that worship is holistic meaning that you worship God with your mind, body, emotions, and dress should be considered part of holistic worship. Of course, he wore a snazzy looking suit every day, but he made it clear that dressing casually went against the grain of holistic worship. He spoke against pastors who dress casually for the Sunday worship service and encouraged all his students to wear their Sunday best when standing behind the pulpit delivering God's word.

Back in the late 80s when I was in Bible seminary just about every pastor wore a suit and tie, including myself, except for a few mavericks that wore Hawaiian shirts. Today there are very few pastors that wear suits on Sunday. Most pastors dress business casual these days, as do most people who attend church—it is overwhelmingly casual. People can wear a designer suit that costs a lot of money, but does it put them in better standing with God? I don't think so.

The Scarlet D

Neil shared with me his experience attending a church in Upstate New York. He described the church as ultra-legalistic. Among the many oppressive things they advocated, he told me how they treated people who had a divorce in their past. If you attend that church and are divorced you have to sit in a separate section of the sanctuary that is specifically designated for those who are divorced. I wondered if the church was trying to punish people who had a failed marriage. Is this their way of branding them with a scarlet D? Where is the grace is this practice? I guess if you have been divorced you are a second-class citizen in this church, and you will be punished for it every time you come to worship on Sunday.

Instruments in Church

Some denominations won't allow any musical instruments to be played in their worship service. It's strange that in the Bible instruments were used regularly: strings, persecution, woodwinds, brass, etc. King David was a gifted musician who played the harp in worshiping God, so where does this idea come from that instruments can't be played in church? It certainly doesn't come from the Bible.

Years ago I was having breakfast with another pastor who was telling me about his attempt to transition his church to a more contemporary venue for his worship service. The church's worship was very traditional, playing hymns on the piano and organ only. He had announced to the congregation that he was going to have a blended service with praise choruses being introduced along with the hymns. He informed the congregation that there would be a guitar and bass played in the service. He wisely gave notice to the church so they had time to process this, and wouldn't be caught off guard when he introduced a more contemporary format for worship.

One long-time member of the church told the pastor, "The day this church has a guitar played in the worship service is the day I leave the church." Sure enough, when the guitar was played he got up from his seat, walked out and never came back. He concluded the church had become worldly because guitars are for rock n roll bands, and should have no place in a worship service. Where does this idea come from that a guitar can't be used to glorify God? Certainly that concept isn't in the Bible.

No TV in This house

Jerry received a new state of the art flat screen TV from his wife for a Christmas present. She thought he would really enjoy it. Prior to this time they didn't have a TV in their house. When Jerry received the TV he thanked his wife, but a few days later said he wanted to return the TV because he didn't think it was appropriate for Christians to have a TV in their home. For him having a TV in his home is accommodating to the world, and doesn't edify anybody watching the trash that is broadcast. While I would agree that there are many things on TV that aren't edifying in any way, shape, or form, there are a lot of good things to watch that are educational and edifying. In his mind TV had no place in the house of believers' in Christ, so they returned the TV.

These are a few examples of legalism that I have personally seen, or that other people have shared with me. There are many others that I could share but I think you get the point. The result is always placing people in bondage. These examples reveal that *legalism is grounded in man-made rules that don't do anything to put one in a more favorable position with God*. Thinking that legalistic practices improve one's position with God is an illusion.

Reading through the above stories reveals how judgmental legalistic people come across. It seems as though the legalists are nitpicking people and placing them under a microscope of judgmentalism. Where is the grace and love in people who carry on like this?

What Message Does Legalism Convey?

When the nonbeliever meets up with a Christian legalist, what impression do they have of the Christian faith? The nonbeliever needs to know that becoming a Christian is all about entering a relationship with Jesus by placing his faith in him. That is first and foremost. A legalistic Christian often gives nonbelievers the wrong picture of what it means to be a Christian. It becomes a religion where I can't do this or that; I have to follow a list of rules. It minimizes the most important thing, which is being in relationship with Jesus!

When someone becomes a Christian they may have a very legalistic believer offer to disciple him. It shouldn't be surprising that the new believer takes on some of the characteristics of his legalistic mentor. Most likely a legalistic mentor will give the new disciple a warped view of what it means to live a righteous life before God. Holiness involves keeping all the rules which might include: wearing a suit and tie, being in the Sunday evening service, not going to movie theaters, or whatever else the mentor deems as important.

I remember talking to a fellow pastor about a person named Joe that we both knew who was attending my church. This individual loved the Lord and served whole-heartedly in the fellowship, but he was incredibly legalistic. My colleague explained to me that a person named Clarence led him to the Lord, whom we also both knew. I don't think there is a more legalistic person on the planet than Clarence. He was a King James Bible only person, Christians have to wear suits and ties to church, if you don't go to Sunday school and the Sunday evening service your commitment to God is questionable, and so forth. For Clarence there was only one way of doing things and that was his way. He was the most intolerant, inflexible person I ever met. It wasn't surprising to see Joe take on some of the characteristics of his legalistic mentor Clarence.

What Message Do Legalistic Parents Give Their Children?

Throughout the years I've been in pastoral ministry it was not uncommon for me to have people attend my church who came out of a legalistic family background. In their adult years many of them had issues to overcome in their relationship with God. Linda was raised by strict Christian parents who imposed many rules on their children. They could not date, go dancing, listen to secular music, no TVs were allowed in the house, they had a dress code to abide by, and were taught that a woman's role is to have children and stay at home. Pursuing a career was considered to be sinful for a woman, for they taught her that was not what God had for women.

Because of her legalistic upbringing she had challenges that had to be addressed in her walk with the Lord later in life. Specifically, she felt that God is only pleased when she adheres to all the rules that were drilled into her head as a child. She was in a legalistic box, so wherever she didn't conform to the rules imposed on her in her upbringing, she felt guilty, as though she was being disobedient to God. She was trapped in a mindset that had little room for grace. Walking with God was a burden for her. She frequently resented her parents for the way they raised her. She often was judgmental of other people in the church who had liberty to dress casually, go to the movies, go dancing, and do the things that she was prohibited from doing when she was growing up. She was greatly conflicted being around believers that had the liberty to do the things that were taboo in her upbringing. It took her years to break out of the legalistic box she was in, but little-by-little she was making progress.

One woman, who attended the church I pastored, came out of a legalistic fellowship and told me that in her previous church, "Everything was legislated for you. You were told what to think, what to do, and what to wear," so being in a church like mine, where that wasn't the case was refreshing for her. She could make decisions for herself and develop her own convictions about things without constantly being told what to do. It was a freeing experience for her, but it took a while for her to adjust to the new found liberty she discovered. There was always the tendency to struggle with guilt if she didn't act like, or think like she had been taught in her previous church. It takes time to break out of the oppressive mold of legalism.

Do Legalistic People Think They Are Legalistic?

If you ask a legalistic person if they consider themselves to be legalistic, I don't think they would regard themselves in that way at all. They would probably say they are conservative Christians, who are staunch defenders of the faith, but legalistic, no way! They may even attend a church that has the word grace in the name of their church, such as Grace Bible Church, Grace Community Church, or Grace Evangelical Church, etc. Legalistic people are often blind to their legalism, just as the Pharisees were. They don't see the box they are in, even though they may feel oppressed by the very rules they try to keep.

Legalistic People Are Typically Unhappy

I have found that most legalistic people are typically very unhappy. Some of the general characteristics I've seen them display is that they are quick to judge other people who see things differently than they do. They often want their standards and practices to be normative for everybody else. They tend to feel uncomfortable around people who are more liberated than they are. Legalistic people feel most comfortable around people who are just like them, but struggle not being critical of other people who don't share their convictions.

Another characteristic is an excessive striving that some legalistic people display in that the things they do for God never seem to be enough. They will often overload themselves with things to do at church to the point where it is too much for them to handle. The role of grace is often minimized in their lives, because they may feel they have to do more to stay in God's favor, and work harder to earn more of God's love. Therefore, they may be some of the busiest people in the church.

The Influence of Secular Culture

The church is to be a change agent in its culture. In fact, the greatest transformative element in any given society is the gospel of Jesus Christ. When an individual becomes a Christian her life undergoes a transformation. When many people in a given society become Christians not only do they individually experience the transformative power of Christ in their lives, but the entire culture in which they live can be transformed. The world will claim more government programs are the answer to societal woes, but Jesus says it is the church that can provide the answer to the problems in any given culture.

Jesus said the church is to be the salt of the earth and the light of the world (Mat 5:13-16). In both these metaphors Jesus was making the point that Christians are to use their influence to impact culture by pointing people to him. If the church is being salt and light in their culture, they should be impacting their society by leading people to Christ. Clearly, Jesus calls the church to be a change agent in its culture—an agent of transformation. However, in America it seems to be the other way around. The secular culture seems to be impacting segments of the church such that the church is being transformed by the world. This is backwards!

For instance, political correctness is something that people have to be aware of these days. In other words, one has to be careful what he says because he will be branded as intolerant, narrow-minded, and so

100

on, if he adheres to a Christian view that the world considers not to be politically correct. One example of this today is the church has been influenced by secular culture's acceptance of homosexuality. The Supreme Court's ruling of legalizing same sex marriages has influenced many Christians to adopt the same view. Today it isn't uncommon for some denominations to ordain gay pastors, and place them in churches. Several years ago, a church that was in close proximity to mine called a gay pastor and his partner to shepherd their congregation. I found it interesting that many of the people attending that church had no problem with that whatsoever.

When the church is influenced by secular culture and begins to adopt the unbiblical views of its society, it has become antinomian. This is what is happening in many churches and denominations in America today. Biblical standards are being discarded in favor of political correctness and the prevailing views of secular culture. *Often legalistic churches and/or believers become that way because they over-react to what is happening in the world and other denominations. Rather than becoming liberal in their theology and practice, they go in the extreme opposite direction and become legalistic. But it is an over-reaction.*

Conclusion

In this chapter we have seen that legalists identify markers of spiritual maturity that are without Biblical foundation. The mature Christian, according to these folks, is one who follows certain man-made rules such as what you wear on Sunday in church, the type of music you employ in worship, and so on. Whether the list of rules imposed on worshipers originates in their church culture, family upbringing, or secular culture the result of living under legalistic codes is spiritual oppression. Striving to keep man-made rules does nothing to put the worshiper in a better standing with God. It robs the believer of joy and makes being a believer in Christ a burden. *For the legalist, spiritual maturity in Christ is based on a false set of criteria that places people in a state of spiritual oppression.*

Chapter 12 ~ Legalism Regarding Preferences

Another form of legalism revolves around how people handle their individual preferences. No two people are exactly alike because everybody is unique, with different tastes, opinions, and viewpoints. Some people like Chinese food, others prefer Italian; some people like jazz while others prefer Country Western music. We all have our individual preferences, for no two people are alike. In the church arena people have individual tastes and preferences as well, and there is nothing wrong with that. God never required everybody to think and act in a uniform way. He wants unity in the body of Christ, but that doesn't mean uniformity in that everybody is exactly alike.

Some church people prefer traditional hymns, others prefer contemporary music, some like liturgical services, others like free-flowing Spirit-led worship. Some people prefer expository preaching while others enjoy a more narrative, story-telling type of sermon, and so forth. There is nothing wrong with having individual preferences. Diversity is a good thing and is one of the characteristics of the body of Christ.

An ugly form of legalism occurs when someone tries to make their personal preferences law for everybody else. For example, a person who desires to have communion every Sunday, because it is a meaningful experience for him, can't understand why everybody else doesn't want to have communion weekly as he does. He thinks his experience with communion should be normative for everybody else in the church. He may tend to be very judgmental of the church leaders for not complying with his wishes, and everyone who doesn't see it the same way he does will be viewed as missing the boat. He's upset because he has a demand on the other worshipers in the church that isn't being met which causes him frustration. However, his demand is rooted in a prideful belief that everybody should have the same experience that he does. Sadly, this sort of thing happens all the time in churches.

It should be obvious from the above example that if everybody in church felt his or her preferences should be normative for everybody else the result would be mass chaos. Everybody would be unhappy because they aren't getting their way. Church would be all about me, and what I want at the expense of everybody else. If this were how a community of believers acted, church would become the most selfish, self-centered community of people in existence.

Formulating One's Belief System

When it comes to personal preferences it is necessary to keep things in perspective. Every Christian should know what they believe and why they believe the way they do. When evaluating one's belief system there are three layers to consider. The first is called the *core*. All believers in Christ regardless of their denominational affiliation, heritage, or upbringing should embrace the core doctrines of Christianity. The core doctrines are the orthodox views that the church has historically held. These are nonnegotiable, should never be compromised, and the believer should be willing to take a stand in defending these core doctrines of the Christian faith. Some examples of core doctrines would include: the deity of Christ, the resurrection, the second coming of Christ, the substitutionary atonement, and the Trinity. These treasures of the faith should never be compromised and aren't to be considered personal preferences, they are the bedrock of Christian beliefs that all believers should embrace.

The second layer, outside the core, is what we would consider matters that aren't crucial to one's salvation, so these are considered *secondary matters*, but still of great importance. This layer would include such things as: different views of the millennium (premillennial, postmillennial, or amillennial), one's view of the rapture (pre-tribulation, mid-tribulation, or post-tribulation), and infant baptism or believer's baptism upon profession of faith. One could include in the secondary layer theological orientations such as Calvinism, Dispensationalism, Lutheranism, etc.   One's view of sanctification, and communion could also be included in this layer.

These items aren't crucial to one's salvation, in the sense that one can believe any one of these views and still be a Christian. The above different views have always been considered to be part of historic orthodox Christianity. On these secondary issues when the historic views on these matters are examined, one will find that Christians that love the Lord, and have a high view of Scripture arrive at different conclusions. Their views can be defended by the word of God, but different groups of Christians will put the data together and arrive at conclusions that stand at odds with other groups of believers.

It must be emphasized that since these issues are not crucial to one's salvation, believers should not exchange blows over these theological positions. When I say these matters are not crucial to one's salvation I mean, for instance, one's view of the rapture (pre, mid, or post) isn't going to determine whether or not he is or isn't a Christian. A better approach is to allow for differences of opinion while having an ongoing intelligent dialogue with those who differ with you. In other words, I can worship with someone who holds to the pre-tribulation rapture, if I maintain the post-tribulation view. Having differing opinions on this matter shouldn't cause two believers to split, exchange blows, and never speak to each other again. They are secondary matters that are distinct from the core, but nonetheless are still important.

A third layer of one's belief system involves *personal preferences* or what I will call *stylistic choices*. These issues are farthest away from the core and should be treated as such. In this layer of one's belief system we would place things such as one's preference in worship: traditional hymns, contemporary praise choruses, etc. The frequency of communion: weekly, biweekly, quarterly, etc.

Other issues would involve the type of church government, the requirements for membership, expository, topical, or narrative preaching. Some would look at the philosophy of ministry set forth by a church such as: seeker sensitive, seeker driven, cell church, attractional, missional, etc. The mode of baptism may be important to some (sprinkling, pouring, or immersion). One's view of women (egalitarian or complementarian), along with the ordination of women could be included in this layer. One's view of tithing, mega church or small church, translation of the Bible used, one's view social drinking,

104

dancing, movies, etc., are all personal preferences. It should be obvious that these are not core issues of doctrine that are essential to one's salvation. These are merely personal preferences. Another way to view personal preferences, or stylistic choices, are to consider them as non-essential issues, far away from the core. Sadly, believers often split over these issues. There should be unity in the core, but tolerance in the non-essentials.

I have just identified three layers of a Christian's belief system. They are as follows:

The *core doctrines of the faith*, which are nonnegotiable, should never be compromised, and should be fought for. Believers' in Christ should unify around these doctrines.

The next layer of one's belief system consists of *secondary doctrines of the faith*, which aren't essential to one's salvation. Christians have different understandings of various issues that are all within the confines of orthodox Christianity. These are things that shouldn't divide Christians, unfortunately at times they do.

The third layer of one's belief system is comprised of *personal preferences*, which are furthest away from the core and reflect a believer's individual choices. Believers shouldn't divide over these things either, but unfortunately sometimes they often do.

Every believer should construct his own personal belief chart identifying what she would place in each tier. This will help believers to consider what they believe and what they consider to be the most important things in their belief system. No two people will do it the same way, but many will be close. This exercise will help believers evaluate what they consider to be most important and stay focused on the majors, without getting sidetracked by focusing on the minors.

If an issue rises to the surface between two believers that causes a great deal of friction they both need to ask themself how important is his issue. Is this a core doctrine of the faith, or is this just their personal preferences that they are in disagreement over? If they are in a dispute about something that is far away from the core, they should both understand that the issue isn't worth fighting for and severing the relationship. A better approach would be for both of them to understand that they will have to agree to disagree agreeably with each other. They can still be friends and disagree because the issue in question isn't in the core.

On the other hand, if two people have an argument over a core doctrine of the faith that is an entirely different matter. For example, if somebody takes the position that Jesus didn't rise bodily from the dead that is a grave theological error that has to be corrected. This is an important issue that has dire consequences for the one embracing that error. In a church context that error can't be perpetuated, for it is false teaching. The elders of the church can't ignore that or gloss over it and take the position "let's be friends, and agree to disagree agreeably."

Below is a sample of a Christian belief system including the Core, Secondary Matters, and Personal Preferences.

THE CORE DOCTRINES

The Trinity
The Deity of Christ
The humanity of Christ
The virgin birth
The substitutionary atonement
The inerrancy of Scripture
The existence of heaven and hell
The resurrection of the body
The second coming of Christ
Faith and repentance for salvation
Salvation by grace
The sacraments of baptism and communion
The ministry of the Holy Spirit
Justification by Faith alone

THE SECONDARY MATTERS

Views on the Millennial Kingdom (premillennial, postmillennial, amillennial)

Views on the rapture (pretribulation, midtribulation, postribulation)

Views on Spiritual gifts (cessationist, continuationist, open but cautious)

Views on baptism (infant, believers only, immersion, sprinkling, pouring)

Views on communion (transubstantiation, consubstantiation, memorial view)

Views on sanctification (Reformed, Pentecostal, Lutheran, Wesleyan, etc.)

Views on eternal security (once saved always saved, loss of salvation)

Views on healing (name it claim it, not for today, God's sovereignty)

Views on theological orientation (Reformed, Pentecostal, Lutheran, Dispensational, etc.)

Views on homosexuality and gender issues

THE PERSONAL PREFERENCES

Frequency of communion (weekly, monthly, quarterly, etc.)

Type of music (hymns, contemporary, etc.)

Type of worship service (liturgical, Spirit-led, traditional, etc.)

Denominational affiliation

Type of church government (Presbyterian, Episcopalian, Congregational, etc.)

Philosophy of ministry (seeker driven, seeker sensitive, cell church, attractional, missional, home church, etc.)

Fasting

Drinking alcohol (social drinking, abstinence, etc.)

Social justice (ministry to the poor, mentally ill, handicapped, homeless, etc.)

Worship arts (creative dance, art, drama, etc.)

Tithing (mandatory, voluntary)

Politics

Approach to missions

Criteria for church membership

Translation of the Bible

Preaching style (expository, topical, story-telling, etc.)

Role of women (ordination, women elders and pastors, no women elders)

Sabbath restrictions (Sunday is continuous with the Sabbath, or no continuity)

Length of Sunday worship service (1 hour, 1.5 hours, etc.)

Christian education (Sunday school, small groups, large groups, Sunday night service)

Keep the Main Thing the Main Thing

It should be noted that there are far more personal preferences than core doctrines and secondary matters. I could probably have thought of some more personal preferences, but I think the point has been made. There are many personal preferences that believers can disagree on. When someone takes a secondary matter (from the second tier), or a personal preference (from the third tier) and moves it into the core, treating it as if it is essential to salvation, big problems can arise from that. Secondary issues and personal preferences should always be kept in perspective for what they are, but sometimes people have such deep rooted convictions about their preferences that they assign a higher place to them than what is warranted, and inadvertently move them to the core. When this happens their belief system is truncated, out of balance, and it leads to legalism! Now a preference or secondary matter becomes a rule for everybody else to follow, and becomes a measure of one's spiritual maturity.

For instance, the church at Corinth had a multitude of problems. One of their issues was that they had taken a secondary matter of speaking in tongues (and all the gifts of the Spirit), and moved them into the core. They assigned a higher place to the gifts of the Spirit than what was warranted. They were judging each other's spirituality based on the gifts they displayed, with some developing an elitist mentality based on the gifts they had (1 Cor 12:21), while others had an inferiority complex because they felt their gifts were of lessor quality than their counterparts, and couldn't make a significant contribution

108

to the church. They felt they weren't needed and of the same importance as others with whom they worshiped (1 Cor 12:15-16).

The result of this was harmful to their church. The gifts of the Spirit had been given to the church for the purpose of building up the body of Christ, but the Corinthians had made them something competitive and divisive. Paul had to offer a corrective and explain that speaking in tongues, and exercising other spiritual gifts are all meaningless if the person isn't using them in love, which the Corinthians weren't doing. He had to take the gifts of the Spirit out of the core, and reestablish love as being the core moral virtue for the Corinthians to display.

Rather than displaying love to one another, their improper placement of spiritual gifts in the core of their belief system created a legalistic environment. You have to speak in tongues to be considered a person of top-notch spirituality. If you speak in tongues hooray for you, but if God hasn't given you that gift you're a second-class citizen at Corinth. Paul would have none of that so he set things straight in Chapter 13 by explaining that love is primary and gifts of the Spirit are secondary. Or to say it differently, the fruit of the Spirit takes priority over the gifts of the Spirit. If you speak in tongues but don't have love you're nothing but a resounding gong or a clanging cymbal (1 Cor 13:1), just noise!

The Corinthians had established a false set of criteria to measure spiritual maturity based on speaking in tongues, and the use of other gifts. Damage will always result when something is placed in the core that shouldn't be there in the following ways: a preference has become a rule for all to follow, or something to strive for, and it becomes a false marker of spiritual maturity, which can breed an elitist mentality that is prideful and belittling to others. This results in legalism.

The Danger of Being Overly Dogmatic

Some people can't be wrong. They see everything in black and white, which means, in their way of thinking, they are right about everything. Some Christians are extremely dogmatic seeing only one way to view an issue; namely the way they view it. Whether an issue is in the core, the secondary level, or just a personal preference, the way they see the issue is the only right way to see that issue. This type of believer is *inflexible*, because he allows no room for someone else to see an issue differently than he does. He is highly intolerant of anybody who disagrees with him on an area of doctrine or practice.

For example, if someone prefers traditional hymns played on the piano and organ, he doesn't see this as a personal preference. This is dogma, the way it should be for everybody. Those who prefer contemporary worship are missing the boat, and he may even consider them to be less than spiritual.

Over the years I've come across many people who fall into that category regarding a host of issues including: church government, worship, strategies for outreach, and more. Having any kind of intelligent discussion with an overly dogmatic, inflexible person is an attempt in futility. There is no reasoning with someone like that, because they believe that their views are right and everybody else is wrong. People of this sort come across as very judgmental, they may be argumentative, contentious, and divisive. People like this need to be in a church where everybody believes the same things they do, across the board, with no variation. This is where they will feel the most comfortable. People who are like this don't distinguish between the *core, secondary issues,* and *personal preferences.*

The Dogmatic Pastor

Over the years I've come across some pastors that are overly dogmatic, inflexible, and intolerant of anybody who disagrees with them even on minor issues outside the core. Some of these are high profile pastors known internationally. I listened to a sermon on the radio of one such pastor while I was driving, and he was advocating that traditional hymns were the only way to go. He bashed contemporary music and considered all forms of modern worship to be the church accommodating to the world. At the conclusion of his sermon, which I disagreed with, I tried to summarize in my thinking what his position was. He considered any form of contemporary music to be accommodating to the world's way of doing things. The only valid expression of worship in a church setting, according to him, should be hymns because they are theologically rich, have stood the test of time, and they focus more on God than contemporary music does.

What this pastor did was place his personal preference (opinion) regarding worship music, and placed it in the core, as if it were a key doctrine of the faith. This is the essence of legalism. He is imposing his preference on his congregation, and listening audience, expecting them to embrace his preference for worship. If they don't they are considered by their pastor to be in the wrong, less than spiritual, or theologically shallow.

A Dogmatic Pastor's View of Sunday

When I was in Bible seminary we had weekly meetings with a professor, called advisor groups. The purpose of this was for fellowship, prayer, and encouragement. On one occasion the professor asked the group of about 10 people what our view was of the Christian Sabbath (Sunday). In other words, what things do you do or not do on Sunday? We went around the circle and everybody expressed their views of how they regard Sunday. I said that I regard Sunday as a special day because I'm doing ministry, I'm in the pulpit teaching, it isn't a day of rest for me because Sunday is a work day for pastors. I don't place any restrictions on myself so if I want to play I play, if I need to work I work. Everybody else said pretty much the same thing.

I couldn't help noticing that one of the other students was having a hard time with what everybody else was saying. He was becoming visibly upset and irritated. When it came to his turn to share his views he spoke very passionately about how he practices the Christian Sabbath (Sunday). His view of the day was that it was a day of rest and relaxation. Family time was the focus of the day, so he allowed no TV to be watched on Sunday. The family hangs out together and they read Scripture and pray together. They don't do work of any type, they have a big meal together, or on special occasions they will all fast, and then go to church for the evening service. He said he teaches this practice to his congregation, because he feels this is the teaching of Scripture. He feels that many of the Sabbath regulations taught in the Old Testament are to be applied on Sunday by Christians.

My thought on his view was that if he chooses to honor God in this way on Sunday hooray for him. I'm sure God is honored and really appreciates his heart's devotion and passion in this matter. The problem is that this man is a pastor and he teaches this view to his congregation. This is a classic example of someone taking a personal preference and trying to make it law for everybody in his church. He is moving his preference into the theological core making it mandatory for all believers in his church. By taking this posture he is placing his congregation under a yoke of legalism.

I remember at the end of the small group I walked away from that experience feeling very disturbed that he would be imposing that view on his church. I wondered if there were other things that he was imposing on his flock, or if there were some things I was trying to impose on my flock that were merely my preferences.

Pastors Steer the Ship

Every senior pastor and his leadership team must be careful to keep the main thing the main thing, which is done by keeping a clear distinction between the core, secondary issues, and nonessential personal preferences. I could go on for many pages about pastors, elders and other key leaders trying to impose their preferences on other people in the church.

Years ago back in the 80s and 90s, the Sunday evening service was on the way out in many churches. Most fellowships had an evening service, but the attendance was beginning to diminish. I remember some of the older saints who had been in Sunday evening church forever were very upset at the lack of interest in Sunday night church. A clear, noticeable attitude developed in many of the hard-core advocates of Sunday night church that if you don't attend this service you're not on board here. For many people it became a false criterion to measure people's spiritual maturity. If you go to church Sunday night you were considered to be one of the committed members of the church, like you're a Green Beret for Jesus. If you don't attend, you're lacking in your commitment to God and your sanctification is questionable. It's as if the subtle message was: true Christians attend the Sunday night service.

It's one thing to enjoy the Sunday night service and derive a benefit from attending the same, but to use it as a way of measuring one's spiritual maturity and commitment to God is totally unacceptable. In churches I pastor I am a big advocate of small groups because they provide connections with other believers, and a platform to study the word of God and pray with other believers. When small groups start up in the fall I encourage people to participate in the group of their choice because it will benefit them spiritually. However, I'm careful to present all the teaching opportunities in the church (small groups, affinity groups, Sunday school) as options for people to take advantage of in their spiritual development. I avoid making it sound like you have to do this or you're being less than what you should be spiritually.

Many churches were noticing that attendance in their adult Sunday school ministry was declining. More people were beginning to attend small groups that were meeting in homes throughout the week at different times, but the older saints mostly attended Sunday school. The newer people weren't interested in Sunday school and gravitated to small groups. Some of the faithful Sunday school attendees were upset with the declining attendance, and began setting forth the subtle message that if you don't attend Sunday school your commitment to Christ is questionable. It was as if the marker of spiritual maturity was attendance in Sunday school. The same situation arose with the mid-week prayer meeting. Those faithful few prayer warriors often were frustrated and upset that more people don't attend the prayer meeting, and some considered the non-attenders to be less than spiritual.

When someone regards a preference as though it should be law for everybody else he has gone overboard, especially when he expresses his displeasure with those who don't see an issue the same way he does. A person like this comes across in a very judgmental way to those who don't share his views. Usually people like this, who project their preferences on others, are typically pretty miserable because not everyone will conform to their way of doing things, leaving them constantly disappointed and frustrated. Preferences should remain nothing more than that, and should never become a test for orthodoxy. It is imperative for believers to identify and distinguish the difference between the core, secondary issues, and preferences. Every believer must understand that no two people are alike and will agree on everything. Because we have personal preferences we must learn to respect each other's views and be tolerant of one another's differences. We can't expect everybody to be just like we are.

Governing bodies of churches should evaluate themselves to make sure they aren't imposing things on the flock they shepherd that place people under a burden of legalism. Over the years I've had many leaders in the church display legalistic tendencies by trying to impose their preferences on others. If after self-evaluation they discover that they are, they should make sure that they explain to their congregation when they are advocating nothing more than their preferences in a given matter, and when they are promoting something in the core that should be binding on everybody.

Your Belief System

Every believer should construct his own personal belief chart. This exercise will help you identify what you believe, and what is most important in your belief system.

#1. Write down your core doctrines, which are nonnegotiable?

#2. Write down your secondary matters that are important, but not crucial to one's salvation.

#3. Write down your personal preferences, which are furthest away from the core.

#4. After completing this exercise do you see some things in your belief system that need to be readjusted? If so in what way(s)?

Chapter 13 ~ The Manipulative Pastor

This is a difficult chapter for me to write. In fact, I've even considered leaving this chapter out of the book, but after much deliberation I feel it's necessary to include it. I've been a pastor for a long time and I love my fellow pastors. My colleagues are good people, who have a tough job, and the vast majority of pastors that I've known have served the Lord with honor and integrity. However, as in any profession, there are those who make mistakes and do things that are inappropriate. The pastor will set the tone for the church. A grace-filled pastor will project that on to his congregation, while a legalistic pastor will project legalism on his church.

A manipulative pastor, who is insecure, has little accountability around him, and wants to control everything is a recipe for disaster. It isn't a question of if he will harm people, it's a question of when and how much damage he will do. From many stories that people have shared with me one-on-one, I've concluded that a controlling, manipulative pastor, who himself is legalistic, can create a toxic legalistic environment in a church. In this chapter I'm going to explain why this is the case by citing many examples.

Fear & Guilt Breed Legalism

Pastors have to be recruiters. Sunday school teachers need to be in place, more AWANA workers are needed to keep the ministry going, ushers are needed, and so forth. It never ends. Pastors are always looking for more volunteers to occupy places of ministry. I don't think I've ever known a fellow pastor who had every position in his church filled: if so it's a rarity. Some pastor's recruit through guilt-trips. Make no mistake about it guilt can be a great motivator. Imagine attending Sunday church and week-after-week your pastor makes impassioned pleas like these:

- If you're not serving in this church God isn't pleased with you

- You're out of God's will if you're not serving and using your spiritual gifts

- You can tell a Christian's level of commitment by the way they serve in their church

- How can you be a Spirit-filled Christian and not serve in your church? It's a contradiction in terms!

- We are in desperate need of workers in _____ but you are not responding to God's call. Some of you are grieving the Holy Spirit.

- If you're not serving you should be attending a church somewhere else.

When a person hears this kind of talk frequently on Sunday they can begin to feel guilty and do things out of guilt and fear, rather than because they really want to. Although that can fill positions, it isn't the right motivation to serve God. Regarding the last bullet point above, one pastor I know announced to his congregation during the Sunday service that everybody in the church should be serving in some capacity. If you are just taking up a seat and not serving, then give up your seat for someone else who serves and find another church to attend. Well, people took to heart what the pastor said and 100 people left the church. That was a devastating blow to the church, and believe me, the pastor never said that again and deeply regretted it. After many apologies and phone calls some of the people came back to the church, but it was a huge setback for that fellowship.

Tom and the Prosperity Gospel

Tom was a new believer who had a bad experience in his church by getting the double whammy of guilt and fear heaped on him by his pastor. He began attending a church that advocated the prosperity gospel. They taught that if a believer tithed, and gave above the tithe, that God would bless the giver 100-fold. They were very bold about promoting this theological position, expecting people to tithe, and telling the people to expect to get blessed financially by God. Tom began the practice of tithing, but didn't see the financial blessing that the pastors told him would come his way. He went to talk with a pastor about it, and was told that God was testing him. He was told to keep giving, be patient, and the financial blessing will come. Tom did what the pastor told him to do, but nothing happened. The 100-fold blessing didn't come back to him as he was told it would.

After a while, Tom went back to the pastor and shared his frustration about the matter. The pastor told him to stay faithful and keep giving, but he encouraged him to give more. He said your breakthrough is coming just keep on giving and God will bless you. God is trying to purge you of all greed, and is testing your faith, so just keep on being faithful with your giving and your financial blessing will come. Tom did just what the pastor told him and continued to give, but he upped his giving to the point where it was hurting him and the blessing still didn't come.

Tom again went to the pastor and shared his frustration with him, and again the pastor encouraged him to continue to be faithful in giving to the Lord's work. Only this time the pastor shifted gears and told Tom that the only reason why God hasn't blessed you financially is because you may have some sin in your life that is causing God to withhold the blessing. So the pastor questioned Tom about any sinful behavior that he may have in his life, or unforgiveness toward someone. Tom was unable to identify any serious sinful patterns of behavior in his life that would cause God to withhold blessings. He thought about people that had hurt him and prayed to God that they would be forgiven, but still the blessing didn't come.

Tom visited the pastor another time and was at the end of his rope. He had given large amounts of money to the church and never seen the blessing come to him that the pastor assured him would arrive because God is faithful. At this point the pastor concluded that the problem was Tom. He said there has to be some unconfessed sin in your life, improper motives, or unforgiveness that is preventing the financial blessing from coming back to you.

118

At this point Tom was totally discouraged and at his wits end. He had given large sums of money, and the pastors blamed him for not seeing the blessing come back to him. Tom left the church and became a dropout for a while feeling overwhelmed with guilt and fear that he wasn't good enough to please God. In fact, the pastor's had suggested that Tom had the curse of poverty on his life.

Through the encouragement of his sister he began attending the singles ministry I was leading and asked me if we could sit down and talk. He shared his story with me and I offered some corrections about their view of the prosperity gospel, but more importantly addressed the thought he was cursed. The pastor had told him that he had the curse of poverty on his life, so I prayed with him and afterwards he felt much better. He felt a burden lifted off his shoulders, and made sure he didn't go to a prosperity preaching church like that again.

The message of the pastors to Tom was giving is mandatory, you have to do this to the point where it hurts, and if you don't realize that financial blessing it's your fault. It can't be God's fault because he is faithful. This isn't just a case of bad theology, this is a case of pastors heaping a load of fear and guilt on Tom and leaving him in the lurch. Tom left the church feeling like a complete failure before God. He had to overcome intense feelings of guilt and fear that he could never please God. Those pastors did a terrible disservice to him, but he moved on with God, got some good counseling, and with help from sincere Christian friends recovered from the bad experience.

Fear and guilt are a deadly one-two combination in the church arena that can knockout well-intended Christians. I mentioned in a previous chapter the pastor who humiliated two women who wore skirts that were above their knees. He had them stand up and announced to the congregation that these two women are dressed like prostitutes. You can bet the other ladies in that church made sure they never wore a skirt that revealed their knees, because they didn't want to be called out in front of the congregation and humiliated. I'm sure the fear of God crept into the women's hearts as they listened to the pastor scold those ladies who had the audacity to show their knees.

Convenient Words From The Lord Breed Legalism

Often in charismatic circles a pastor will allegedly receive a word from the Lord and will share it with his congregation. Since it was the Lord's word through the pastor, if you don't line up with his word you're not lining up with God. I'm not implying that if a pastor announces to his church that God has spoken to him, and is leading him in a certain direction for his church that it should automatically be dismissed. I am, however, suggesting that when a pastor claims that God has spoken to him it should be carefully evaluated. Such things to consider are the following: was the pastor the only one who received this word? Was this shared with the elders of the church and are they on board with it? Did they have a time of prayer and discussion about this word to test it?

Sometimes people sit under the leadership of a pastor who uses prophetic words to manipulate his congregation into buying into a new program he wants to develop in his church, or to raise money for a new initiative, etc. I want to make it clear that in no way am I suggesting that all charismatic / Pentecostal pastors are manipulative. I've seen non-charismatic / non-Pentecostal pastors that were manipulative, so every denomination, and every theological persuasion will have some manipulative pastors.

When the pastor claims to have received a word from the Lord, it may be nothing more than a word from the pastor under the guise of it being from God. Be cautious when a pastor repeatedly claims God spoke to him and demands that everybody line up with his word, otherwise you're not lining up with God. This could be a legalistic ploy in that he is imposing something on his church, and demanding obedience to a word that originated with him, not God.

One woman shared with me that her pastor once announced to his congregation during Sunday worship that if you're not on board with what we're doing in this church, than you're not on board with God. I've heard other pastors and leaders in their churches spread the word that every time the doors of the church are open you should be here. Really! People have practical matters that prohibit them from being in church every night, like work, family responsibilities, personal time, and so on. If I'm not in church every time the doors are open than I'm less than what I should be before God. Really! God will love me more if I'm in church every night! This idea breeds a legalistic environment.

An Elitist Spirit Breeds Legalism

Another red flag to be deeply concerned about in pastoral leadership is an elitist mentality. I remember listening to a pastor of a mega church deliver his sermon and he said, "This is the best church in the whole world." That comment was rooted in his sinful nature, not the Holy Spirit. God loves all churches and all believers, regardless of which church they attend, or denomination they affiliate with, or how large the church is, so to proclaim that his church is the best church in the world is prideful and is something that should be repented of.

There is a high profile pastor, who has his sermons broadcast on the radio once said that his church is the only Bible believing church in the entire city. What? He thinks he's the only pastor who has it right in the entire city, and every other pastor has it wrong. There are many fine pastors who are faithful to God's word in that city, so his statement is without foundation and was the product of his elitist, prideful sin nature.

Some pastors will bad mouth other denominations that see issues differently than they do, and tell their congregation to have nothing to do with those people. It's as if the only true Christians are the ones attending this church, and all other denominations are apostates to be avoided. A woman informed me that in her previous church one Sunday the pastor announced to his congregation after a long-time member left the fellowship to attend another church, that everybody should shun him and have nothing to do with him. Apparently, he has committed the unpardonable sin by leaving his long-time church to attend another one.

Control & Power Breeds Legalism

Power corrupts, but absolute power corrupts absolutely. Some pastors, and others in positions of leadership, have a problem with pride, and enjoy being in charge, but in ways that are inappropriate. They may be overbearing and come across in a dictatorial fashion. They may like to throw around the fact that they are in authority in the church. Often times leaders will say to their congregation something to the effect: you need to be submitted to my leadership, it's Biblical.

The Bible does say leaders are to be obeyed, which is clearly stated in Hebrews 13:17-18:

> Obey your leaders and submit *to them*, for they keep watch over your souls as those who will give an account. Let them do this with joy and not with grief, for this would be unprofitable for you. [18]Pray for us, for we are sure that we have a good conscience, desiring to conduct ourselves honorably in all things.

It's important to note what else is said along with obeying and submitting to leaders. They have to give an account to God for the way they shepherd the flock, and exercise pastoral leadership. So when the pastor says you need to obey and submit, he should be mindful that he needs to obey and submit himself to God, and give an account to him. A pastor can't expect his congregation to submit to his leadership if he isn't submitted to God's leadership in his own life.

In v. 18 the author requests prayer that he and his entourage would "conduct ourselves honorably in all things." Certainly, "all things" would include the way they exercise pastoral oversight of their church. They can't be bullies, who throw their weight around and demand total obedience from the congregation. The authority God has given leaders should be used in a servant's spirit, with humility to build up the people, not be a dictator over them.

There is a chain of command in the church, for God is a God of order not chaos, but leaders are called to lead in a way that is distinct from the world's way of doing things. Our example of leadership is to lead like Jesus, exuding a servant's spirit (Mark 10:45).

Unfortunately, over the years I've seen people who appear to be humble servants of Christ, but when they are placed in a position of authority something happens to them—they go viral. They become proud, authoritative, and demanding rather than being the humble servant that Jesus was. Every leader should do an evaluation of the way he conducts himself and ask probing questions such as: Am I using my God-given authority to build people up? Am I being harsh and prideful in the use of my leadership position? Am I setting an example to the flock of humble service to God? Am I in this for personal recognition or to serve God and his people? Am I willing to be accountable to God and other leaders in my pastoral oversight?

When a pastor looses his perspective on his God-given authority and reads Hebrews 13:17-18 as permission from God to assert his authority, without noting the other things said, he may find himself being a little pushy, bossy, and overly aggressive in his dealings with people.

On one occasion I was helping a church work through some leadership issues that revolved around the senior pastor and his relationship with other key leaders. As I listened carefully to what was said it became obvious to me that the pastor had some control issues. The other leaders were feeling stifled by the pastor. He said, "I'm the leader and God works through me. In the Bible God always works through the leader." Apparently he felt that his power was absolute, and the other committed workers felt devalued by him. His need to control everything was hurting the church in that decisions about various operational matters had to be made, but he wasn't always there to make those decisions. He wouldn't delegate authority to other workers to make those types of decisions, which was stifling the church. Rather than listening to what people were telling him he was defensive and claimed, "I'm the pastor, God works through me, not you."

This bred a legalistic environment in that everybody had to line up with him and his dysfunctional, dictatorial, leadership style. The other committed workers were frustrated, felt devalued, and unappreciated by him.

Pastoral Insecurity Breeds Legalism

Sometimes a pastor may be excessively controlling to the point where he is stifling the body. When a pastor is hyper-controlling of all the ministries there can be several reasons why this is the case. *One reason may be that at some point in his past he was burned by someone and bears the wounds of that situation.* For instance, I know a senior pastor who was betrayed by his associate, who secretly recruited a large number of people to leave the church and be part of his new congregation that he was founding. When the senior pastor caught wind of this he confronted his associate and asked him if there was any truth to this. The associate didn't say a word to him; he just got up and walked out of the room.

That was a crushing blow to the senior pastor, who had to clean up the pieces of a church split, deal with the loss of revenue from decreasing offerings, and deal with the sting of betrayal. The pastor questioned his leadership abilities and wondered where he went wrong. He concluded that he gave way too much freedom to his associate, so he over-reacted to this situation and became controlling of people and situations. He was trying to protect himself and his family from being hurt in the future, like he was by his associate. The scares from this situation ran deep, taking a long time for him and his wife to heal from this devastating scenario.

There are times when people in the church may hurt the pastor's wife or kids and he becomes overly protective of them. He tries to protect them by being controlling of circumstances and people.   His motivation may be nothing more than trying to look out for his family. God only knows how many pastors' wives have been severely hurt in a church setting. I remember at one district conference I attended years ago, the pastors were huddled in groups of about 10 people for a time of prayer. One of the pastors had a very troubled look on his face as he requested prayer for his wife. He explained to his colleagues that she had been very hurt by some people in the church and it was next to impossible for her to go there.

I know a pastor who was voted out of office in an ugly congregational meeting while his son was in grade school. That had a profound effect on the young lad as he struggled with what happened and resented the way his dad was treated. There are many pastors' kids that bear scares from watching their parents go through ugly church conflicts and take a lot of blows. This sort of thing is very sad to consider but it happens, and as a reaction to these kinds of things pastors can become controlling to protect their families.

Another reason why a leader may become overly controlling is that he doesn't have much *confidence in the people around him*. He doesn't unleash people to do ministry because he figures nobody can do the ministry as good as he can, so he basically tries to do everything himself. His fear is that if he deploys people to do ministry the quality control level will suffer greatly, so he does everything himself. His actions hurt the body because he isn't letting people serve and contribute to the edification of the body by using their spiritual gifts. His estimation of himself is higher than it should be, and his estimation of the people around him is lower than it should be.

Another reason for a pastor to be overly controlling is *insecurity*. When a pastor has quality people who are very gifted coming into his church, that are willing to serve there are several ways that he can react to this. One way is he can praise God for the influx of gifted people coming into the church, get to know them and utilize them in building his church. On the other hand, if the pastor is insecure he may be threatened by gifted people coming into the fellowship, because they might be able to do things better than he can. He fears that they might be better Bible teachers than he is, or counselors, administrators and so forth, so he restricts people from serving and hurts the church because of it. He's afraid that someone might outdo him and make him look bad.

King Saul was insanely jealous of David. It seems as though David was better than Saul at everything, and King Saul couldn't deal with that because of his insecurity. What he didn't realize is that if he would have honored David and given him all the praise and accolades that he deserved, the people would have respected and loved Saul for that. When a pastor gives people permission to serve and recognizes them for their work, the people will respect the pastor and love him for it. The people are glad to serve under a pastor like that because they feel valued, and appreciated as his colleagues, rather than feeling as if they are sources of irritation to him.

Pastor Lenny

Pastor Lenny had a revolving door in his church. He had a multitude of talented people who kept showing up in his church: musicians, teachers, administrators, and so on. However, he couldn't keep them. The ones who stayed long-term were the initial core that he started the church with, and a few others. People would come into the church, stay for a while and then leave. His standard MO with people was to get to know them, make promises to train them for ministry, but when it came to the point where it was time to let them serve he wouldn't unleash them. He would say they need more training, or it wasn't the right time of the year to start this ministry, or come up with some other battery of excuses. The result was that people would get very frustrated because they were willing and able to serve, but he never gave them permission to do so. After a while they would leave and go elsewhere.

There were times when he did give permission to someone to start a new ministry, and it was showing signs of traction, then he would abruptly end it. He would explain that the Lord was leading him in another direction, or that the ministry didn't fit into the overall vision of the church, or whatever. The result was that more people would leave because they felt hurt, frustrated, and unappreciated.

Why he was so controlling of people was probably a combination of all three factors mentioned above, but make no mistake about it, he was a control freak. Whether his control issues were rooted in past hurts, insecurity, or low confidence in the people around him, his actions hurt the church and many of the people.

Another issue people in the church had with Pastor Lenny was that nobody could keep up with him. In staff meetings he would say one thing, then at the next weekly staff meeting he would completely reverse his position on an issue. Things constantly changed, nobody

126

could follow him, but nobody ever said anything to him. Where was his leadership team to hold him accountable and keep him on task?

The Dynamic Sunday School Class

One church I had familiarity with had started a new Sunday school class that was totally volunteer led. The class was taught by a gifted teacher and grew rapidly. The attendance quickly soared to about 60-70 people, which was amazing when you consider the church had about 300 people on any given Sunday, plus there were other classes offered at the same time. The class was vibrant and the ministry that was taking place was touching people's lives. This was a totally a lay-led initiative and served as a great example of deploying people for ministry; allowing them to use their spiritual gifts to strengthen and encourage the body of Christ.

After a time the pastor and board of elders made a decision to terminate the class to everyone's amazement. Why would the governing body of the church shut down a class that was growing, meeting the needs of the people, and edifying the body? There was never a satisfactory explanation given to the congregation as to why the class was cancelled. People speculated that the only reason the board of elders would shut down a class that was growing and meeting the needs of people was because the leadership of the church was threatened that they didn't have control of it. It was a grass roots initiative begun with the permission of the elders, but they or the pastor were threatened by the success of the ministry, so rather than letting it continue they shut it down. They abruptly halted the work of the Holy Spirit in that class because they couldn't control the ministry. People were shocked and upset that the class ended, but technically speaking, this was more of an affront to the Holy Spirit than it was to the people.

How interesting it is that when God—the Holy Spirit—shows up and does a great work in an area of the church the leadership feels threatened, so rather than rejoicing at the work God is doing they shut it down. It just doesn't make sense, but those sorts of things happen when pastors are insecure, controlling, and easily threatened.

Lack of Accountability With the Pastor

In some churches pastors are King. Whatever they say goes. In other churches the board controls things so much that the pastor can't get anything done. They always feel stifled and unable to provide leadership because their board wants to be in control. Extremes of this nature in leadership are to be avoided, for control of the church should be somewhere in the middle.

When a church calls a pastor they are calling him to set forth a ministry and vision for the church. They should give him the freedom to do that, all within proper lines of accountability. I've known too many pastors that resigned their position and went to another ministry because they were controlled by their board to the point where they couldn't set forth their vision and were frustrated. They came into the church with a set of fresh eyes, and could see very clearly where things needed to change for the church to have a bright future. Their board wasn't in favor of the proposed changes, so after years of trying to unsuccessfully convince their board that change was necessary they were tired, worn down, battered, bruised, and left disappointed.

The opposite scenario can occur as well. A board is excited about having a new pastor and has high hopes that he will set forth a vision and ministry that will give the church a promising future. They let the pastor get settled into his new position, unpack his books, and wait patiently for him to set forth a vision for the church, but it never comes. They discover their new pastor, that they had pinned their hopes on, is a low energy maintenance man, who isn't the visionary they thought he was. They are disappointed and wonder if they made the right choice.

Scripture teaches that there is always a plurality of elders that oversee the church. The mantle of leadership doesn't rest on one person's shoulders (1 Peter 5:1). God in his wisdom knows that if one man has all power he will most likely have a failure of some sort because of his sinful nature. That is one reason why God has assigned the oversight of a local church to a plurality of elders. If the pastor of the church is doing things, such as pastor Lenny mentioned above, it is the elder's job to talk with him about it. They need to keep him on track and help him be the best that he can be for God and the church.

There are Scriptural principles that explain how this should be done (Mat 18:15-18; 1 Tim 5:19-20). All too often in churches where the pastor is King, the board of elders says nothing when the pastor goes off track. It may be that they don't have the energy to go through a rough confrontation, or the knowhow to do it, so they let it slide and do nothing. All this does is perpetuate the dysfunction of the church, and by not saying anything to the pastor they are doing him and the congregation a disservice.

Conclusion

Pastors are human beings like everybody else and occasionally we make mistakes. But when a church becomes dysfunctional because of leadership there can be much harm done to the people. Some of the markers of dysfunctional leadership that can breed a culture of legalism are using fear and guilt as a means of manipulating people. Displaying an elitist mentality that suggests this church has it right, but the other ones in the city are playing catch up. Another marker of dysfunctional leadership is excessive control to the point where the work of the Holy Spirit is thwarted in the church.

An insecure pastor can be very controlling of people, situations, and stifle the growth of the church. A lack of accountability existing between the pastor and his leadership team is a huge red flag. Prophetic words from God can be used in a very manipulative way to promote man-made agendas. All the above dysfunctions can create a toxic legalistic church. Pastors and elders have been given authority to shepherd their flock, but they must use their authority in a humble servant's spirit to build people up not tear them down.

Chapter 14 ~ Legalism in Keeping One's Salvation

There is another way that legalism's ugly face presents itself, which involves keeping one's salvation. In this form of legalism the believer understands that he was saved by God's grace, having nothing to do with his good works or anything that is inherently good in him. However, now that he is saved he believes he must generate good works in order to stay saved. In other words, maintaining his salvation is contingent on his ability to manufacture good works. This believer lives with an underlying fear and insecurity in his relationship with Christ.

One doctrinal issue that believers have had different views about over the millennia is whether or not a Christian can lose his salvation. It is well beyond the scope of this book to do an exhaustive treatment of this issue, so a brief summary of the positions will be offered.

One view is that once someone is saved she can never lose her salvation. She is *eternally secure* in her relationship with Christ (John 10:28-30; Rom 8:29-30; 38-39).

Another position is that in the case of willful and deliberate apostasy the believer can lose his salvation. In other words, if a believer deliberately renounces his standing with Christ and chooses to walk away from him he can lose his salvation (Heb 6:1-8).

The position I take is that once someone is born again and in relationship with Christ, that relationship will be retained for all eternity—it can never be severed. Once saved the person will always be saved.

Those who maintain the possibility of losing their salvation may feel a sense of insecurity in their walk with the Lord, and may have a need to prove to themselves, and God, that they are saved by manufacturing good works. They totally understand that their salvation was by grace—God's free gift to them—but they strive rather than resting in the assurance of their salvation. In their minds they are entertaining an error that says, "I have to work hard at being a good person to stay saved."

The apostle Paul had a situation with the Galatian churches that is similar to the scenario that I've just described. First, I'll do an analysis of the passage then bring it home to the modern reader with a number of pertinent applications.

You foolish Galatians, who has bewitched you, before whose eyes Jesus Christ was publicly portrayed *as* crucified? ²This is the only thing I want to find out from you: did you receive the Spirit by the works of the Law, or by hearing with faith? ³Are you so foolish? Having begun by the Spirit, are you now being perfected by the flesh? ⁴Did you suffer so many things in vain—if indeed it was in vain? ⁵So then, does He who provides you with the Spirit and works miracles among you, do it by the works of the Law, or by hearing with faith? (Galatians 3:1-5)

Paul writes this passage in a style known as diatribe, which is a rhetorical device that shows opposing views to be illogical. He asks them a series of questions that appeal to their conversion experience.

Question 1: You foolish Galatians, who has bewitched you? (Galatians 3:1)

Paul seems to be utterly amazed at the Galatians' thought process to the point where he considers them foolish—as if someone cast a magical spell on them. The word foolish is a translation of the Greek word *anoétos*. This word doesn't mean stupid; rather it refers to people who don't think through a matter in a logical fashion. Paul is implying the Galatian believers weren't thinking clearly regarding spiritual matters because they have embraced a false gospel presented by the Judaizers (false teachers).

Paul had taught them the true gospel when he was with them, now they are defecting from the gospel of grace and going backwards to a

131

gospel of law. They are forfeiting their freedom in Christ and placing themselves under the oppression of legalism based on the Law of Moses, ceremonial rules, and dietary regulations that the New Covenant has made obsolete because Christ fulfilled them. The Galatians were going backwards in their spiritual experience to a place where they would substitute their freedom and joy for a form of religion that was powerless, and would take away the joyfulness of life that they once enjoyed in knowing Jesus.

The fact that the Galatians have deserted the true gospel of Christ for a false gospel is so bewildering to Paul he wants to know "who has bewitched you?" Magic in the ancient world was commonly practiced. Malevolent powers would be called upon in casting spells on people. Paul is thinking the only possible explanation for the Galatians' deserting the gospel he taught them must be that someone cast a spell on them. Paul could be implying that there is a demonic component to the Galatians' departure from the true gospel of grace, for Satan is the father of lies (John 8:44), and false doctrine does have a demonic component to it (1 Tim 4:1).

Although there may have been a demonic influence involved with the false teachers, the truth of the matter is that the Galatians should have known better. Paul taught them the true gospel of grace, therefore they should have had the ability to discern the false teaching instantly and walk away from it. Instead, they let themselves be misled by the false teachers and submitted themselves to the false gospel of works righteousness. They were duped into thinking that Jesus' sacrifice wasn't enough for their salvation, so they had to add works such as circumcision, following dietary regulations (basically becoming Jewish) in order to be saved.

This deprecates the all-sufficient efficacious sacrifice of Christ. So Paul reminds them of the centrality of the cross, which was a main part of his teaching when he was there: "before whose eyes Jesus Christ was publicly portrayed *as* crucified?" In Paul's gospel presentation he presented Jesus as the only means of atoning for sin and the Galatians' accepted the message, believed, and were born again believers in Christ.

The words "publicly portrayed" is the Greek word *prographó*, which was a word used of posting notices on a placard in public places for people to read. Paul is making the point that when he preached to them it was as if he placarded Jesus before the Galatians, so they could publically see the centrality of Jesus' crucifixion with crystal clarity. The word crucified is written as a perfect passive participle, which indicates the crucifixion was an event rooted in history with ongoing results in the present. In other words, the cross never stops being efficacious in atoning for sin. The blood of Jesus is just as powerful today to forgive sin, as it was the day he died. The cross of Jesus continues to be effective as the eternal payment for sin such that any sinner, in any era of history that places their trust in Christ will be forgiven. This fact makes the desertion of the true gospel by the Galatians even more ridiculous, and baffling to Paul.

The Judaizers were advocating that to become part of the covenant community they needed to be circumcised, thus advocating faith in Jesus plus works were necessary for their salvation. How could cutting away a piece of flesh make one acceptable to God, when Jesus paid the full penalty for our sins? It seems preposterous to take such a view.

Question 2: This is the only thing I want to find out from you: did you receive the Spirit by the works of the Law, or by hearing with faith? (Galatians 3:2)

Paul appeals to the Galatians' experience regarding their reception of the Holy Spirit. Paul isn't therefore questioning whether or not they are true believers, because he acknowledges that they have received the Holy Spirit. This is one of the markers of believers' in Christ; they are people in whom the Spirit resides (Ro 8:16; Eph 1:13-14; 1 John 4:13; 3:24). The false teachers were claiming that to become true believers they had to be circumcised, so that the combination of faith in Christ plus circumcision would qualify one to be accepted by God. They felt only Torah observing Jews could receive the Spirit.

The question Paul asks isn't theological it is experiential. Did they receive the Spirit by "works of the Law" or "by hearing with faith?" Paul considers these two different spiritual orientations, which stand as polar opposites. The answer to this should be obvious: they heard the gospel and responded with faith in Christ and received the Spirit. The fact that they received the Spirit by faith also supports Paul's argument that they are justified by faith alone in Christ. This should be a no brainer to the Galatians. If they remember their conversion experience it should be obvious to them that it was by God's grace through faith that they were justified, declared righteous in God's sight, and received the Spirit. Good works wasn't even remotely close to being in the picture of Paul's gospel—it's all grace through faith. If the Galatians jog their memories and answer "yes" to this question that ends the debate right there, but Paul has more to say about this matter.

Question 3: Are you so foolish? Having begun by the Spirit, are you now being perfected by the flesh? (Galatians 3:3)

There are two parts to this question. Paul returns to their irrational thinking, which he brands as "foolish" (same word as in v. 1). The Galatian believers began their life in Christ "by the Spirit." The Spirit is the source of life that enables Christians to live faithfully for Christ. Without the Spirit the power source for godly living is eliminated, hence Paul's admonition for believers to be filled with the Spirit (Eph 5:18). Paul tells the Galatian believers later in his letter that they are to live by the Spirit (5:16), be led by the Spirit (5:18), bear the fruit of the Spirit (5:22-23), and keep in step with the Spirit (5:26). He is the source of godly living and victory over the temptations to sin. The Galatians had a good start in their new life in Christ, but when they succumbed to the influence of the false teachers, they changed directions in their spiritual experience.

"Having begun by the Spirit are you now being perfected by the flesh?" The Greek word *sárks* is translated flesh, and in Pauline vocabulary usually refers to unregenerate man living apart from faith in Christ. However, the flesh is still a force to contend with in the lives of believers. The "flesh" and "Spirit" are viewed as warring against one another (5:16-18), thus even though one has been born again that doesn't mean that the flesh is totally inoperative. The believer lives in spiritual tension between the flesh and Spirit, which is a recurring theme for Paul.

134

That Paul says "are you now being perfected by the flesh" indicates that the Galatians were going backwards into the wrong spiritual realm in their sanctification. "Spirit" and "flesh" stand as polar opposites. The Spirit is the realm in which believers live, whereas flesh is the realm in which man outside of Christ lives. The Spirit and flesh are two different domains, two different spiritual orientations in life, two different periods of time (before and after becoming a believer), or two different eras (the Old Covenant then the New Covenant). Paul views life in the flesh as life under the law, which means the Galatians' are going backwards to the old era and are no longer focusing on living in the Spirit. Casting aside the provision of grace and the fullness of the Spirit to do the works of the law to gain God's approval is spiritually outrageous. God has already approved of the Galatians through their faith in Christ's efficacious sacrifice. They are already in a right standing with God, which can't be improved upon.

The New Living Translation (NLT) translates *sárks* "human effort" rather than "flesh." In this understanding of the text "human effort" could refer to circumcision (and other works of the law), which would be the initiation into Judaism for the Gentile proselytes. Either way the meaning is very similar because for Paul life in the flesh was life under the law, and those who live under the law commit to the works of the law, which is human effort (NLT).

Question 4: Did you suffer so many things in vain—if indeed it was in vain? (Galatians 3:4)

The word "suffer" is the translation of the Greek word *paschó*, which can also mean: to experience hardship and pain. It appears that Paul is alluding to the Galatians experience of persecution after they became Christians, probably at the hands of the Jews (Gal 4:29). If they suffer as a believer in Christ there is some purpose in the hardship they endured. However, if they go back to Judaism, and keeping the law, their suffering for Christ was for nothing. If they turn their backs on the Spirit, and go back to the works of the law, all their experiences of the Spirit will have been for nothing—it was all in vain.

Paul hasn't completely closed the door on the Galatians because he says: "if indeed it was in vain?" He's leaving room for the possibility of the Galatians to come back to their spiritual senses and sever their ties with the false teachers and their false gospel. Paul is hopeful that the Galatians will get back on track and walk in grace.

Question 5: So then, does He who provides you with the Spirit and works miracles among you, do it by the works of the Law, or by hearing with faith? (Galatians 3:5)

The word "provides" is a translation of the Greek word *epichorēgéō,* which doesn't bring out the full nuance of the Greek word. It means to supply with great generosity and abundance. It is written as a present participle, which denotes continuous action. The word was used of husbands making vows to their brides to provide bountifully for them, as well as patrons who would donate money to fund the arts, and patriotic citizens to donate some of their wealth to the government. God continuously supplies us with the abundance of the Spirit, much like a mighty flowing river that never runs dry. Such is God's provision of the Holy Spirit to his people.

The two verbs: God "provides" the Spirit and "works" (*energéō*) miracles indicate God's activity among the Galatian believers. By mentioning miracles Paul is pointing to the outward manifestation of the Spirit. They already have the internal witness of the Spirit, which causes them to cry out Abba (Ro 8:15-16; Gal 4:6). Precisely what miracles Paul is referring to is unknown. It could be to their conversion experience, their success in evangelism, and more, but it sounds like miracles were common occurrences among them.

The answer to the last question is obvious: God gives the inexhaustible resource of the Spirit and works miracles among them because of their faith in Christ, not through compliance to the Mosaic Law. God accepts all people; Jew and Gentile through faith in Christ, there are no exceptions to this rule. He doesn't just give the Spirit to Torah observing Jews; he gives the Spirit to anybody who has faith in Christ for his salvation.

By appealing to the experience of the Galatians Paul has shown them the error of their ways. By this point one wonders if the Galatian believers are hanging their heads in shame thinking, "what have we done?" Has Paul shocked them back to spiritual reality, such that they can renounce the false gospel of legalism and go back to the true gospel of grace that Paul preached to them?

To come to the point of realizing the abundance of God's grace through Jesus' death on the cross, become part of the New Covenant community of believers, receive the gift of the Holy Spirit and all the other benefits that accrue to believer's in Christ was the experience of the Galatians. However, they were going to throw all this away because of the influence of the false teachers. They were going back to keeping the law, thinking that Jesus' sacrifice wasn't sufficient for their salvation; so they embraced the gospel of legalism and added works in order for God to accept them. This is the epitome of going backwards in their spiritual experience.

Appealing to Experience

Usually theologians and Bible scholars don't like to talk about one's experience for fear that it leads to emotionalism, and sensationalism that isn't grounded in reality. For that reason theologians like to point to Scripture to make their points, rather than appealing to people's experience. This is not what Paul does here, which seems to be uncharacteristic for him. He directly appeals to the Galatians' spiritual experience and essentially argues backwards to make his Scriptural and theological points. This proved to be a great strategy in getting the Galatians to think about correct theology.

Everybody has defining moments in life such as: getting married, graduating from college, having your first child, launching your business, and so forth. Certainly, one of the most important defining moments in life has to be when you became a Christian. Some people have dramatic conversions while others have more mundane testimonies of how they met Jesus. Christians enjoy sharing their testimonies, which is often a requirement for church membership. Some churches take time in their Sunday morning worship service to have people share their testimony, or utilize a small group setting to have people share their personal experiences with Jesus.

Apparently the Galatian believers had a rather dramatic conversion experience. They received the Holy Spirit and apparently witnessed miracles in their midst (Gal 3:5). Paul preached the gospel to them when he took sick, and the Galatians treated him exceptionally well in providing care for him. Paul wants them to jog their memories and think about when they heard him preach the gospel and they received Jesus into their hearts. From time-to-time all Christians should reflect on their conversion experience, and consider how their life in Christ began.

As the Galatians reflect on the questions Paul asks them about their conversion, they should realize that becoming a Christian had nothing to do with keeping the Law of Moses, following any moral code, being a good person, or anything to do with inherent goodness about themselves such that God would accept them on the basis of their personal merit. It was all grace through faith, having nothing to do with their works.

One of the benefits of rehearsing your testimony is that it brings God's grace to the surface and makes one realize that their relationship with Christ is God's gift to them. As I reflect on how I became a believer in Christ, that's the one thing that stands out in my mind. I had nothing to bring to the table by way of personal goodness such that God accepted me and forgave me for my sins. In fact, I was alone in my apartment, in a state of despair, trying to figure out how someone can be content and fulfilled in life. I wasn't coming up with any answers and my life wasn't working for me. I began having flashbacks in my mind to when I was in grade school attending a Presbyterian Church. Images of the pastor kept coming into my mind, as I saw myself sitting in the pew and I was perplexed as to why these images were coming into my mind's eye.

It hit me like a ton of bricks! I was thinking about why my life wasn't working, how I could possibly be content and fulfilled, when I realized that I missed the whole point of life: I had rejected God and was doing my own thing. It was at that moment I realized that everything I was taught in Sunday school about Jesus was true. I remembered John 3:16, which was the only verse I could recite. I committed my life to Christ at that moment, experienced the new birth, and felt a

138

tremendous burden lifted off my shoulders. I had finally figured out how one can be content and fulfilled in life, which happens only by knowing Jesus.

As I reflect on my conversion experience, quite often, I realize that God reached his hand down from heaven and saved me. There was nothing I did to merit his favor, it was all God reaching out to me, and it was his grace poured out all over me. Claiming that my salvation was rooted in any inherent goodness I possessed is totally unwarranted, because I didn't have any inherent goodness—neither does anybody else. My conversion experience is a picture of God's grace, which makes me grateful to God for showing me mercy.

As people reflect on their testimony they should hopefully come to the same conclusion. The Galatians should be realizing that their conversion was all God's grace. The strange thing about the Galatians is that they began their life in Christ by his grace and received the Holy Spirit, but through the influence of the false teachers didn't continue their life in Christ by grace. It's as if the Galatians were living in the Spirit, then slammed on the brakes, reversed direction and began living by the law. They began by grace, but didn't continue in grace, they shifted gears to the works of the law. This course of action makes no sense when they compare it to their conversion experience. God gave them the Spirit by faith, not works, so why would they think they have to add works to be accepted by God now?

Conclusion

In this chapter we have looked at the Galatian believers and seen how they went off track by going back to works, rather than continuing on in the Holy Spirit in their sanctification. We have discussed how the role of the Holy Spirit is minimized in many people's lives because they are doing things in their own strength for reasons that are suspect to God. The point of application for everyone to take away from this passage is: *one doesn't get saved by doing good works and one doesn't stay saved by doing good works.* The Christian life is all God's grace from beginning to end!

Some believers are duped into thinking they have to manufacture good works to keep their salvation, which is not correct. The relationship between faith and works is very simple. They are like two links of a chain that are inseparable. Where true faith in Christ exists in the human heart, faith will burst forth in good deeds. True faith can't be hidden, suppressed, shackled, contained, or imprisoned; faith will just naturally manifest itself in good deeds. The apostle James said faith without works is dead (James 2:26). One of the natural consequences of being a Christian is that good deeds will be evident in the believer's life. The proof of one's faith and continuing relationship with Christ is that good deeds will naturally occur that are done in the power of the Holy Spirit.

For those who are running on the treadmill of trying to manufacture good works to improve their standing with God, or keep their right standing with God, they need to be freed from this striving? John MacArthur makes a makes an insightful comment:

> The validity of good works in God's sight depends on whose power they are done in and for whose glory. When they are done in the power of His spirit and for His glory, they are beautiful and acceptable to him. When they are done in the power of the flesh and for the sake of personal recognition or merit, they are rejected by Him. Legalism is separated from true obedience by attitude. The one is a rotten smell in God's nostrils, whereas the other is a sweet savor.
>
> The prayer offered in humble faith, seeking God's will and glory, is pleasing to the Father, whereas a prayer uttered by rote or to impress God or other people is anathema to Him (Luke 18:10-14). Going to church to worship God sincerely with fellow believers is pleasing to Him, whereas going to the same church service and being with the same fellow believers is not acceptable to Him if done in a self-righteous, self-serving, legalistic spirit (MacArthur, p. 68).

Good works will not improve our standing with God, for Jesus has already provided us with a right standing before God that can't be improved upon! As we live the Christian life with Christ, through the Spirit, we naturally want to please God by being obedient. Through the enablement of the Spirit, believers are to be obedient, for God's glory, not their own. MacArthur's quote above provided a keen insight that all believer's should take note of: *Legalism is separated from true obedience by attitude.* Believers need to do an attitude check periodically so they make sure their motives for serving God are not corrupted by the need for recognition, one-upmanship, or trying to keep themselves in good standing with God.

The Christian life begins in the Spirit, who is received the moment we place our trust in Jesus to save us. The believer continues on in the Spirit for the duration of his life doing good deeds as the Holy Spirit leads and empowers. This will naturally happen so there is no need for believers to try and produce good works in their own strength, as if they have to prove to themselves, and to God that they are saved. In the next chapter we will discuss the importance of knowing with certainty that you are saved and in a right relationship with God, through Christ.

Chapter 15 ~ Assurance of Salvation

When a sinner is born-again and receives eternal life he can never lose his salvation. In other words, once God imparts eternal life to the believer he will never take it away from her. This is known as *eternal security*. Nothing can sever a believer's relationship with Jesus (Rom 8:38-39), so at the moment of his death he goes directly to heaven and is in the presence of the Lord (Phil 1:23).

Assurance of salvation is a different matter. One may have received Jesus into his heart and been born-again, but doesn't have confidence in his status with God. He isn't sure whether he is saved, so doubts linger in his mind making him feel insecure in his relationship with God. *Assurance of salvation is the confidence that the believer has in knowing, beyond any shadow of doubt that he is saved—in a right relationship with God.*

It isn't uncommon for people to question whether or not they are truly saved. In fact, I've had many people over the years come to me and express their concern regarding their status with God. Some people are distressed because they aren't sure whether they are truly born again, and ask me the question: "Pastor Bruce, how do I know if I'm really saved?" They tell me that they aren't sure and live with a sense of insecurity about their relationship with God. It causes them much spiritual trauma and anxiety.

When someone has assurance of their salvation they are fully persuaded that their sins are forgiven, and that they are in a right standing with God. They don't doubt whether or not they are saved because it is a certainty to them. This is a subjective matter with each believer. One can be born again, it is a fact, but in their thought-life they aren't sure about this reality. Objectively speaking it is a fact that he is born again and saved, but subjectively speaking the person lacks assurance of his secure status with God.

Assurance of one's salvation is rooted in fact not feelings and emotionalism. Scripture indicates that it is possible for a person to know they are saved. The apostle John made this point very clear: "These things I have written to you who believe in the name of the Son of God, so that you may know that you have eternal life" (1 John 5:13). In John's first letter he compiled a list of proof tests that reveal characteristics of those who are truly born again. Reading through his letter can be a profitable exercise in growing in your level of confidence that you are saved.

Assurance of one's salvation is rooted in the following objective facts revealed in Scripture:

> For God so loved the world, that He gave His only begotten Son, that whoever believes in Him shall not perish, but have eternal life. (John 3:16)

> For this is the will of My Father, that everyone who beholds the Son and believes in Him will have eternal life, and I Myself will raise him up on the last day. (John 6:40)

The above passages reveal that to have eternal life one must believe in Jesus. Once you believe in Jesus you will not perish, there is no need to fear going to hell, for having eternal life means that you will meet up with Jesus in heaven. Having assurance of salvation will be greatly facilitated by pinpointing the exact moment that you placed your trust in Christ. For those who have had dramatic conversions it is easy to do that. That is my case for I can remember with crystal clarity the exact moment I got saved. Others may have a more difficult time identifying this moment. For example, people who grow up in church and place their faith in Christ at a very early age may have a problem identifying the specific moment when they placed their trust in Jesus for their salvation.

When one believes in Jesus he is born again, or regenerated which means the same thing. Consider the following passages:

> Jesus answered and said to him, "Truly, truly, I say to you, unless one is born again he cannot see the kingdom of God." (John 3:3)

> He saved us, not on the basis of deeds which we have done in righteousness, but according to His mercy, by the washing of regeneration and renewing by the Holy Spirit, [6]whom He poured out upon us richly through Jesus Christ our Savior, [7]so that being justified by His grace we would be made heirs according to *the* hope of eternal life. (Titus 3:5-7)

Jesus said one must be born again to access the Kingdom of God (cf. John 3:5). In the Titus passage above regeneration is the same as being born again. Many people claim to be believers in Christ but haven't been born again, which means they aren't true believers. A profession of faith that is genuine will lead to a sinner being born again. There are many people sitting in pews in their sanctuaries that think they are born again, and claim to believe in Jesus, but haven't been regenerated. Each person must be certain that they have been born again.

> My sheep hear My voice, and I know them, and they follow Me; [28]and I give eternal life to them, and they will never perish; and no one will snatch them out of My hand. [29]My Father, who has given *them* to Me, is greater than all; and no one is able to snatch *them* out of the Father's hand. [30]I and the Father are one." (John 10:27-30)

The above passage is one of the strongest texts in all of Scripture to support the position of eternal security. Once sinners enter a relationship with Jesus he imparts eternal life to them, so that they will never perish (go to hell). Jesus provides a word picture of himself and the Father holding the believer in their hands, such that nobody, even Satan, can take them away from their protective care.

> For those whom He foreknew, He also predestined *to become* conformed to the image of His Son, so that He

would be the firstborn among many brethren; [30]and these whom He predestined, He also called; and these whom He called, He also justified; and these whom He justified, He also glorified (Romans 8:29-30).

One of the hallmarks of Christian doctrine is justification by faith alone. Once the sinner is declared righteous in God's sight and has Christ's righteousness imputed to him, there is no evidence in Scripture to suggest that this declaration is reversible. Once God declares the sinner righteous it is binding for all eternity. God doesn't declare someone unrighteous after he declares him or her to be righteous. He doesn't change his mind because of something lacking in their behavior. The above passage in Romans indicates those whom God justifies he will take all the way to glorification, which is living in the perfected state in the resurrection body. God will keep the believer in his hands all the way through eternity. If you have been justified by faith in Christ, it is a certainty that God will take you all the way to glorification.

One of the characteristics of true believers is that they will endure to the end of their natural lives in the faith. This is known as *perseverance*. God will keep the believer all the way to the end as Peter brings out in his letter:

> to *obtain* an inheritance *which is* imperishable and undefiled and will not fade away, reserved in heaven for you, [5]who are protected by the power of God through faith for a salvation ready to be revealed in the last time. (1 Peter 1:4-5)

God keeps the believer by his power all the way to the end where he will realize his inheritance in heaven. However, the Christian's role is faith, trusting in God as he goes through life, and God will keep him all the way to the end. We see God and man working together as God preserves the believer, while the believer exercises faith.

Reasons People May Lack Assurance

It is necessary for believers to be confident in their relationship with God by having assurance that they are saved. Lack of assurance can hinder one's growth in Christ and cause unnecessary spiritual crisis. *Assurance is the realization and internalization that one possesses eternal life.* People will lack assurance of their salvation for several reasons, one of which is they can't identify the exact moment when they placed their trust in Christ and were born again.

People who have a dramatic conversion experience can remember the exact moment they became a believer in Christ. By dramatic conversion I mean someone who believed in Jesus and may have experienced a physical healing, been set free from a bad habit, and things of that nature. For people who have had that kind of experience the moment of their conversion is crystal clear to them— they can tell you the date, the location, the time, etc. The details are vivid for them. However, for others it is very difficult to pinpoint that exact moment in life when they became a believer. They didn't have a dramatic conversion so they aren't sure when it took place. When they compare their conversion experience with those whose conversion was more dramatic they may be left wondering if theirs was genuine. God knows when the exact moment was when that person was regenerated, even though it is unclear in the person's mind when it occurred.

A second reason one may lack assurance of his salvation may stem from the belief that a true believer can lose his salvation. Those who are raised in a tradition that advocates the position that believers can lose their salvation will inevitably lack assurance at times.

A third reason one may lack assurance is when a serious sin is established in the believer's life, and becomes habitual. He can't gain victory over the sin and constantly struggles in his sanctification in this area of his life. He then begins to wonder if his inability to gain victory over this sin is because he isn't really saved. Doubt enters his mind and he feels insecure in his relationship with God. A believer can have sinful habits in his life, have ups and downs in his spiritual experience, and may even backslide at times throughout his life, but that doesn't mean that his relationship with Christ has been severed. He is still justified by faith and righteous in God's sight, but is struggling in his sanctification.

People in this situation, which I believe to be many believers, are usually carrying an extreme load of guilt, feeling like they can't please God because of the sin in their life. In scenarios like this one must be cautious of the counsel he provides someone in this tender situation. To tell someone who is in bondage to a sin that they may not be truly saved, because if they were they wouldn't be struggling with this bad habit, only heaps a bigger load of guilt, condemnation, and judgment upon the struggling individual. It might make for a nice pat answer, and an airtight systematic, but in a real life counseling situation telling someone that they may not be a Christian only makes things worse.

A fourth reason one may lack assurance is the manner in which they got saved. Questions linger in the new converts mind regarding things such as: does my salvation become effective only after I'm baptized? I prayed privately, but do I need to make a public profession of faith to be saved? I didn't go forward at the end of the worship service, so does this mean I'm not saved? Then there is bad theology that people are exposed to that serves only to confuse new believers and causes them to question their salvation. Things such as you have to speak in tongues to be a genuine believer. You have to be a member of a church to be truly saved. You're not saved until you take communion. This is one reason new believers should immediately start reading Scripture and place themselves in a church that teaches the word of God, which enables the new believer to begin his journey of discipleship. This course of action will help clear away confusing misconceptions about one's salvation.

It should be noted in this discussion of *assurance of one's salvation* and *eternal security* that the term *eternal security* can be greatly misunderstood. One may hear the gospel presented in a way that doesn't emphasize the need for repentance, and commitment to Christ for the duration of one's life. The gospel may have been diluted such that the hearer is led to believe that once he makes a decision for Christ that's all he needs to do to go to heaven. He is misled into thinking that he has eternal security.

Wayne Grudem comments on this tragic situation:

> The phrase eternal security can be quite misleading. In some evangelical churches, instead of teaching the full and balanced presentation of the doctrine of the perseverance of the saints, pastors have sometimes taught a watered-down version, which in effect tells people that all who have once made a profession of faith and been baptized are "eternally secure." The result is that some people who are not genuinely converted at all may "come forward" at the end of an evangelistic sermon to profess faith in Christ, and may be baptized shortly after that, but then they leave the fellowship of the church and live a life no different from the one they lived before they gained this "eternal security." In this way people are given false assurance and are being cruelly deceived into thinking they are going to heaven when in fact they are not. (Grudem, p. 806)

Pastors must give an accurate gospel presentation that emphasizes faith, repentance, and life-long commitment to Christ (perseverance) so that people understand what God expects of those who want to become a Christian. Many people today carry a false sense of security because they have been duped into thinking they are saved, and eternally secure when in point of fact they are not.

Perhaps, this is why at evangelistic rallies many people come forward, pray the sinner's prayer and leave the auditorium thinking they are going to heaven. After going to church for a while they don't see any real change in their life so they drop out of fellowship, concluding "I tried the Christian life but it didn't work for me." What probably happened was the individual in question made a quick emotional decision to trust Christ, but without understanding the need for repentance and life-long commitment to Jesus his conversion wasn't genuine. This is one reason why many of the people that come forward at evangelistic rallies to receive Christ become dropouts.

148

I knew of a pastor that ended every service with an altar call where he invited those who wanted to receive Christ into their lives to come forward. He would lead them in a prayer and afterwards proclaim that you are saved and going to heaven. I have always found altar calls of this type to be troubling because nothing was said about a life of discipleship, sanctification, or the need to persevere to the end.

The story of Troy Boswell

Troy had a drinking problem but became a believer in Christ and the Lord took away his desire for alcohol. It was a miraculous work that God did in his life by setting him free. He was grateful to God for giving him grace and wanted to excel in his walk with the Lord. As Troy progressed in the Christian life he told God that if he ever went back to drinking that God should blot his name out of the book of life.

Ten years after he began his new life in Christ he experienced some hard times in the crash of 2008 and began to drink again. He started to alienate himself from church, other believers, and was trying to live the Christian life all alone. There were little compromises that occurred over that period of time that had a cumulative effect, such that little compromises turned into bigger ones. He began to drink more, which began a downward spiral, where he began to feel overwhelmed with a sense of shame and guilt.

He went back into the world, and his drinking took the same place it did before he became a Christian. He drank to medicate himself as a means of coping with his difficult life. It was a downward spiral of guilt and shame. Troy found himself right back where he was before he was saved, but he has the knowledge of his prior experience with God, and desired to be in that place with the Lord that he was before he started drinking again. Now Troy carries two loads of guilt: one is the guilt of going back to drinking, the other is the guilt of feeling he let God down. He began to feel that God had abandoned him and that he lost his salvation.

He felt God's grace and acceptance of him was contingent on his behavior (this is legalism). His logic was: "If I was a true believer this sin wouldn't be in my life." For 15 years he was struggling with drinking and everyday he felt he was lost and out of God's grace. He felt there was no hope of ever being restored to God, he thought he was going to hell, and even became suicidal. Even in reading the Bible he kept coming across passages, like in Hebrews, that convinced him he'd lost his salvation. He felt as though there was no hope in ever coming back to God and being restored.

Troy's Restoration

One day Troy got a phone call from an old friend, and brother in Christ named Lou. They hadn't seen each other for many years and this started a work of restoration in his life. After he talked with Lou he stopped drinking—cold turkey. God miraculously removed his desire to drink and set him free such that he doesn't even think about drinking any more. Now he is in the process of gaining assurance that he is truly saved and secure in his relationship with God. The hole in his life that only God can fill is being filled. He realizes his need to get back into church and be in fellowship with Christians and establish supportive relationships. He is reading his Bible, praying, and growing in the assurance of his relationship with Christ.

He questions at times, whether it was God who did this work in him of drawing him back, or whether it was just by his own strength, totally independent of the Holy Spirit that he stopped drinking. At times he's not sure and kept asking himself: "Did God do this work in me, or did I do it myself?" Answering that question came with great difficulty because he just wasn't sure. We encourage Troy to see the hand of God at work in setting him free from the alcohol, we encourage him to offload his guilt, remember that Jesus died for his failures and they are all forgiven. He has a tendency to beat himself up, place a lot of guilt on himself, which causes a great deal of spiritual trauma for him. Thank God that Troy is back on track with God and growing in his assurance of salvation.

One of the symptoms of someone who lacks assurance of their salvation is that they may strive excessively to do good works to prove to themselves that they are saved. They may be motivated by guilt, insecurity, and be driven to commit to good works for the wrong reasons. This becomes legalistic and burdensome.

Those who lack assurance or have a fear of losing their salvation will often commit to good works to keep themselves in good standing with God, like the Galatian believers mentioned earlier. This is the wrong motivation and is unnecessary. This also becomes a burden of legalism. Believers need to have peace and rest in the knowledge that God will keep them all the way to the end. Having a mental image of the Father and Jesus holding you in their hands should give the believer a sense of safety and security in their relationship with God (John 10:27-30).

Bad Theology

Another position I've heard propagated is the belief that when someone sins they lose their salvation. I remember talking to a good friend of mine who told me that when he was attending some youth rallies in summer camp the speaker would threaten the students with loss of salvation. If you drink a beer, or fire up a Marlboro you're not a true Christian and you're going to hell. This is really bad theology, but if you grow up under this type of preaching it can produce a great deal of spiritual anxiety. It's almost as if there is no room for human weakness and failure. There is a complete absence of grace. If you sin you're going to hell.

An old friend and colleague in ministry, named Jim was discussing eternal security with me. He told me that he knew of several pastors who taught their congregations that every time you sin you lose your salvation. I thought, "What, you've got to be kidding!" If you grow up under this type of teaching, how can you have any assurance of your salvation? This is theology at its worst, and places people under a crippling burden that they can't possibly keep. It breeds a culture of legalism.

When Does Behavior Become legalistic?

When someone serves God it boils down to the attitude of the heart. I've been discussing the person who lacks assurance of his salvation, and the Galatian believers who began by the Spirit, but were moving on in their walk with the Lord through the flesh. On any given Sunday there are a lot of people who are serving the Lord in their church: teachers, children's workers, ushers, parking attendants, nursery workers, kitchen workers, and more. As one watches the people being busy doing their ministry it makes a pastor happy to see all the people serving. By outward appearance everybody looks pretty much the same, but looking inward to the heart, which only God can do, is where you find the motivation to serve God.

One person is serving God because he loves the Lord, wants to please him, and put himself in a position to be used by the Lord to impact other people's lives, all for the glory of God. He is using his spiritual gifts to help build up the body of Christ, and feels fulfilled knowing that he is making a contribution to the church. He is happy to let the Holy Spirit work through him to build up the people that he is interacting with. No doubt, this person is pleasing God and has the right motivation in serving.

Another person is serving but with an entirely different motivation. This believer is serving because he feels he has to, and may even resent it. He may resent the pastor that recruited him for the position he's in, and he may even resent God. He feels that he must be doing something in his church because God will love him more if he finds a place to serve. He may even feel that he is proving to himself and God that he is truly saved by working in his church. The one who serves with this attitude will find little joy in his ministry. He is stuck in a legalistic mindset that tells him to work to earn God's love—the essence of legalism.

Two believers are serving with entirely different motivations. They may look the same on the outside, but inwardly there is a world of difference between the two of them. The first is letting God use him, and the Spirit work through him, while the second is working in his own energy to prove something to himself, or God. Possibly his motivation is to rack up brownie points with God and others, but the Spirit's role is minimized in his life. Guilt may be a motivating factor in serving and striving for God, but this is legalism—working to earn more of God's love.

Conclusion

In this chapter several important terms were introduced that are pertinent to our discussion of legalism. We discussed the importance of having *assurance of your salvation,* which is knowing with confidence that you are in a right relationship with God. Another term is *eternal security,* which means that one's relationship with Christ can never be severed. Finally, the term *perseverance* was introduced, which means the believer will endure in the faith for the duration of his life. One who is lacking assurance of his salvation, or believes in the possibility of losing his salvation, may be striving to prove to himself and God that he is truly saved. He may feel that in order to keep his salvation he has to manufacture good works, but he does so in his own strength, rather than through the power of the Spirit. I highlighted the importance of doing an attitude check to make sure that you are serving God with the right motivation, and letting the Holy Spirit work through you for the glory of God.

This brings us to the end of Part I. Several varieties of legalism have been discussed including: Legalism that blocks the way of salvation, legalism in one's sanctification, legalism regarding one's preferences, and finally, legalism in keeping one's salvation. I have set forth the premise that legalism establishes a false set of criteria to measure spiritual maturity that has little or nothing to do with the Bible. The markers of spiritual maturity legalists identify are man-made, rooted in one's upbringing, church culture, or secular culture, but are not founded on Scriptural principles.

In part II of this book I'm going to point out the markers of spiritual maturity that the Bible identifies. In doing this the reader will see how drastically far off course legalists go.

Part II - The Biblical Markers of Spiritual Maturity

Chapter 16 ~ The Journey of Sanctification

If there were a pill that people could take to cure them of legalism, it would be a strong dose of sanctification. That is the best remedy for legalism that I am aware of because as one studies what the Bible presents as markers of spiritual maturity, it won't take long to see how far off course legalists are in their understanding of what constitutes a mature believer. It is important for every disciple of Christ to know what the Bible presents as the markers of spiritual maturity so that they can be freed of any legalistic tendencies in their life. Additionally, they need to know what picture the Bible presents of spiritual maturity so they can progress as Scripture directs them.

The Journey Begins

When someone becomes a Christian they begin their life-long journey where they are to grow in the faith and become a mature disciple. This is a process that each believer goes through where they are rooted and established in the faith and become more Christlike. The theological term for this process is *sanctification*.

Scripture is filled with a multitude of moral imperatives that encourage the believer to be holy (1 Pet 1:15-16), bear the fruit of the Spirit (Gal 5:22-23), become imitators of God (Eph 5:1), follow the example of Jesus (John 15:15), become mature believers (Eph 4:13), and so on. All these injunctions refer to the believer's sanctification. The Greek word *hagiasmos* is translated sanctification in our English Bibles. The root of the word means "to cut" or "to separate" or "to set apart." The words holy, holiness, and saint come from the same root. *Therefore sanctification describes a process whereby the believer is being separated from sin and becoming more Christlike.* This process is progressive and ongoing for the duration of the believer's life. That sanctification is progressive means that throughout the believer's life she will become more-and-more separated from sin, thus

155

sanctification is a life-long process where the believer is being progressively transformed into the image of Christ.

The Goal of Sanctification

The goal of the believer's sanctification is nothing short of moral perfection. It is a high and lofty goal to shoot for. In the Sermon on the Mount Jesus said:

> **Therefore you are to be perfect, as your heavenly Father is perfect. (Matthew 5:48)**

The perfection Jesus is advocating is a moral / ethical perfection in keeping his commands, but there is something more to it than that. The goal of keeping the law, or obeying God's word, isn't just about keeping the rules. It's about being transformed into the image of God, which will lead the disciple on the road to becoming mature and living obediently. As sons and daughters of the Father, Jesus' disciples must emulate their Father and become like him, with the resources he provides (Matt 10:24-25; Rom 8:29; 12:1-2; 2 Cor 3:18; Gal 5:22-23). Jesus requires his disciples to be a mirror image of their heavenly Father.

The Law (the Old Testament) and all the moral imperatives in the New Testament are a reflection of God's character. Therefore, it shouldn't surprise us that God's standards call for nothing short of perfection. Imagine a God whose law didn't reflect perfection, and didn't require his subjects to live on higher moral ground than everybody else. In the Sermon on the Mount Jesus was speaking against the faulty righteousness of the Pharisees. True righteousness isn't measured by their standards; it is God who sets the standard of righteousness. If God's standards were anything less than a reflection of his moral perfection there would be something drastically wrong with that picture. Wayne Grudem makes the following observation about the believer's goal in sanctification:

> When Jesus commands us to be perfect as our Father in heaven is perfect (Matt 5:48), this simply shows

that God's own absolute moral purity is the standard toward which we are to aim and the standard for which God holds us accountable. The fact that we are unable to attain that standard does not mean that it will be lowered; rather, it means that we need God's grace and forgiveness to overcome our remaining sin. Similarly, when Paul commands the Corinthians to make holiness perfect in the fear of the Lord (2 Cor 7:1), or prays that God would sanctify the Thessalonians wholly (1 Thess 5:23), he is pointing to the goal that he desires them to reach. He does not imply that any reach it, but only that this is the high moral standard toward which God wants all believers to aspire. (Grudem, p. 751)

Is Perfection Attainable in This Life?

Throughout church history there have been groups that believed sinless perfection is attainable in this life. However, that goes against the teaching of Scripture. Even though believers have been born again and infused with spiritual power they are still living under the curse (Gen 3:14-19). Christians are not fully redeemed from their fallen nature at this time. When the Lord Jesus returns all believers will be living in the perfected state—in glorified, resurrection bodies. At that time sin will be a thing of the past. There will not even be the possibility of a believer sinning in the perfected state. The moral attributes of believers will be perfectly aligned with the moral characteristics of God the Father in the glorified state.

Believers are on the road to becoming Christlike and like their heavenly Father, but that goal isn't attainable in this life. This means that believers live in tension. On the one hand, they have been given spiritual life through the new birth, and have the Holy Spirit living within them to help in their spiritual development. On the other hand, believers are still under the curse, and struggle with the power of the sin nature (Rom 7:14-25), and wait expectantly for the day of their redemption at the return of Christ (Rom 8:19-21).

Living in tension between the old order of life under the sinful nature, and the new order of life in the Spirit is a constant in a believer's life. There will be times in one's spiritual growth where they may see great progress. There will be other times when they seem to be going nowhere in their sanctification because of the weakness of the flesh (Gal 5:16-17). Sanctification is like an ongoing battle where there will times of great victory, times of disappointment, and times where it seems mundane.

The fact that God has set perfection as the standard for all believers should cause Christians to rely on his grace. Independent of God's resources the believer will go nowhere in his sanctification, which should cause us to be humble before God and rely on his enablement. Because God has set such a high standard for our spiritual development some people may conclude: since it isn't possible to achieve that goal in this life why even bother trying? They might give up concluding it's too difficult for me. This, of course, is the wrong response.

As we consider the moral perfection of Jesus, as he lived among us and demonstrated what a perfectly sinless life looked like, we should stand all the more amazed at him. This should cause us to draw near to him in worship, and look forward to the day when we are fully redeemed and conformed to his image.

Our Part and God's Part

Both God and man play an active part in the process of sanctification. In Paul's letter to the church at Philippi he said something that is crucial to understand regarding our sanctification in 2:12-13:

> So then, my beloved, just as you have always obeyed, not as in my presence only, but now much more in my absence, work out your salvation with fear and trembling; [13]for it is God who is at work in you, both to will and to work for *His* good pleasure.

In v. 12 the believer is commanded to "work out your salvation." The Greek word *katergázomai* is translated "work out" in our English Bible. This is a compound word consisting of two Greek words the first being *katá,* which means: down, or exactly according to. The second Greek word is *ergázomai,* which means: to work, or to accomplish. Putting both words together the meaning is to "work down to an end," or "to work to an exact definite conclusion." The preposition *katá* intensifies *ergázomai,* so the idea of the word is that the believer is to *work to a precise end* in his salvation. In the context of the passage under consideration Paul is talking about the believer's sanctification.

Salvation is a broad and spacious word that can refer to the moment a sinner becomes a believer and is reconciled to God. It can also be used synonymously of sanctification, as it is here, and it can also refer to the believer's final salvation at the end of the age.

Believers are to "work out" to a precise end their sanctification. They must keep in mind the goal of perfection to which they are challenged to attain. They make a contribution to this process by working. There are no shortcuts in growing as a believer in Christ. When someone becomes a Christian it is important to develop the right habits, disciplines, and practices that promote godliness. This is commonly referred to as *spiritual formation.*

Wayne Grudem makes a comment about spiritual formation that is noteworthy:

> The New Testament does not suggest any short-cuts by which we can grow in sanctification, but simply encourages us repeatedly to give ourselves to the old-fashioned, time-honored means of Bible reading and meditation (Ps 1:2; Mat 4:4; 17:17), prayer (Eph 6:18; Phil 4:6), worship (Eph 5:18-20), witnessing (Mat 28:19-20), Christian fellowship (Heb 10:24-25), and self-discipline or self-control (Gal 5:23; Titus 1:8). (Grudem, p. 755)

The way a believer "works out" his salvation is by developing the right habits that will promote spiritual growth. The above-mentioned things should be considered disciplines that will bear fruit in the believer's life. It is through regularly practicing these things that one will make gains in his sanctification. There is no easy path to travel in growing as a believer, it takes hard work, but it is well worth the effort.

God's Role in Sanctification

In the Philippians passage man's role in sanctification was discussed above, now we will direct our attention to God's contribution to the believer's sanctification. Note the 2:12-13 passage again:

> So then, my beloved, just as you have always obeyed, not as in my presence only, but now much more in my absence, work out your salvation with fear and trembling; [13]for it is God who is at work in you, both to will and to work for *His* good pleasure.

Verse 12 deals with man's role, while v. 13 describes God's role in our sanctification. Notice that v. 12 describes man's role as "working," while v. 13 describes God as "working" in the believer. Both God and man are working together in sanctification. God's "will" and "good pleasure" refers to his desire to see the believer mature and become godlier. God is taking us in a direction throughout this life to assist us in our moral development. However, God uses the spiritual disciplines we practice to do the work in us. Man can't produce the fruit of the Spirit, only God can do that, but he does use the things we do to help us grow. The reason we can "work out" our salvation is because God is "at work" in us.

It is entirely the work of the Holy Spirit to produce spiritual fruit within the believer (Gal 5:22-23). However, as the believer reads the word of God, prays, worships, serves, and so forth, God is using those activities to do his work. It is totally appropriate therefore, to say that *progressive sanctification is a cooperative effort between God and man, with God's part being dominant.*

160

Referring to the role that God and man play in the believer's sanctification Millard Erickson offers the following observations:

> Since sanctification is the work of the Holy Spirit one might conclude that sanctification is completely a passive matter on the believer's part. This is not so, however. While sanctification is exclusively of God, that is, its power rests entirely on his holiness, the believer is constantly exhorted to work and to grow in the matters pertaining to salvation. For example, Paul writes to the Philippians: "Work out your own salvation with fear and trembling; for God is at work in you, both to will and to work for his good pleasure" (Phil 2:12-13). Paul urges both practice of virtues and avoidance of evils (Rom. 12:9, 16-17). We are to put to death the works of the body (Rom. 8:13) and present our bodies a living sacrifice (Rom. 12:1-2). So while sanctification is God's work, the believer has a role as well, entailing both removal of sinfulness and development of holiness. (Erickson, p. 971)

It is exciting to consider that God is at work in us to change and transform believers' lives. Because of that we should work out our salvation with "fear and trembling." God the Holy Spirit is within us, which should cause believers to have a healthy holy fear as they go through life becoming more Christlike. The believer's journey shouldn't be taken lightly since God the Holy Spirit is working in us. This should bring about a holy sense of awe, or as Paul says, "fear and trembling" as each believer "works out" his salvation. Without God being at work in us, our journey in sanctification would rest solely on our human efforts and get us nowhere.

Sanctification Through Trials

Certainly God works through our spiritual disciplines to bring us to maturity, but he also works through the trials that may come into our lives. Trials are a normal experience for Christians, and God works through the trials we face to produce greater levels of holiness in us.

Going through trials will strengthen the believer's faith, which results in more dependence and reliance on God. James tells us that we should consider trials to be a source of joy because God uses them to do his transforming work in believer's lives (James 1:1-8).

Peter wrote to Christians that were suffering under the persecution of Nero—the Roman Emperor. He considered the suffering they were enduring to be a testing of their faith, and God's cleansing activity in purifying the church (1 Pet 4:12-19).

God often engineers trials for believers as he sees fit. Consider the test of Abraham's faith that God brought his way when he commanded him to slay his son Isaac (Gen 22:1-2). Abraham passed the test of radical obedience and God blessed him, along with future generations of believers because of it (Gen 22:16-18; Galatians 3:6-9).

Sanctification Through Sickness

God often works in believer's lives through physical pain and sickness to produce greater levels of holiness. Think of the physical suffering that Job endured and the test of faith that he went through. Job endured hellacious pain and suffering through physical maladies which took him to his limit of endurance, but God used this to do a work in his life of producing greater holiness and dependence. He grew substantially in his walk with the Lord through his sufferings. It was God who initiated this trial in his life (Job 1:8-12; 2:3-7).

King David wrote about how times of sickness in his life to drew him closer to God (Ps 32; 38). There is a relationship between sin and sickness (1 Cor 11:30). Sin that goes unencumbered can have a weakening effect on a fellowship of believers and individuals. God often uses sickness in the lives of believers to get their attention regarding matters of sinful behavior to bring them to acknowledge their sin, repent, seek forgiveness, and bring them to a deeper level of trust.

The apostle Paul was given a thorn in the flesh to keep him humble, which was something that facilitated his usefulness to Christ in his ministry (2 Cor 12:7). Even though he prayed three times that the Lord would take the thorn away, the answer he received was "My grace is sufficient for you, for power is perfected in weakness" (2 Cor 7:8-9). Although we don't know with certainty what the thorn in the flesh was, Paul wanted it gone, which is why he asked the Lord to take it away. Paul came to see that the thorn was beneficial to him spiritually because it increased the flow of God's grace into his experience; keeping him humble and more useful to Christ. For that reason Paul was content to boast about his weaknesses, because he understood they became the channel through which God's power would be displayed in his life.

Paul suffered greatly in his ministry as an apostle of Christ (2 Cor 11:23-30). God worked through the suffering that he endured to produce greater levels of godliness and trust in his life (2 Cor 4:7-18). He saw his present sufferings as momentary light afflictions that were producing a transformation that will be completed in the realm of glory. The present afflictions that he was enduring, and other believers as well, pale in comparison to the greatness of what will be realized in the heavenly state (Rom 8:18).

Sanctification Through God's Discipline

The author of Hebrews wrote about God's discipline, which is something that every believer in Christ will receive. In fact, one of the characteristics of a true believer is that he receives God's disciple. This is proof that God loves him and that he is a legitimate child of God (Heb 12:5-8). God disciplines us just as our earthly fathers disciplined us, but God's discipline is perfect and always without error. We may not always agree with the way our earthly parents disciplined us, and in fact, they may have made some costly errors in their parenting. The purpose for God's discipline is clearly stated in Hebrews 12:10-11:

> For they (earthly fathers) disciplined us for a short time as seemed best to them, but He *disciplines us* for *our* good, so that we may share His holiness. [11]All discipline for the moment seems not to be joyful, but

sorrowful; yet to those who have been trained by it, afterwards it yields the peaceful fruit of righteousness.

The purpose of God's discipline is to produce greater levels of holiness and righteousness in the believer. The author of Hebrews was writing to a group of Jews who became Christians and were suffering persecution. For that reason many were so discouraged they were abandoning the Christian faith and were reverting back to Judaism. The author wanted these struggling believers to know that God loves them, and they should consider their hardships as God's discipline, which serves the purpose of producing more holiness in them. He was encouraging them to hang in there and endure in the midst of their difficulties.

Christians grow in their sanctification because God is at work in them—his role is dominant. He uses the spiritual disciplines that we practice to produce Christlike character. He works through tests of faith and trials that come into our lives to develop deeper levels of holiness in us. God also disciplines us for the purpose of becoming more holy and righteous, and it is always done for corrective purposes and in love.

Sanctification is Different For Each Person

Some believers will attain a greater level of sanctification in this life than others, which can be correlated to the degree that they "work out their salvation" by engaging in spiritual disciplines. It makes sense that one who regularly engages in Bible reading, prayer, fellowship, serving in church, and so on, will make gains in his sanctification. The believer who doesn't do these things will not progress at the same rate as his counterpart who does.

It's similar to athletes who train for their sport. If you take two baseball players with equal ability, and one trains diligently but the other one doesn't, who will be the better player? Obviously, the one who rigorously trains will be the better baseball player.

God works uniquely in each individual. A person who is bedridden with a physical malady may not be able to practice all the spiritual disciples mentioned above, yet the Spirit of God works in them to produce a sweet spirit and a godly disposition. I've known believers that were confined to wheelchairs and lived with very poor health, but through their affliction and close union with God attained great levels of sanctification. Certainly, God purifies believers through their sufferings.

Who can presume to know how God is working in the lives of people who are bedridden with physical maladies, or have handicaps, chronic illnesses, chronic pain, and so forth. There are those who may contend that the body of Christ needs to pray for healing for these people so they can be restored to health. Others may contend that is it the work of the Devil to keep them sick, so he needs to be rebuked and commanded to take his hands off God's people. Others may contend that when a believer is sick she is out of God's will. There are some circles of Christians who contend that God guarantees that believers can walk in perfect health this side of heaven if they have the faith to believe for that.

I'm in favor of praying for people who are sick, asking God to bring healing into their life. However, God may be doing a special work through the above things that is the precise vehicle through which he is producing greater levels of trust, holiness, and spiritual fruit in their lives. In this sense their physical malady may be considered a gift (James 1:17). This is a hard truth to understand, but the point is that God works in each believer as he sees fit, with the goal in mind of bringing us to deeper levels of holiness, trust, and Christlikeness.

God wants all believers to grow and works equally in assisting them in their spiritual growth, but in unique ways to each believer. God doesn't show favoritism by working to a greater degree in one person and in a lesser degree in another. He desires that everybody grow to maturity. He gives the same resources to every believer, so in that sense when it comes to sanctification there is a level playing field. Whether it is though spiritual disciplines, trials, tests of faith, God's discipline, or sickness God is at work to transform us and develop fruit in believers.

What About Lapses?

Some believers may have a lapse in their spiritual growth, and even appear to have fallen away from the Lord. It isn't uncommon for believers to experience low points in their journey with Christ and some may become dropouts. I've encountered many Christians who have had a period of time where they dropped out of fellowship with other believers, appeared to be disinterested in following Christ, drifted into the world, and reverted back to sinful behaviors. After a period of time they came back to the Lord and got on track spiritually. After repentance, or some kind of experience with God they normalized their relationship with the Lord. Some people may have long periods of time where they don't openly follow Christ, for others it may be a short interval of time, still others may never have a lapse. Every person is different. Thank God that he grants people repentance and helps people get back on track.

When a believer has a lapse in his spiritual experience and appears completely disinterested in walking with Christ, that doesn't mean he has lost his salvation such that God has thrown the towel in on him. Once a sinner receives Jesus into his heart by faith and is born again, I don't think it is possible to lose his salvation. However, the quality of one's walk with Christ can be less than what it should be. The Holy Spirit can be grieved and the fruit of one's salvation may not be evident in the person's life. God the Holy Spirit will tug on the person's heart and influence them to repent of sin and normalize their relationship with him.

Usually when a believer does have a lapse they will be miserable because they are grieving the Spirit, and God is bringing conviction on them to repent. Often when a believer checks out spiritually they aren't useful to God as they could be if they were walking with him.

Ultimately speaking, only God can look into the depths of the human heart and see faith or the absence of the same. Only God can know who is a believer and who isn't. All people can do is look at the fruit that a person displays, and listen to their testimony, but only God knows the heart. Why one person makes great gains in sanctification while another one doesn't is a bit of a mystery.

The Story of Henry Far

Henry started attending my church, through the influence of a mutual friend, and appeared in the membership class I taught. I was so happy to see him excited about his faith and getting plugged into a church, which is something he hadn't done for a long time. At the end of the five-week class everyone shares their testimony with some of the elders present. Henry shared his testimony, which was extremely difficult for him. He was in his mid 60s and he shared how he had become a Christian over 30 years ago, but after a while he had a lapse in his walk with the Lord. He and his wife went into partying, drinking, smoking and dropped out of church. The lifestyle they developed took them right into the world, such that they appeared to be completely disinterested in living as Christians should.

After many years of living in rebellion against God he came to a point where he did some serious soul-searching about the direction of his life, and decided to come back to the Lord. He was finally responsive to Holy Spirit tugging on his heart to bring him back to where he should be with Christ. Henry stopped all the partying, drinking, smoking, and began to get back on track with the Lord, which led him to my church.

As he shared his testimony he had tears running down his cheeks as he told us how filled with remorse he was for throwing over 20 years out the window through his partying, rather than walking with God. Henry couldn't relive those twenty years, but God brought him back to where he should be. He also shared that the years spent in partying away from God were terrible times that he wishes he could have back. Henry is grateful that God has forgiven him for his long lapse and restored him.

The point of sharing Henry's story is that some Christians will have lapses in their walk with the Lord (sanctification) that last for varying intervals of time—some very long some very short. When a lapse does occur that doesn't mean the believer has lost his salvation and God has abandoned him. The Holy Spirit will tug on his heart to bring conviction to him so that he can repent and get back on track with the

Lord. God will always reach out in his love to bring a believer back to where he needs to be.

Past Experiences Related to Sanctification

Some people become believers out of traumatic circumstances. For example, some people may have had abusive backgrounds where they suffered emotional abuse, physical abuse, sexual trauma, drug or alcohol addiction, and so on. Some things run in the family line and are genetically transmitted such as: anxiety, depression, alcoholism, and more. It is wise for each person to have an understanding of their family history regarding these matters. They may discover that they are at greater risk than other people regarding these issues. When a person comes out of a troubled background of this nature they have much to overcome. They may need much help from the body of Christ to realize healing of their emotions through extensive Christian counseling and prayer. An individual may have gone deep into sinful behavior making it a battle to refrain from those things. The power of Christ can set people free from addictions, bring healing of emotional trauma, do a great work in people separating them from sin and developing the fruit of the Spirit. My point is these people have much to overcome in their journey of maturing as a believer.

On the other hand, there are nonbelievers that grow up in emotionally healthy stable families. Their parents gave them love, provided well for them such that they grow up to be emotionally healthy people as well. They can relate well to others, are free of harmful habits, and are productive in life. When they become a believer in Christ they have less to overcome in their sanctification journey than people who got saved out of the above-mentioned traumas.

Conclusion

In this chapter the term sanctification was introduced, which is a term that all Christians should be familiar with, because it describes the growth process that disciples go through. Sanctification is progressive in that the believer becomes more-and-more separated from sin throughout his life, and it is a life-long process. Both the believer and

God play a role in sanctification with God's role being dominant, in that only God can transform the believer and produce spiritual fruit in him. However, the believer must develop good habits and disciplines that will lend themselves to bearing fruit. God works through the spiritual disciplines of the believer such as Scripture reading, prayer, worship, meditation, serving, and so on. Developing good habits and spiritual disciplines are known as spiritual formation.

God disciplines his children, uses trials, and tests of faith to bring believers to deeper levels of maturity, and works in unique ways in each person. Reading about the lives of God's people in Scripture demonstrates how they grew through difficult circumstances, trials, and tests of faith that God engineered for them. Some believers will attain a greater level of holiness in this life than others. Each believer's growth process is totally unique, for no two Christians will grow in the exact same way.

Also discussed was the issue of believers having a lapse in their sanctification, where they appear to be disinterested in walking with the Lord, and drift into the world as they live in a way that isn't pleasing to God. When that happens, that doesn't mean they have lost their salvation, for the Holy Spirit will tug on their hearts by bringing conviction to them, so that they repent and return to the Lord. Some people may have lapses of long periods, some for short periods, and some believers won't have any lapses at all.

In contrast to the legalists, the primary marker of spiritual maturity the Bible presents is God transforming the individual into the likeness of Christ (Rom 8:29). This is the essence of sanctification. Believers are to display the moral virtues that God displays, which is what Jesus meant when he said "be perfect as your heavenly Father is perfect" (Mat 5:48).

Chapter 17 ~ The Role of the Holy Spirit

The Holy Spirit plays a crucial role in the believer's sanctification. Christians have the Spirit of God living within them, for if one does not have the Spirit of God resident in them they do not belong to Christ (Rom 8:9). Scripture instructs disciples' of Christ to be filled with the Spirit (Eph 5:18), rather than grieving the Spirit (Eph 4:30). In this chapter we will discuss what it means to be filled with the Spirit, how the believer can be filled with the Spirit, and what it means to grieve the Spirit. The filling and grieving of the Spirit should be viewed as not just individual experiences, but as part of the corporate life of the church. In other words, the entire church is to reflect the fullness of the Spirit, and the entire fellowship should not grieve the Spirit.

We begin our discussion of this topic by looking at an insight that Wayne Grudem offers on the Spirit's role in our spiritual development:

> But it is specifically God the Holy Spirit who works within us to change us and sanctify us, giving us greater holiness of life. Peter speaks of the "sanctification of the Spirit" (1 Pet 1:2), and Paul speaks of "sanctification by the Spirit" (2 Thess 2:13). It is the Holy Spirit who produces in us the "fruit of the Spirit" (Gal 5:22-23), those character traits that are part of greater and greater sanctification. If we grow in sanctification we "walk by the Spirit" and are "led by the Spirit" (Gal 5:16-18; Rom 8:14), that is, we are more and more responsive to the desires and promptings of the Holy Spirit in our life and character. The Holy Spirit is the spirit of holiness, and he produces holiness within us. (Grudem, P. 754)

Man can't manufacture the fruit of the Spirit; only God—the Holy Spirit—can do that. It is the Holy Spirit who makes us more Christlike, separating us from sin so we are more conformed to the moral

170

character of the Lord Jesus. Crucial to Grudem's statement above is what the apostle Paul says in Ephesians 5:18:

And do not get drunk with wine, for that is dissipation,
but be filled with the Spirit.

The Greek word *plēróō* is translated "filled." There are several interesting features about the way the word is written in Greek. First, it is written in the imperative, which means it is a command. Secondly, it is plural so this applies to all believers. Being filled with the Spirit isn't just for the elite Christian, it is a directive for all believers to be filled, thus it should be a normative experience for every Christian. Thirdly, it is written in the present tense, which carries with it the sense of continuation in the Greek language. Therefore this verse could be translated "keep on being filled with the Spirit." Paul is not talking about an event; rather he's talking about a continual process, or relationship with the Holy Spirit. Fourthly, it is written in the passive voice, which means the believer is receiving the action of the Spirit filling him.

When something is written in the *active voice* the believer is *doing* something, but since this is written in the *passive voice* the believer is *receiving* something. In other words, when the conditions are right in the person's life, the Holy Spirit moves on the individual and fills him. The believer receives the action of the Holy Spirit. A Christian can't fill himself with the Spirit; he has to be filled by the Spirit. Since Paul writes this as a command it requires an *active response* on the part of the believer to be filled, but it is a *passive experience* because the Spirit moves upon the believer and fills him. This may seem like a contradiction in terms: requiring an active response, but being a passive experience, but this is how it is written in Greek.

What is involved in the active response on the believer's part? There are some clues given in the verse under consideration (Eph 5:18). Paul makes a contrast between being drunk with wine, which leads to dissipation or debauchery, and being filled with the Spirit. When someone drinks too much alcohol they are under the influence, and their behavior reflects that state. Paul says being drunk leads to debauchery and all kinds of immoral behavior. In other words, one's

171

behavior is changed because they are under the influence of the beverage they are drinking. They are in a sense controlled by the alcohol, for they are inebriated.

Following Paul's analogy, being filled with the Spirit is like being under the influence of the Spirit. When controlled by the Spirit the believer's behavior will change. Under the Spirit's control believers will display the fruit of the Spirit and behave in a Christlike fashion. The *active response* of the believer begins with the *desire* to be controlled by the Spirit. Believers must surrender their will to God and want to give him control of their life. The words submit, surrender, desire, dedicate, consecrate, longing, craving, etc. all express the idea of giving your will over to God and letting him have his way in your life. It's like being in a car with the Holy Spirit, and letting him drive the car while you are in the passenger's seat. You give yourself over to the direction the Spirit wants to take you.

When you surrender your will to the influence of the Spirit he will fill you. You will receive the action of the Spirit filling you. This is the passive side of being filled with the Spirit. To review, being filled with the Spirit requires an *active response* on the believer's part by having the desire to surrender your will to the Spirit and give him the control of your life, but it is a *passive experience* in that the Spirit fills you.

Caution must be taken in presenting a formulaic approach to being filled with the Spirit. For example, someone might say step one requires confession of sin. Step two requires prayer. Step three requires reading Scripture. Step four requires worshiping through song, and then the believer will be filled. There is no formula to be followed that will magically cause one to be filled with the Spirit. Certainly, the above-mentioned things may assist a believer in being filled with the Spirit, but Scripture gives no precise formula to be followed in being filled, and it is different for every person.

Some believers may find listening to worship music gets them in the mood to surrender to God. Others may find reading Scripture helpful, others may find a time of silent meditation the most helpful in being filled. It's different for every person, but the key principle is the desire to give the control of your life to the Holy Spirit, letting him have his way with you.

Repeated Fillings

When a sinner becomes a believer he instantly receives the Holy Spirit in his heart. This is a one-time event. However, there can be repeated fillings of the Spirit. An example of this is Stephen, who is described as a man full of faith and the Holy Spirit (Acts 6:5). When he gave his talk to the Sanhedrin (Acts 7:55) he is described as being "full of the Holy Spirit." On the day of Pentecost when the Holy Spirit was sent to occupy the hearts of believers in the Upper Room, they are described as being filled with the Spirit (Acts 2:4). When Peter gave his talk to the Sanhedrin he is described as being "filled with the Spirit" (Acts 4:8).

The conclusion to be drawn is that the reception of the Holy Spirit is a one-time event, but there can be repeated fillings as needed. When God places a believer in a situation where he has a ministry task to perform such as sharing his testimony, delivering a message, sharing the gospel, etc. the Spirit will fill him to empower him to do that task. God doesn't require us to do ministry in our own strength, he will fill us with the Spirit to empower the ministry he calls us to perform. Jesus told his disciples that they would be called upon to testify about him, but when that happens they shouldn't worry about what to say because the Spirit will speak through them (Mat 10:17-20).

This is comforting to know and should give believers confidence as they do ministry because the Holy Spirit will fill them so they can minister in the Spirit's strength. Whether one is teaching Sunday school, preaching a sermon, leading a small group in his home, or doing administrative work in the church the Spirit will empower believers by filling them.

The normative experience for all believers is to be filled with the Holy Spirit. Christians should develop sensitivity to the Spirit's presence in their lives, realizing that he is the power source for accomplishing the things God calls him to do. He is the source of our holiness and empowerment for daily life.

How Full of the Spirit Can One Be?

When it comes to the fullness of the Spirit there are several illustrations that are commonly used. One is the glass of water. In this illustration being filled with the Spirit is like water being poured into a glass that becomes full then the water spills over. The idea being that when the believer is filled, he can't contain the fullness of the Spirit. The Spirit spills over (out of him) so that the one filled with the Spirit spills over love and kindness, and the fruit of the Spirit. Although this illustration is commonly used and may be helpful, there is another way to illustrate the filling of the Spirit.

Wayne Grudem uses the analogy of the filling of the Spirit being like filling a balloon with air (Grudem, p. 782). A balloon already has air in it, but more can be added and is contained within the balloon. The believer doesn't become so full of the Spirit that he can't contain the Spirit within him. It isn't as if the believer that is filled with the Spirit is bursting at the seams and the Spirit is oozing out of him. The Spirit doesn't spill over; he stays with the believer and there can be more invasive fillings of the Spirit throughout the believer's life. Both of the above illustrations are helpful.

As a believer grows throughout his journey with the Lord and is becoming more Christlike, separated from sin, he can experience deeper fillings of the Spirit, which can produce more fruit in his life. In other words, being filled with the Spirit isn't equal for all believers. The filling is *potentially* equal for all believers, but based on the quality of one's walk with the Lord he may experience more fullness of the Spirit than one that is grieving the Spirit. Only Jesus is described as having the Spirit without measure (John 3:34). Some may experience more invasive fillings than others, which produce greater levels of godliness. Going back to the balloon illustration above, as the believer matures he is like a balloon that expands with more air (the Spirit) being put inside. Of course, all spatial illustrations of the filling of the Spirit come up short because being filled is a spiritual phenomenon that can't be described by the laws of physics. This is merely an illustration to explain a spiritual truth.

Grieving the Spirit

Ephesians 5:18 informs the reader that all believers are to be filled with Spirit. This should be the normative experience for every Christian. The Spirit can also be grieved, which is what believers don't want to have happen, as is clearly stated in Ephesians 4:30:

> **Do not grieve the Holy Spirit of God, by whom you were sealed for the day of redemption.**

There are several things that are noteworthy about this verse. In Greek this is written as a command, so believers are to be cautious not to grieve the Spirit. It is also written in the present tense so this describes a continuous practice. That the Spirit can be grieved testifies to the personhood of the Holy Spirit, for only a person can be grieved. The Spirit isn't an "it", or a "thing", or a "force", he is a person: God the Holy Spirit.

How does someone grieve the Holy Spirit? All kinds of ungodly behavior will hurt the Holy Spirit. The fact that the believer is sealed with the Holy Spirit indicates that when he is grieved through sinful behavior, he doesn't depart from the believer. The fact that the Holy Spirit resides within the believer should provide incentive to live a godly life and refrain from sinful activities that grieve him. Every time believers sin they do so in the presence of the Spirit. In the Ephesians passage (4:25-32) the dominant sin Paul mentions that grieves the Spirit is sinful speech. When believers in the community of faith are doing the things mentioned in vv. 29 & 31, it not only tears down the body of Christ, having harmful effects on their fellowship, it also grieves the Holy Spirit:

> Let no unwholesome word proceed from your mouth, but only such *a word* as is good for edification according to the need *of the moment*, so that it will give grace to those who hear. [30]Do not grieve the Holy

175

Spirit of God, by whom you were sealed for the day of redemption. ³¹Let all bitterness and wrath and anger and clamor and slander be put away from you, along with all malice. (Ephesians 4:29-31)

The command not to grieve the Spirit is sandwiched in between vv. 29 and 31. The catalogue of sins mentioned are those that grieve the Holy Spirit, which is similar to Paul's injunction to not give the Devil a foothold (4:27). Ungodly behavior opens up space for the Devil to wreak havoc in the fellowship of believers, as well as grieving the Spirit. Sins that divide the body of Christ usually originate with Satan, while the work of the Holy Spirit is to unify and edify believers. The Devil tries to destroy, while the Holy Spirit always builds and unifies God's people.

Paul is alluding to Isaiah 63:9-10 in his warning to the Ephesian believers not to grieve the Spirit:

in all their affliction He was afflicted, And the angel of His presence saved them; In His love and in His mercy He redeemed them, And He lifted them and carried them all the days of old. ¹⁰But they rebelled and grieved His Holy Spirit; Therefore He turned Himself to become their enemy, He fought against them.

Isaiah is describing how in God's love and mercy he redeemed them from Egypt and led them through the desert, but they rebelled and grieved the Spirit (Ps 78:40-41). The Ephesian believers seem to be walking in the footsteps of their ancestors. Through God's love and mercy they have been redeemed, but in their journey of faith they are also rebelling and grieving the Spirit like their ancestors. This is serious business because in v. 10 of the passage above it says that, "He (the Spirit) turned Himself to become their enemy, He fought against them." This is probably an allusion to the disciplinary action of God upon the disobedient people. This statement should not be taken lightly because God the Holy Spirit will certainly discipline believers in the New Covenant community when necessary (Acts 5:3; 9). Paul is speaking against ongoing sinful practices in the lives of the Ephesian believers, which deeply grieve the Spirit, and open up the church to God's disciplinary action to get them back on track.

In both the filling of the Spirit and the grieving of the Spirit Paul is talking about relationships within the church. A community of believers can be filled with the Spirit, or they can grieve the Spirit. Paul's emphasis isn't so much on the individual believer being filled; it seems to be more about corporate life in the church. He's picturing the entire Ephesian church as being filled with the Spirit, or the entire church grieving the Spirit. Peter O'Brien's comment about grieving the Spirit is worthy of consideration:

> His (Paul's) injunction is striking, for it refers not to a direct attack on the Spirit but to believers engaging in sinful activities mentioned in the previous verses (especially harmful speech) which destroy relationships within the body and so mar the Spirit's work in building Christ's people (cf. 2:22; 4:3, 4). Anything incompatible with the unity or purity of the church is inconsistent with the Spirit's own nature and therefore grieves him. (O'Brien, p. 348)

In building up the people the Spirit's work can be frustrated when he is grieved. The commands to be filled with the Spirit, and not to grieve the Spirit, are to the entire church.   Thus they must, first and foremost, be carried out in each believer's life. The implication is that each believer should have awareness that his actions affect the entire body. Believers should not engage in any type of ungodly behavior that impedes the work of the Spirit in his own life and in the life of his church.

Conclusion

In this chapter we have discussed the crucial role the Holy Spirit plays in the life of believers. The normative experience for all believers, and for every local church, is to be filled with the Spirit. He is the power source for everything that a Christian, and a local church, is called to do. He empowers us to do whatever ministry God calls us into, he gives us the ability to resist the temptation to sin, and he produces holiness in us. We have also discussed the importance of not grieving the Holy Spirit. Through sinful behavior in the body of Christ the Spirit's influence can be minimized. Paul spoke of both the filling of the Spirit and the grieving of the Spirit, not just in individual terms, but in terms of corporate life in the church. Every local church is a Temple of the Holy Spirit (Eph 2:21-22), and every individual Christian is also a Temple of the Holy Spirit (1 Cor 6:19).

The reader should be seeing that the Bible emphasizes the work of God transforming the individual into the image of Christ. It is God— the Holy Spirit—working within the individual to separate him from sin and move him in the direction of being more like Christ. Every believer should be filled with the Spirit, for he is the power source for godly living, and life transformation. The legalist minimizes God's role and places an emphasis on behavior that has nothing to do with the Spirit's work in a person's life.

In the next chapter we will discuss the virtues that the Spirit of God produces in individual believers. This will give us specific examples of Biblical markers of spiritual maturity, in contrast to what legalists identify.

Chapter 18 ~ The Fruit of the Spirit

But the fruit of the Spirit is love, joy, peace, patience, kindness, goodness, faithfulness, ²³gentleness, self-control; against such things there is no law. (Galatians 5:22-23)

The fruit of the Spirit are supernatural virtues that are produced by the Holy Spirit, which means fruit isn't a work of man. As the believer is filled with the Spirit and lives a life that is more-and-more surrendered to the Spirit greater levels of fruit will be evident in his life. Note that it is the fruit (singular) of the Spirit not fruits (plural) of the Spirit. The fruit are different aspects, or virtues of the Holy Spirit that will be produced in the believer.

Understanding what these virtues are will help Christians assess their progress in sanctification. The fruit of the Spirit can serve as markers of one's spiritual development. There are different ways the fruit of the Spirit are broken down or categorized. The most common is to group them in sets of three.

Scot McKnight makes an interesting observation about the works of the flesh and the fruit of the Spirit that are mentioned in Galatians 5:19-23:

> Most importantly, the lists here of the works of the flesh and the fruit of the Spirit are not abstract listings, nor are they comprehensive. Rather, they are context specific. In the context of church conflict, the observer will find the manifestation of the flesh in such things as factionalism and will find that the Spirit, when in control, will produce such things as love and patience. In other words, we interpret these lists incorrectly if we take them out of their context and pretend that they are complete listings of either the flesh or the Spirit. These are the kinds of things Paul

wants to focus on because he is concerned with conflict. Had he written to the Ephesians, he would have had other items in both lists. (McKnight, p. 270)

McKnight's point is well taken. The nine fruit of the Spirit are not to be taken as a comprehensive list of virtues that the Spirit produces in believers. When comparing Paul's list with Peter's list of Christian virtues in 2 Peter 1:5-7 the lists are different. Paul begins with love while Peter ends his list with love. Peter mentions moral excellence, godliness, and perseverance but Paul doesn't. Certainly, the Holy Spirit is involved in cultivating the virtues that Peter mentions. One of the primary virtues believers are to display is humility, but neither Paul nor Peter mentions that virtue on their list. To conclude that the Spirit has nothing to do with producing humility in believers would be incorrect. For whatever reason Paul and Peter didn't mention humility because it wasn't crucial to their argument.

In Colossians 3:12-15 Paul has another list of virtues that are different than the fruit of the Spirit in Galatians 5:22-23, and Peter's list in 2 Peter 1:5-7. On this list in Colossians Paul mentions humility and compassion. The Holy Spirit is involved in producing godly virtues in believers, beyond those listed in Galatians 5:22-23. Therefore, the following conclusions can be made about the fruit of the Spirit:

- The list of nine fruit of the Spirit is not an exhaustive list of virtues that the Holy Spirit develops in believers.

- The fruit Paul mentions is specific to the context at Galatia.

- Paul's emphasis is on handling conflict in his Galatian congregations.

- Where believers display the fruit of the Spirit peaceful harmonious relationships will result, bringing unity in the church.

- There is overlap in meaning with some of the terms.

- Some of the virtues are difficult to define because there are no one-to-one English equivalents for the Greek terms.

- The fruit of the Spirit should be viewed in contrast to the works of the flesh (Gal 5:19-21).

Below are the three lists previously mentioned. Note the similarities and differences in the lists. Also, note the differences in the order of the virtues mentioned.

Colossians 3:12-15
Compassion
Kindness
Humility
Gentleness
Patience
Bearing with. . .
Forgiving each . . .
Love
Peace

Galatians 5:22-23
Love
Joy
Peace
Patience
Kindness
Goodness
Faithfulness
Gentleness
Self-control

2 Peter 1:5-7
Moral excellence
Knowledge
Self-control
Perseverance
Godliness
Brotherly kindness

Love

The Holy Spirit is involved in cultivating all these virtues in believers, not just the ones mentioned in Galatians 5:22-23. These virtues should be studied and developed in all Christians. They serve as markers of godliness and spiritual maturity. One can ask himself if he sees these characteristics in his life, and other people can bear witness to these traits or lack thereof. Fruit is grown! It takes time to grow a fruit tree and harvest produce. Spiritual growth is generally very slow as well.

At this point we turn to a discussion of each fruit of the Spirit (Gal 5:22-23), which I will refer to as Spirit-produced virtues.

Spirit-Produced Love *(agápē)*

That love is mentioned first should not come as a surprise, since earlier in Galatians Paul said that love fulfills the law (5:13-15). People are to use their freedom in Christ to love and serve one another, which will facilitate avoidance of conflict and create unity in the church. Love is a primary virtue of the Christian. Jesus identified love as the feature of Christian relationships that would cause the world to take note of us (John 13:34-35). Our love should emulate God's love, which is self-giving for the benefit of others. In other words, God sets the standard for love that we are to strive for. Spirit-produced love isn't a touchy feely type of love, it is love that is expressed in action. It is a way of life for a believer. Christians give love, first and foremost, to people in the body of Christ, secondarily to those outside the community of faith, even to one's enemies (Mat 5:44). Spirit-produced love goes beyond the human capacity to love, it is not of this world, which is why the believer can love even his enemies, pray for them, and turn the other cheek when assaulted (Mat 5:39).

Spirit-Produced Joy *(chará)*

Christians experience a gladness of heart, a sense of elation and bliss that is independent of their circumstances. Spirit-produced joy stems from one's relationship with Christ, such that even in dire circumstances like persecution, joy can be a constant element in a believer's life. When a sinner receives Jesus into his heart there is an accompanying sense of exhilaration that goes along with his salvation. Receiving God's forgiveness and all the benefits that come from knowing Christ is cause for great joy.

As the believer goes through his life, regardless of what circumstances may be presented to him joy can be a constant, even in the midst of difficult trials, deprivation, imprisonment, persecution, tragedy, and so forth. Being in relationship with Christ brings into the heart a joy that remains.

In the world's way of thinking joy is found by acquiring more money, nicer things, lavish vacations, and so on. That may be the case, but this type of joy is fleeting and temporary. It is like a thrill that fades away until the next purchase is made, vacation is taken, or new adventure is pursued. Spirit-produced joy is not of this world and will reside in the believer's heart throughout the duration of his life. Peter describes this type of joy as being inexpressible and full of glory (1 Peter 1:8). It is inexpressible in that words can't describe the inner exuberance believers have. That is why Christians will often spontaneously begin praising the Lord, singing worship songs, offering thanks to God, and more, even in difficult times.

Another example of Spirit-produced joy is the apostle Paul, who demonstrated an amazing level of joy when he wrote Philippians. Most people would think that being under house arrest and out of commission regarding planting churches, which is what Paul loved to do, would cause Paul much grief and rob him of joy. However, that wasn't the case. Paul seems to be overwhelmingly joyful when he wrote this letter, and serves as an example of how Spirit-produced joy transcends circumstances in life.

Spirit-Produced Peace *(eirếnē)*

The Hebrew equivalent of the Greek word is *shalom* which means peace, wholeness, prosperity, and wellness. In the New Testament "peace" is used as a greeting, just as "shalom" is used the same way in the Old Testament. Peace has several different meanings in the New Testament such as being at peace with God through Jesus Christ (Ro

5:1). In this usage of the word it refers to being reconciled to God through Jesus (John 14:6). It can refer to peace between people in the sense of having harmonious relationships in the body of Christ (Col 3:15). It can refer to peace between Jew and Gentile unified by common faith in Christ (Eph 2:14-15; 17).

The Greek word translated peace comes from a root that means "to tie" or "to tie together into a whole." When things get crazy and one finds himself in difficult circumstances the Spirit ties together your emotions and keeps you on an even keel so that you aren't frazzled. Spirit-produced peace results in an inner tranquility that helps one cope with difficult circumstances. The apostle Paul referred to the "peace that surpasses all understanding" (Phil 4:7), which stands in contrast to anxiety. When the believer marshals his faith and commits his cares to God, the Spirit imparts peace and tranquility that is not of this world, which is why Paul says the peace of God surpasses understanding. He commands Christians not to be anxious about anything.

Joy and peace are paired together (Rom 14:17; 15:13). Jesus gave his peace to his disciples (John 14:17), told them to remain in his love (John 15:9), and wanted them to experience his joy (John 15:11). The early church may have used love, joy, and peace as a triad in their everyday conversation, just as faith, hope, and love were used (1 Thess 1:2).

Spirit-Produced Patience *(makrothymía)*

This term is translated a number of different ways in our English Bibles, such as: patience, forbearance, longsuffering, steadfastness, and endurance. Patience is an attribute of God, which he displayed in great measure toward the objects of his wrath (Ro 2:4-5). This term is relational in nature. The one who possesses this characteristic doesn't "blow up," or lose his temper, when working with difficult people. Rather, he bears up and goes the extra mile refusing to retaliate. He keeps his anger under control, and keeps the relationship intact. Given the conflict that existed in the Galatian churches, one can see where this virtue would be necessary in bringing conflict scenarios to conclusion.

184

In the English language, patience is often disconnected from relationships. For example, if someone is waiting for the bus to come they might get on edge because the bus is five minutes late, which causes them to become impatient. The Greek term isn't used in this way, it is people focused. Spirit-produced patience helps preserve relationships even in difficult circumstances.

Spirit-Produced Kindness *(chrēstótēs)*

It is difficult to come up with a precise definition of this Greek term because there is no English equivalent. It means something like having a useful, easy, pleasant, gentle disposition. In the Romans 2:4-5 passage God's patience and kindness are linked together. It is God's kindness that influences sinners to repent.

Believers are to display kindness to one another (Col 3:12, Eph 4:32), which is described as a quality of love (1 Cor 13:4), and, like love, is expressed in action (Luke 6:35). One can see how kindness and patience are complementary. In going the extra mile with difficult people one can retain an easygoing disposition. Spirit produced kindness gives one the ability to keep his composure in difficult circumstances with people, while having a Spirit-produced easygoing way about him.

Spirit-Produced Goodness *(agathōsynē)*

The definition of this term is: intrinsic goodness, especially as a personal quality, with stress on the kindly side of goodness. The word describes an attitude of generosity and kindness toward people. The term may be the antithesis of "envy" listed in the works of the flesh (Gal 5:21). Patience, kindness, and goodness are Spirit-produced virtues that help keep relationships intact.

Spirit-Produced Faithfulness *(pístis)*

This word can be translated "faith" or "faithfulness," so the context must determine which is the best translation option. In the context of this passage the emphasis of the fruit of the Spirit is keeping unity and relationships intact. Therefore, the best option is to translate the word faithfulness. Spirit-produced faithfulness results in loyalty, and deepens commitments made to other people. It is best to see faithfulness as a quality displayed in personal relationships. Faithful people don't break fellowship with other believers easily. They are loyal and hang in there in difficult times.

God expects us to be faithful in keeping our commitments, so there is an element to faithfulness that is directed toward God. Faithfulness is a characteristic of believers in that they need to discharge their duties being reliable and dependable as faithful stewards of Christ. The one who displays the Spirit-produced virtue of faithfulness will be responsible in keeping his commitments, will be dependable and can be counted on to show up when he says he will, and whose word can be accepted without reservation. This person is trustworthy.

Spirit-Produced Gentleness *(prautēs)*

This word is often translated meekness. It is another word that is problematic to grasp because no exact English equivalent exists. In our culture when we think of someone who is gentle or meek, it might conjure up negative connotations. Meekness and gentleness might not be considered to be virtuous by many people in our modern world.

In classical Greek the word, and its derivatives, describe a person in whom strength and gentleness reside together. William Barclay says:

> the man who is meek has every instinct and every passion under perfect control. It would not be right to say that such a man is entirely self-controlled, for such self-control is beyond human power, but it would be right to say that such a man is God-controlled. (Barclay, William. *Ephesians*. Daily Study Bible. Studylight.org)

The idea Barclay presents is that meekness refers to one who has *strength under God's control*. As one submits himself to God's will, God strengthens him to be obedient. Ronald Fung offers additional insights into this Spirit-produced virtue:

186

As an ethical grace in the believer's life, "gentleness" may be described as a humble and pliable forbearance towards others, regarding even insult or injury as God's means of chastisement (cf. 2 Sam. 16:11) or training (cf. Num. 12:3). It thus implies, but is not identical with self-control. (Fung, p. 270)

In keeping peace and unity in one's church this virtue would be very helpful.

Spirit-Produced Self-Control *(egkráteia)*

The last Spirit-produced virtue is self-control, which overlaps in meaning with gentleness above. The Greek word is derived from two words: *en*, which means "in the sphere of" and *krátos*, which means "dominion" or "mastery." Therefore, the idea of the word is "dominion from within." This self-dominion or self-mastery enables one to keep his sinful passions in check and resist temptations as they appear. The Spirit produces self-control in the life of a believer: it isn't manufactured by sheer will power a person can marshal. Fung describes self-control as "the mastery of the self and the fashioning of one's life in the way which God desires" (Fung, p. 271). In a conflict rich environment one can see the benefit of having this virtue.

This brings us to the conclusion of the Spirit-produced virtues Paul mentions in Galatians.

Conclusion

Every believer must surrender his life to the will of God and desire to be filled, letting the Spirit have control of his life. As that happens, the believer can experience greater levels of fruit that the Spirit produces in him. The fruit of the Spirit is about character development—about becoming like Christ. A mature Christian would have a balance of these virtues in his personality, for Jesus had displayed all these virtues in a balanced fashion, and, of course, the believer is to emulate him. These virtues are the benchmarks of spiritual maturity that one should look for in other people and in their own life. Where a congregation is Spirit-filled and people are manifesting the fruit of the Spirit these virtues will preserve the unity of the body, help keep the church conflict free, and enhance the relational life of the gathering of believers. The fruit of the Spirit are not an exhaustive list of Spirit-produced virtues; they are specific to the context of the conflict-laden Galatian churches (cf. Col 3:12-15; 2 Pet 1:5-7).

What makes a believer mature and growing in his spiritual development is the work of the Spirit in his life. The Bible doesn't measure spiritual maturity by whether the believer does or doesn't drink alcohol, wear floor-length skirts, or go dancing on Saturday nights. Spiritual maturity is measured by the work of the Spirit in transforming the believer into the likeness of Christ (Rom 8:29). In the next chapter we will direct our attention to the role that Jesus plays in the believer's sanctification.

Chapter 19 ~ Jesus in Bearing Fruit

Bearing spiritual fruit is Trinitarian in nature. God the Father works in the believer both to will and to work for His good pleasure (Phil 2:13). The Holy Spirit produces the fruit of the Spirit in the believer (Gal 5:22-23), and the Lord Jesus plays a part as well, which will be the focus of the next three chapters. Thus growing as a believer involves all three members of the Godhead, who each play a significant role. In John 15 Jesus is talking with his disciples for the last time before he is crucified. This chapter is part of what is commonly referred to as his "Farewell Discourse" (John 13-17). Usually the last things someone says before their death are very important and will be remembered by the listeners.

Jesus was concerned that his men would continue in their spiritual development after he left them. He would rise from the dead, then ascend into heaven, and the Holy Spirit would be poured out on the day of Pentecost to reside in the heart of every believer. Without Jesus being with them bodily, he was concerned that they would continue to grow and thrive spiritually. As they began to spread the gospel and fulfill the Great Commission they would face severe pressures, trials, persecution, demonic attacks, spend time away from their families, and more. Under all this pressure would they implode? Would they burnout and self-destruct? Would they have moral failures? Would they give up and go back to fishing?

Jesus gave them some information that would help them stay on track spiritually and continue to bear fruit. This passage (John 15:1-17) is filled with nuggets of gold regarding disciples' spiritual growth, and should occupy a prominent place in any discussion of sanctification.

"I am the true vine, and My Father is the vinedresser. ²Every branch in Me that does not bear fruit, He takes away; and every *branch* that bears fruit, He prunes it so that it may bear more fruit. ³You are already clean because of the word which I have spoken to you.

⁴Abide in Me, and I in you. As the branch cannot bear fruit of itself unless it abides in the vine, so neither *can* you unless you abide in Me. ⁵I am the vine, you are the branches; he who abides in Me and I in him, he bears much fruit, for apart from Me you can do nothing. ⁶If anyone does not abide in Me, he is thrown away as a branch and dries up; and they gather them, and cast them into the fire and they are burned. (John 15:1-6)

Jesus introduces a metaphor of a vineyard. There are several characters featured in the metaphor that need to be identified. Jesus calls himself the "true vine." God the Father occupies the role of the "vinedresser." The "branches" are individual believers, and the "vineyard" is the gathering of believers. A vineyard is designed to produce grapes (fruit). Jesus uses this metaphor to drive home some important concepts about being a fruitful Christian.

The Messiah is probably drawing from the vineyard metaphor in Isaiah 5:1-7. In that passage Israel is God's vineyard (the vine) that was supernaturally planted and cared for, but it didn't produce good grapes as it was supposed to, because of their defective spirituality. This brought God's judgment to bear on them. Jesus wants to make sure that his disciples don't walk in the footsteps of their ancestors by being an unfruitful vineyard.

The identity of Jesus as the "true vine" is quite significant. As the Messiah, all of God's plans come to fruition in him. Jesus is the fulfillment of the Law and prophets who brought the entire Old Testament revelation to its intended goal. Since Jesus is the "true vine" he, in a sense, replaces Israel as the national people of God. Now God's people bear that identity through their identification with a man—Jesus. No longer are God's people associated with a geographic location—the Promise Land. Through Jesus, God's people are now transnational composed of Jews and Gentiles who place their faith in him. God's plan now focuses on a man, not a national entity. Carson makes a noteworthy comment:

> . . . Jesus claims, 'I am the true vine', *i.e.* the one to whom Israel pointed the one that brings forth good fruit. Jesus has already, in principle, superseded the

190

temple, the Jewish feasts, Moses, various holy sites; here he supersedes Israel as the very locus of the people of God. (A similar contrast between Israel and Jesus is developed in various ways in the Synoptics: *e.g.* in the temptation narrative, Mt. 4:1-11 par). (Carson, p. 513)

If Jesus is the true vine, then what constitutes the false vine? Jesus isn't rejecting Judaism; he sees the false vine as the corruption brought about by the religious authorities of his day. He is rejecting all their oral traditions, which made Israel an unfruitful vine. The spiritual leaders didn't recognize Jesus as the Messiah, thus cutting themselves off from him and the heavenly Father. Jesus and his disciples now take the place of Israel as the new people of God—the vine and the branches. Unlike Israel this new vineyard must and will be fruitful.

God is the vinedresser or gardener. In growing grapes the role of the vinedresser can't be underestimated. For the first three to five years of a new vineyard 90% of the growth is trimmed back at the end of every growing season, before they produce any grapes. A vineyard requires constant attention through pruning, fertilizing, watering, weed control, and so on. In growing a fruitful vineyard having a skilled vinedresser is crucial. With God occupying the role of vinedresser, he never makes any mistakes in caring for the vineyard. He is the most skilled gardener that exists, and because of that the potential for believers to bear fruit is limitless.

Grapes will only be as good as the vine (the stock). A single vine can produce as much as 80 lbs. of grapes in a season. A healthy vineyard can produce fruit for as much as one hundred years. With the branches (believers) being connected to the vine (Jesus) they are united to the best possible stock, which gives them the potential to produce top quality fruit. With God as gardener and Jesus as the vine the branches are supplied with every resource needed to bear high-end fruit in their spiritual development. How should we understand fruit? What exactly does Jesus mean by fruit?

In this passage the fruit mentioned is the byproduct of remaining in Jesus. If the disciple does this he will be fruitful. The fruit produced is prayer (vv. 7; 16), love (vv. 9-10; 12-13; 17), obedience (v. 10; 14; 17), and joy (v. 11), which are all dependent upon the branches remaining in Jesus. Apart from the dynamic connection the branch has with the vine there will be no fruit produced (v. 5). The spiritual fruit a branch produces is supernatural and can't be produced by man. Fruit goes beyond the things mentioned in this passage and should include the fruit of the Spirit (Gal 5:22-23), the virtues that Peter identifies (2 Pet 1:5-8), and another list from the apostle Paul (Col 3:12-15). Also included in fruit should be the believer's witness and all that is included in living the Christian life Jesus calls for. We might say that: *bearing fruit is making progress in everything that Jesus calls us to do* (Mat 28:20).

Every branch in Me that does not bear fruit, He takes away; and every *branch* that bears fruit, He prunes it so that it may bear more fruit. (John 15:2)

Jesus describes the work of God (the vinedresser) in pruning. Where there are branches that are unfruitful, or diseased they will be cut off so that they don't infect the rest of the plant. This is a crucial role of the vinedresser and ensures that the vineyard will be productive. Every branch that does bear fruit the vinedresser prunes so that it will be more fruitful. There are two types of pruning that take place: one is to remove the diseased or dead branches, the other is to prune the fruitful branches to make them more productive. Branches, also called tendrils, can grow incredibly fast reaching lengths between twelve and twenty feet. When they grow this long they are diverting resources away from the production of grapes, so the gardener cuts them back so they can divert the nourishment from the vine into grape production.

When God sees growth in a believer's life he automatically responds by pruning. How should this pruning be understood? It could refer to God's disciplinary activity in the believer's life for the purpose of making us better disciples, and strengthening us where we are weak. It can also refer to tests of faith to strengthen character, increase dependency on God, or remove things from our life to enable us to be more focused on God. It is through reading God's word that believers are purged of worldly attitudes that conflict with living in God's

192

vineyard, and gain a greater level of sanctification. God prunes ungodliness from us as we read his word, and let it have its effect on us (John 15:3).

In a face-paced society such as ours more activity, more things to do, and keeping busy is often considered better, for it makes people more productive. People will often fill up their schedule so that they have no margin, which can cause burnout, and loss of productivity and fruitfulness. God has a way of clearing the path so that we can focus on what he deems important at various times of life. Often activities that we spend our time on detract from our ability to bear fruit, and God may remove them as a benefit to us. God's pruning can be a painful process, but it is always done in love to make us more fruitful, and useful in serving the Lord.

You are already clean because of the word which I have spoken to you. ⁴Abide in Me, and I in you. As the branch cannot bear fruit of itself unless it abides in the vine, so neither *can* you unless you abide in Me. (John 15:3-4)

The disciples are already "clean" which is a translation of the Greek word *katharos*, a form of the same word translated prune in v. 2. Jesus is referring to the spiritual quality of the disciples. They are clean and bearing fruit because they have accepted the teaching of Jesus that he imparted to them. The word Jesus spoke to the disciples has made them clean (v. 3), which means they have the life of the vine flowing through them, and are being nourished by him. This seems to indicate that one of the ways in which God prunes is through his word, which is like a pair of supernatural pruning sheers. The word of God is one of the greatest agents of sanctification for the believer (Psalm 119; John 17:17; James 1:21-25; 1 Peter 2:2).

The word "abide" is the Greek word *menó*, which is often translated remain, or continue. This is written as a command in Greek so the believer's responsibility is to abide in Jesus. As the believer does that Jesus also abides in the believer, thus pointing out the vital connection between the branches and vine. There is a mutual indwelling of the believer with Christ, and Christ with the believer. As the branch stays connected to the vine, and receives nourishment from the same, the branch will be healthy and productive. As the believer stays connected to Jesus he will be bearing fruit and developing spiritual maturity. Apart from the connection with Jesus it is impossible to develop fruit.

I am the vine, you are the branches; he who abides in Me and I in him, he bears much fruit, for apart from Me you can do nothing. (John 15:5)

The believer who abides in Jesus will experience Jesus abiding in him. Abide is *menó*, (same as in v. 4) which is a present participle denoting continuous action. Abiding in Jesus means to have an active, moment-by-moment, trust in him, and awareness of his presence in your life. The believer is to stay connected to Jesus everyday through prayer, reading his word, and other spiritual disciplines. This is the formula for being a fruitful believer—stay connected to Jesus. The disciple and the Lord are in a cooperative relationship in the process of bearing fruit (Phil 2:12-13). The Lord's part is dominant, he takes the initiative, and the disciple responds. As the believer remains in Jesus, he will experience more intimacy with him because Jesus will abide with him. The indwelling is thus a mutual experience. Rodney Whitaker provides a value insight about what it means to remain (abide) in Jesus:

> But the disciples themselves must make an effort to *remain*. Remaining is not simply believing in him, though that is crucial, but includes being in union with him, sharing his thoughts, emotions, intentions and power. In a relationship both parties must be engaged. The divine must take the initiative and provide the means and the ability for the union to take place, but it cannot happen without the response of the disciples. (Whitacre, p. 376)

Abiding in Jesus is having an active on-going relationship with him, the result of which will be fruitfulness and more intimacy with him.

If anyone does not abide in Me, he is thrown away as a branch and dries up; and they gather them, and cast them into the fire and they are burned. (John 15:6)

The branches that don't abide in Jesus are discarded and used for firewood. This takes us back to v. 2 where Jesus said: "Every branch in Me that does not bear fruit, He takes away." This provides the interpreter with a problem in understanding how to handle this verse. How can a branch be "in Jesus" and not bear fruit? Jesus said that anyone who abides in him will bear fruit—it is a certainty. There are several ways that people understand the identity of the branches "in me" that don't bear fruit.

One way is to see these branches as believers who actually lose their salvation. Since they are "in Jesus" they must be true believers who have fallen away and broken the connection with Jesus so they have lost their salvation.

A second way to see these branches is as professing believers who aren't really born-again. It is maintained by some people that although Judas followed Jesus he didn't really believe in him, thus he is one of the branches who is cut off. The rest of the disciples are abiding in Jesus, unlike Judas. The problem with this view is how can Judas be described as being "in Jesus" since he was never a believer in the first place?

A third way of understanding the unfruitful branches *in Jesus* is believers that suffer loss of rewards on judgment day. At the Judgment Seat of Christ, the believer will be saved but will suffer loss of rewards (1 Cor 3:12-15; 2 Cor 5:10). This seems to be the most unlikely option.

A fourth way of understanding the branches that are cut off from Jesus are the religious leaders of the day that rejected him. They were the vine (Israel) but failed to recognize Jesus as the true vine, so they are cut off. The entire religious system advocated by the spiritual authorities is on the way out, with Jesus bringing in the new way of knowing God, which is through faith in him (John 14:6). Many of the Pharisees and scribes couldn't make that radical a transition to accepting Jesus as the Messiah, so they are the branches in the vine (Israel) that are cut off. The problem with this view is the phrase *in me:* those Jews were never *in Jesus* in the first place, so how can they be cut off from him?

Interpreting a metaphor is always challenging. Caution must be taken in assigning a precise meaning to every detail in the narrative. Don Carson brings this out as he comments on the *in me* language:

> It is more satisfactory to recognize that asking the *in me* language to settle such disputes is to push the vine imagery too far. The transparent purpose of the verse is to insist that there are no true Christians without some measure of fruit. Fruitfulness is an infallible mark of true Christianity; the alternative is dead wood, and the exigencies of the vine metaphor make it necessary that such wood be connected to the vine. (Carson, p. 515)

Carson correctly points out the main idea of the verse is the fruitfulness of true Christians. It is impossible to think that a branch can be connected to Jesus (the vine) and not bear fruit, for that would bring Jesus' credibility into question. Debating who are the branches *in me* that are cut off and thrown into the fire comes to a point of futility. It is better to see, as Carson has pointed out, the transparent purpose of the passage is that the true believer will bear fruit. Those who may have been in close proximity with Jesus, like Judas, appear to have never had divine life in the first place, since they failed to persevere to the end.

Vineyards were common in Israel; therefore Jesus' teaching would hit home to his audience. The point of the metaphor is being fruitful by staying connected to Jesus. If the disciples are remaining in Jesus they will be fruitful, not only in their own lives, but they will be able to successfully fulfill the Great Commission. Therefore, the idea of the passage isn't so much on who is saved and who isn't, or who the true branches are in distinction from the false branches. Nor does this passage deal with the possibility of the believer loosing his salvation.

196

The main idea of this Scripture is how to be fruitful and useful to Jesus in serving him.

Points of Application

This portion of Scripture has provided the reader with many applications and insights regarding sanctification. Through the vineyard metaphor there are many things about sanctification that are helpful for the disciple of Christ to understand.

Spiritual growth is a slow process. New plants are pruned for three to five years before they produce any grapes. While each believer grows at different speeds, generally speaking, spiritual growth is slow, just like producing grapes. Don't expect to be a mature Christian over night because progressive sanctification is a life-long process.

Producing a high-yield vineyard requires a lot of care and attention in the form of irrigation, fertilizer, pruning, and more. Disciples also require a lot of care and attention. In fact, the production of grapes is totally dependent on the care provided by the farmer. The same is true of believers in Christ. The ability to be fruitful is directly related to the supernatural care provided by God—the vinedresser, and Jesus the true vine.

Producing grapes requires a highly skilled vinedresser to do the work of pruning. If I'm the owner of a new vineyard I'm not going to hire a rookie to do the pruning. I'm going to spare no expense at finding a highly regarded vinedresser to ensure that I'll have a high-yield vineyard down the road. With God doing the pruning in our lives, he never makes a mistake. He is the ultimate expert at pruning the believer such that they will be more fruitful.

Pruning can be a painful experience, but God does this for our benefit so that we may mature as believers. God prunes through discipline to make us better people and more useful to him. God may prune us through trials that come into our lives and test our faith. God may remove things from our life that interfere with our spiritual development, such as hobbies, people, jobs, and so forth.

The branches are connected to the vine and receive their nourishment. If the vine is unhealthy, certainly the branches will be sickly and not yield good grapes, or any at all. Believers are connected to Jesus, who is the best vine in existence. Jesus will provide the believer with nourishment and life-giving energy, such that he will be fruitful. Given the fact that we have the best vinedresser caring for the vineyard, and disciples are connected to the best vine in existence, the potential for being a fruitful Christian is unlimited. This should be a source of encouragement to the believer as he considers the progress he can make in his sanctification.

The branches are commanded to abide in Jesus. This requires a response on the part of believers. As the disciple displays a moment-by-moment trust in Jesus he is being supernaturally nourished and will be fruitful. In fact, it is a certainty that those who are connected to Jesus will bear fruit to some degree. It is not possible to be a branch abiding in Jesus and not bear fruit. Every disciple needs to keep the connection with Jesus intact. Jesus is always available to the believer, but if in our everyday life we are disconnected from Jesus because of busyness, improper priorities and so on, the problem is on our end, not with Jesus.

As the believer abides in Jesus the Messiah responds in like fashion. He abides in us, so there is a mutual abiding between Jesus and the believer. This gives us great fellowship and intimacy with the Lord. If you want to experience more of the Lord in your life abide in Jesus, and he will do the same with you.

The point of this passage isn't to produce fear and doubt in the believer about whether or not he will lose his salvation and be thrown into the fire. It is important to keep in mind that this is a metaphor, so one must be cautious not to assign meaning to every detail. The main point of the passage is how to be fruitful and useful to the Lord.

Conclusion

In this chapter we have seen that bearing fruit is contingent upon the disciple staying connected to Jesus. It is a certainty, not likelihood, that one who abides in Jesus will bear fruit to some degree. It isn't possible to be abiding in Jesus and not bear any fruit. One is mindful of the Great Commission passage where Jesus said one of the characteristics of disciples is that they should be taught to obey everything I have commanded (Mat 28:20). Certainly, bearing fruit involves making progress in everything that Jesus commanded his disciples to do. It should be a source of encouragement for believers to study this passage because it reveals the potential for bearing fruit is enormous.

In the next chapter we will delve into the next section of John 15, which will point out some of the specific fruit disciples will bear as they stay connected to Jesus.

Chapter 20 ~ Fruit From Abiding in Jesus

Jesus has told the disciples that in bearing fruit it is imperative to continuously abide in him. As the believer does that, fruit will definitely be realized in his experience. In this section (John 15:7-11) Jesus explains what some of the specific fruits are that will appear in the believer's life from abiding in him.

If you abide in Me, and My words abide in you, ask whatever you wish, and it will be done for you. ⁸My Father is glorified by this, that you bear much fruit, and *so* prove to be My disciples. (John 15:7-8)

Jesus makes a great promise to his disciples about abiding in him and his words. He sees abiding in him as equivalent to abiding in his words. The Greek word *rhémata* is translated "words" in v. 7, which is a different Greek word than the one found in v. 3. The "word" Jesus spoke to the disciples that has already made them clean is the Greek *logos* (v. 3). The difference between the two words is that *rhémata* refers to the individual sayings of Jesus that, put together as a whole, constitute his word (*logos*). To abide in Jesus' words means the disciple must saturate his mind and lodge his words deep into his heart. This isn't done for intellectual stimulation it is done for life transformation, which should lead to obedience to his word.

This indicates that the word of the Lord should occupy a dominant place in a believer's life. The promise relates to prayer. If the believer is abiding in Jesus and his word he may: "ask whatever you wish, and it will be done for you." The disciple's prayer requests must be in conformity to God's will. In the context of the passage the asking should be in relation to bearing fruit. As the believer prays about his spiritual development, Jesus promises that the prayer will be answered.

One of the focal points of a believer's prayer life should be asking God to assist him in his growth as a disciple—his sanctification. Jesus said, "ask whatever you wish," meaning that anything pertaining to one's fruitfulness is fair game in prayer. When the disciple has Jesus' words abiding in him, it makes sense that the content of his prayers will reflect the word that abides in him. He will be praying God's word to fruition in his own life.

It is necessary to see the connection of this passage with John 14:12-14, where the disciples pray in Jesus' name and he will grant the requests in relation to doing greater works in ministry, so that the Son brings glory to the Father. Praying in Jesus' name is the same as praying Jesus' words that abide in the heart of the disciple. One prays in Jesus' name by praying that which is consistent with his message, character, and mission.

Jesus always brought glory to the Father. When disciples bear much fruit God the Father is glorified. As he does the work of the vinedresser by pruning the branches, and he sees them producing fruit, he is pleased. All the care and tending to the branches that God does produces maturity in the believers. God is glorified because the fact that the branches produce fruit proves the authenticity of their status as Christ's disciples. Bearing fruit is growing in all that is required of a disciple for witness, life transformation, and everything else God requires of us. The proof of a branch being in a vital connection with the vine (Jesus) is the fact that he is bearing fruit. God is glorified through the Son as his disciples grow. Growing as disciples is how Jesus brings glory to the Father. God is honored when his Son is honored.

One of the ways believers have assurance of their salvation is to look at their life and evaluate the fruit that they see over the time they've been a Christian. If they are connected to Jesus they will have developed some degree of fruit, thus proving that they belong to him.

Just as the Father has loved Me, I have also loved you; abide in My love. [10]If you keep My commandments, you will abide in My love; just as I have kept My Father's commandments and abide in His love. (John 15:9-10)

Believers are commanded to abide in Jesus (John 15:4), abide in his word (John 15:7), and now they are commanded to abide in his love (15:9). Jesus received the Father's love without restriction because he wasn't tainted by sin as humans are. In the same way that Jesus received God's love, Jesus has loved the disciples. In v. 9 both occurrences of "loved" are in the aorist tense, which pictures remaining in his love as a completed act. In other words, when the disciples' lives are viewed as a whole, it is like a snapshot of God's love residing in the heart of the disciple.

How did Jesus abide in his Father's love? He kept his Father's commandments and consequently abided in his love. The disciples' ability to abide in Jesus' love is contingent on their obedience to his commands. The fruit of obedience lends itself to enhancing one's experience with Jesus. Thus, there is a connection between one's obedience and the ability to have Jesus' love glowing in his heart. Obedience opens the door to receiving God's love. Conversely, lack of obedience inhibits the experience of God's love in the disciple's life. Jesus, as the sinless Son of God, never disobeyed the Father, so his ability to receive his Father's love was never restricted. His reception the Father's love was a constant in his life.

These things I have spoken to you so that My joy may be in you, and *that* your joy may be made full. (John 15:11)

Another fruit that the disciple can realize in his experience is joy. The ground of Jesus' joy was obedience to the commands of God, regardless of how difficult or costly obedience may have been. The author of Hebrews says: "who for the *joy* set before him endured the cross" (Heb 12:2). One derivative of obedience is the experience of joy. Jesus imparts "my joy," but this is not a carte blanch distribution, it is rather given as the disciple obeys Jesus' commands. For those who think a life of obedience is dull and restrictive, Jesus gives his joy into the obedient heart of the one who is willing to forsake all to follow him.

Human joy in a fallen world is temporary, fleeting, allusive, and shallow at best. On the other hand, when Jesus imparts his joy into the heart of an obedient believer, the disciple's joy becomes complete and is made full. His joy goes over the top and overflows. This type of joy transcends circumstances so that even when in dire straights the disciple can be filled with the supernatural joy of Jesus. This is a timely message for those who are looking for happiness and meaning in life through all kinds of activities including: sports, relationships, academics, partying, etc. Joy that comes from obedience to Jesus, and from sharing in the life of Jesus and the Father, far exceeds any kind of joy the world can deliver. God didn't intend the Christian life to be a dull, boring, and burdensome existence.

Insights Regarding Sanctification

The role of prayer can't be underestimated in one's sanctification. If the disciple is abiding in Jesus and his word, he can ask for anything and it will be done for him. The asking for anything, in the context of this passage, is asking for things pertaining to bearing fruit. A disciple of Christ should develop the practice of praying about his own spiritual progress, for Jesus has promised to answer those prayers. He has a vested interest in his people's spiritual growth.

In some circles of Christianity, unfortunately, the discipline of prayer has been butchered. With the influence of the prosperity gospel prayer is often selfishly driven and focuses on one's needs, wants, and comforts. Some circles of Christianity will claim that one measure of a mature Christian is that he will be increasing in prosperity throughout his lifetime. This means more money, possessions, and a more comfortable lifestyle are one measure of a believer's maturity. If one doesn't see these things appearing in his life he is deemed to have some kind of spiritual problem. Perhaps it is lack of faith, or an area of sin in his life that blocks the blessing of God from coming to him. People will often take this passage totally out of context and make it mean that Jesus will give you whatever you want, like a blank check that you fill in and he'll bring it to you.

Jesus placed two contingencies on his promise to ask for anything regarding fruit bearing: one is abiding in him, the second is having his word abide in the disciple. Then the prayer(s) will be answered. One can't go wrong if he prays God's word for his life. This is the type of prayer that honors God, and indicates that the disciple is of a kindred spirit with Jesus regarding what's important. Having Jesus' word abide in you involves more than knowing the content of the Bible. It is letting the word of God so saturate your mind that you begin to think the thoughts of God. Your mind is occupied with God's agenda and you begin to pray those things to become real in your life.

Two spiritual disciplines that should be instilled in every Christian are Scripture reading and praying for one's spiritual maturity. It also stands to reason that one can pray for his brothers and sisters in Christ regarding their spiritual development, and God will honor those prayers as well. The gathering of believers should be a praying community that has a prayer focus on being a fruitful assembly. A community of believers that is thriving spiritually, walking in the Spirit, displaying the fruit of the Spirit, and loving one another as Jesus instructs, will have a vibrant witness to the world. Every believer should have a prayer focus on his personal growth, and those of his friends, and entire church.

God is glorified as the disciple grows. The most important thing that God wants for each believer is to thrive spiritually. We all set goals for ourselves in life and establish priorities. On the top of the list of our goals should be the concern to glorify God by being a fruitful believer. Many of the things we value in life, and invest our time and energy in, pale in comparison to what God considers important. On judgment day when the Lord evaluates our lives one of the primary things he will look at is the stewardship of our spiritual life (2 Cor 5:10). Did we take it seriously and grow as a disciple? Our earthly treasurers aren't that important. The things we did to touch people with God's love, and the transformation of our character into the image of Christ are the things that are essential to God, thus they should be a priority to every believer.

Assurance of salvation

Many people struggle with having confidence that they are saved and in a right relationship with God through Jesus (cf. chapter 15). One way that a person can be certain he is a disciple is to look at the fruit that he developed since receiving Jesus into his heart. A true disciple will bear fruit, to some degree, because he is connected to the vine. In one's spiritual growth it is important to have a sense of confidence in knowing beyond any shadow of doubt that he is saved and going to heaven. Ask people who know you very well if they see a change in your life over the time you've known Christ. They can serve as good indicators of your spiritual growth.

Things to evaluate regarding bearing fruit are the following:

- Do I see a change in my attitudes toward sin?
- Do I have a desire to please God?
- Do I see a difference in my relationship with the world?
- Do I see different behavior developing since I've known Jesus?

Abiding in Jesus' Love

Jesus has instructed his disciples to abide in his love. The continuous experience of having God's love glowing in your heart, rather than bitterness and anger, or whatever sinful vices one may have to overcome, is the preferred state to be in. Jesus abided in his Father's love, and tells us we can accomplish abiding in his love the same way he was able to abide in his Father's love. The pathway to remaining in Jesus' love is obedience to his commands. If the disciple wants to experience more of God's love in his heart he must be obedient. This should provide incentive to followers' of Christ to live as Jesus instructs us to live. There is an exchange that takes place here: the disciple offers his devoted obedience to Jesus, and Jesus' love fills his heart. As Jesus' love fills the disciple's heart more devoted obedience is produced. Therefore there is reciprocity between the disciple and Jesus in obedience and the experience of his love.

The Experience of Joy

Who among us doesn't want to have their hearts filled with joy? Obedience shouldn't be burdensome, for the apostle John said his commands are not burdensome (1 John 5:3). There is a sense of joy that comes into the heart of a disciple through obedience. This should serve as another incentive to the believer to do as Jesus instructs us. Jesus also offers the disciple his peace, which is distinct from the peace the world offers (John 14:27).

Jesus gives his disciples the triad of love, joy, and peace in the Farewell Discourse. This is a gift beyond description. So many people's emotional lives are a train wreck. Jesus offers supernatural love, joy, and peace that can reside in the heart of a believer. In one's journey of sanctification these are virtues that should be coveted because they add a wonderful dimension to life. In the most difficult circumstances of life love, joy, and peace can be a constant in a believer's heart. These virtues transcend circumstances and are to be considered a gift that Jesus gives his people.

Conclusion

This chapter has examined some of the specific fruit that comes from the believer being connected to the vine (Jesus), such as experiencing Jesus love, joy, obedience, and prayer. Jesus promised to answer our prayers regarding our spiritual development, so that the Son can bring glory to the Father. The disciples' prayers must be based on Jesus' word, which should be deeply rooted in the hearts of his people. Christians must align their thoughts, spiritual aspirations, and agendas with Jesus' word. As believers pray God's word to fruition in their lives Jesus responds and answers these prayers. It is imperative that Christians pray this way for themselves, their friends, family members, and people they worship with. Each local church should be a praying community that focuses on prayers for the maturity of the body, and of course, every believer.

Chapter 21 ~ Fruitful Relationships

Jesus transitions his talk to how the disciples should relate to one another. What needs to characterize their relationships in the band of brothers is mutual love—that is, the sharing of divine love with each other. Jesus has already told his men that the distinctive feature of the community of believers that the world will take note of is love (John 13:34-35). The Christian life is a life of love on both the vertical dimension, between God and man, and horizontal dimension, between men. The community of Jesus' disciples should excel at living in love and expressing it to one another. Jesus says some pertinent things about bearing the fruit of love, which are essential to our discussion of sanctification.

"This is My commandment, that you love one another, just as I have loved you. [13]Greater love has no one than this, that one lay down his life for his friends. [14]You are My friends if you do what I command you. [15]No longer do I call you slaves, for the slave does not know what his master is doing; but I have called you friends, for all things that I have heard from My Father I have made known to you. [16]You did not choose Me but I chose you, and appointed you that you would go and bear fruit, and *that* your fruit would remain, so that whatever you ask of the Father in My name He may give to you. [17]This I command you, that you love one another. (John 15:12-17)

Jesus gave his disciples many commands to be followed, but in v. 12 he seems to be giving a summary of all his commands in one by saying "my commandment." He calls for his disciples to love another in the same way that he loved them. His example of love is to be emulated by all his followers. The gathering of believers is to be characterized by mutually expressed love for one another. In other words, disciples' of Christ live a lifestyle of love that mimics Jesus' love. Jesus raised the bar of love through his sacrificial lifestyle, which has become the standard to be followed by his disciples.

He gives an example of the highest form of love that one can produce in v. 13, which he refers to as "greater love." He is referring to his imminent death on the cross, where he is laying down his life for his friends—his disciples. Self-sacrificial love is the highest form of love that Jesus identifies. Placing the welfare of others above yourself and doing what's in the best interest of other people is what Jesus considers "greater love." This is the type of love that is to be cultivated and shared in the Christian community.

Jesus calls his disciples his friends. It appears that there is a shift in the relationship that Jesus had with his men that is taking place, where they transition from slaves to friends. Students of a rabbi were called servants in those days. The Greek word *doulos* can be translated "slave" or "servant" depending on the context. The NASB translates the word "slave" in this passage. No longer does Jesus refer to his disciples as slaves he calls them friends, which typically wasn't done by a rabbi. Jesus' friendship isn't automatically given. The contingency is that Jesus considers them his friends if they obey him. The sign of true friendship on behalf of the disciples is that they obey Jesus' commands. Jesus doesn't consider those who disobey him his friends. Thus, friendship with Jesus is a two-way-street.

He considered them his friends because he shared with them all that the Father revealed to him. He withheld nothing from his disciples, and entrusted them with the gospel. This is an amazing thought to consider for Jesus was the medium through which the band of brothers received everything that God wanted the disciples to know. This is the sense in which Jesus says "all things I heard from my Father I have made known to you."

The word "friend" is a translation of the Greek word *phílos*. This word carries a much deeper meaning than the English word for friend. It is not an exact one-to-one equivalent. It is related to the word *phileo,* which means to love. The Greek term for friend expresses an intimate relationship that goes beyond the English definition of friend. Such is the relationship that Jesus has with his disciples.

You did not choose Me but I chose you, and appointed you that you would go and bear fruit, and *that* your fruit would remain, so that

208

whatever you ask of the Father in My name He may give to you. [17]This I command you, that you love one another. (John 15:16-17)

Jesus chose the disciples; they didn't choose him. He chose them for service as his apostles, so this isn't a reference to salvation. What Jesus is saying to his men is true for disciples of all ages. Once a sinner becomes a believer in Christ, serving in some capacity should be a normal part of the life of a disciple, just as is bearing fruit. Whitacre makes an insightful comment about the fruit that Jesus appointed his disciples to bear:

> The primary expression of this fruit that Jesus speaks of here is the love within the Christian community. The fruit that remains is thus the love that flows from, and bears witness to, life in union with God. This love has come into the world in Jesus and now is to remain in the world in the community of his disciples. This divine love manifested within the church will bear witness to Jesus before the world (17:21, 23), which will enable some to find eternal life and will also reveal judgment of those who reject it. (Whitacre, p. 280)

The reference Jesus makes to the disciples' fruit remaining (v. 16): "your fruit will remain," is considered by Whitacre to be the ongoing love that remains throughout the ages in the gathering of believers. The divine love shared between Jesus and his disciples can never become a closed-off community that isolates itself from the world. Christians aren't called to be a holy huddle they are called to mission—to take his love to the world.

The primary fruit that emerges here is that which comes from spreading the gospel. Although the fruit that has been discussed throughout chapter 15 is comprehensive, in that fruit bearing involves growing in all that God requires of the disciple in the Christian life, fruit bearing must culminate in reaching people with the gospel. One of the characteristics of divine love is that it reaches out to touch those who are estranged from God. Therefore, God's people who share in divine love will be driven to reach out and share his love with nonbelievers. God reaches out and so should those who have God's love in their hearts. How can fruitful believers not reach out to the world? If they don't that would be an indication of their unfruitfulness, and lack of engagement with divine love.

The disciples can take courage in the fact that as they embrace the mission they have prayer as a vital resource. Jesus said: "so that whatever you ask of the Father in My name He may give to you" (v. 16b). Jesus has linked the production of fruit to the prayers of his disciples (14:12-14; 15:7-8). As the gathering of believers in all ages deploys for mission they can pray that their efforts will produce "fruit that will remain." As disciples pray in Jesus' name the Father will honor those requests that are consistent with his character, his word, and his mission.

Jesus ends this section by tying together what he's said about fruit bearing, especially the fruit of love (v. 12), by reiterating his command to love one another. Reading through chapter 15:1-17 reveals that the word "love" appears nine times. The word "fruit" appears eight times. It is safe to conclude that the fruit of love occupies a central place in this passage.

It is imperative that the disciples excel at living in the divine love and having a mutual expression of the same with each other. After the day of Pentecost the disciples would be sent into hostile territory to spread the gospel. Jesus proceeded to tell the disciples that as they went into the world they would be persecuted, suffer all kinds of abuse, and even be martyred. The world hates disciples and has hated Jesus as well (v. 18).

Thus, all the commands to love one another stand in stark contrast to the hatred the disciples will receive from the world (v. 18). If the disciples are going to have success in fulfilling the mission of spreading the gospel, they must be fruitful branches connected to the vine. They must individually stay connected to Jesus and be fruitful, and they must as a community share the divine love so they don't implode, self-destruct, and fail at accomplishing their mission. They will face unbelievable pressures in their ministry that will push them to their limits. If they stay connected to Jesus and tend to their own spiritual lives, bearing fruit through Jesus, they will stay the course and emerge victoriously.

Insights Regarding Sanctification

There are many things to consider from this passage (John 15:12-17) that are pertinent to our discussion of sanctification. The primacy of love rises to the surface in this passage. This is a challenging passage for any disciple. When I read some parts of the Bible I'm left shaking my head thinking I can't do what is required of me. This is one of those passages. Jesus is telling us to love those in the gathering of believers the same way he loves us. This is a high standard that we are to strive for. If we participate in the divine love, the love of Jesus and God the Father, it must be expressed to our brothers and sisters in our church.

Jesus' love is self-sacrificial. The world's concept of love isn't even remotely close to Jesus' love. The world's view of love may be sexual, self-centered, and convenience-based. Jesus' love is expressed in outward action. The greatest demonstration of God's love was sending Jesus to atone for our sins, and the greatest act of Jesus' love for the Father and mankind was dying on the cross. He made the ultimate sacrifice. Obviously, not every Christian is called to die for someone else, but the principle to take away is believers need to show action-packed love expressed in deeds, which are at times sacrificial. Loving people may require a sacrifice of time, energy, money, and so on. This is the "greater love" that Jesus is challenging us to emulate. This type of love comes from being united with Jesus, as the branch is to the vine, and is supernatural in nature.

In this chapter, which contains so much information on sanctification, it is imperative that we don't miss the climax of fruitful Christian living, which is participation in mission. If we ask ourselves what constitutes a mature believer and establish a set of criteria that includes one who reads their Bible, goes to church, attends a small group, and serves in some capacity at church, but leave mission out of the equation we error. All the fruit a believer produces should be for the purpose of participating in God's mission to reach the world. In what sense would someone be a mature Christian if he never reaches out and shares the divine love they live in? The question for every believer to ask herself is: "do I see my life moving in the direction of living on mission for Jesus?"

Jesus has called his disciples to bear fruit that remains (v. 16). The question for each believer to consider is: when I die and go to heaven what fruit did I leave behind me? What fruit remains in other people because of my influence on them? Who did I share Jesus' love with that was greatly impacted? What acts of kindness did I do for other people to demonstrate Jesus' love? Did I introduce someone to Jesus that is now impacting others for Christ? Hopefully, every believer will be fruitful in his spiritual development and have fruit remaining in the lives of people he left behind.

The believer's prayer life is essential to the development of fruit in his experience. As Christians penetrate the world to spread the gospel it must be done with prayer. In fact, the battle is won through prayer. A prayer-less believer is like going into battle with no ammunition in your weapon. As believers reach out to those who don't know God it must be done through prayer.

John 15:1-17 has revealed some crucial things about growing as a believer in Christ. Most importantly Christians are to abide in Christ and keep the connection with Jesus intact and healthy. As that happens fruit will be evident in the believer's life.

Conclusion

The focus of Part II of this book was to identify the Biblical markers of spiritual maturity. The way to break out of the prison cell of legalism is to understand the Biblical teaching on sanctification. A mature Christian is one who bears fruit, which is supernatural in nature because it is God's work in the believer. Fruit is the product of the Trinity's life-transforming work in the community of believers. Spiritual maturity is about character development that is in line with Jesus' character, for the believer is in the process of being conformed to his image (Rom 8:29). The markers of spiritual maturity identified by

212

legalists are miles apart from the markers of spiritual maturity that Scripture identifies. There are legalistic churches that may do some teaching on the fruit of the Spirit, but that isn't the emphasis of their criteria of the markers of a mature believer. Note the contrast below:

Biblical Markers of Spiritual Maturity
Love
Joy
Peace
Patience
Kindness
Goodness
Faithfulness
Gentleness
Self-control
Compassion
Humility
Moral Excellence
Knowledge
Perseverance
Godliness
Brotherly Kindness
Prayer
Missional Living

Legalistic Markers of Spiritual Maturity
Don't drink
Don't smoke
Don't chew tobacco
Don't watch certain movies
Don't go dancing
Don't play video games
Don't play contact sports
Women must wear skirts below the knee
Women must not wear cosmetics
Women must not go to the beauty salon
Women must not wear jewelry
Men must wear a suit and tie
Don't read secular books

Attend the Sunday night service
Avoid people in other denominations
Don't listen to secular music

It should be obvious that legalists have the wrong picture of spiritual maturity. The presence or absence of certain behaviors are used by legalists as markers of spiritual maturity, but these things have little or nothing to do with God transforming a person's life into the image of Christ. The criteria they establish to measure spiritual maturity are nothing more than man-made rules. Many more things could be added to the legalists' list above.

Along with a powerful dose of sanctification, another antibiotic that can help cure the disease of legalism is a strong dose of teaching on the topic of *liberty* believers have in Christ. It is to a discussion of this topic that we now direct our attention in Part III of this book.

Part III - The Liberation of Christians

Chapter 22 ~ Jesus Christ the Liberator

As World War II was winding down the Allied forces were liberating one town after another as they were closing in on Nazi Germany. The people would welcome the solders that liberated them with open arms as they gained their freedom. The women would offer hugs and kisses to the soldiers as they embraced them as heroes and liberators. After all, who doesn't want to be free?

One of the greatest things about being a Christian is the freedom that we have been given as one of the benefits of Christ's sacrifice. *Jesus Christ is the greatest liberator of all!* Understanding the Biblical teaching on liberty can be like walking out of a prison cell. It can be like taking spiritual handcuffs off your wrists. Understanding the concept of Christian liberty can make the believer happy, joyful, and enable him to truly experience the abundant life that Christ offers us. Breaking out of legalism can be greatly facilitated by understanding the concept of Christian liberty. The apostle Paul wrote extensively about liberty in his letter to the Romans.

The book of Romans is a theological masterpiece written by one of the greatest theologians of all time—the apostle Paul. He presents theological complexities that scholars have been trying to unravel and understand for millennia. The debate over the precise meaning of the apostle's writing is still raging on today in modern scholarship with those who are advocating the *New Perspective* on Paul. When we come to chapter 14 in Romans it appears that Paul isn't presenting a theological complexity, he is rather dealing with a very practical issue, but one that is difficult to solve.

How can Jewish Christians who have all kinds of scruples about the types of food they eat, go to church with Gentile converts who don't share the same scruples about food, and have fellowship together? After church when they have a potluck the Gentiles will eat anything: pork, ham, sausage, you name it, they'll eat it. Most Jewish Christians eat Kosher. They won't eat pork, bacon and a host of other things that their Gentile brothers in the Lord will eat; in fact, eating that stuff is repulsive to them. When they have a potluck, do the Jews sit on one side of the room with separate tables for them to place their food on, and Gentiles on the other side of the room with tables for their food? Do they eat separately with a line drawn down the middle of the room with Jews on their side and Gentiles on the other side? If they do, that sure doesn't promote the unity of the body.

Paul had to figure out a way for these two groups to get past their food differences, and other things, so there wouldn't be Jewish Christians, and Gentile Christians, that don't mingle and have any type of fellowship. Paul wants to build community, and see the body of Christ strengthened, but how can unity be promoted without requiring uniformity? How can people from drastically different cultures, with a wide variety of preferences, which at times are at odds with each other, worship God together and share the love of Jesus with one another? This is no easy task to accomplish!

The cultural divide between Jew and Gentile was huge and can't be underestimated. Jews had many Sabbath restrictions, observed their festivals, dietary laws, and more, but the Gentiles had no interest in getting involved with those things. The thought of Gentiles receiving the Spirit was amazing to the Jews, who thought that only Torah observing Jews would receive the Holy Spirit (Acts 10:44-45).

How can people of different ethnic backgrounds share a common faith in Christ, and a common community identity without loosing their own cultural distinctives is the issue Paul had to deal with. How can unity be fostered and retained, without destroying one's heritage, and how can differences be tolerated without causing the unity of the body to disintegrate? Furthermore, every church consists of people with differing levels of maturity. There are those in every congregation who have the liberty to engage in certain practices because of their understanding that food regulations, holy days, and Sabbath regulations have all been fulfilled in Christ, therefore, they understand that they don't have to abide by those stipulations. On the other hand, some believers who have grown up practicing these things don't have the liberty to stop observing them, because they are deeply

217

ingrained in their conscience. How can those believers who have the liberty not to practice these things have fellowship with those who insist that they must be observed?

The liberated believers may tend to look down on those who aren't, while the non-liberated brothers may tend to view their liberated counterparts as taking too many strides in their liberty, and are judging them as being ungodly. This type of situation will surely cause divisions in the body of Christ and inhibit the work of the Holy Spirit in strengthening the church. Paul presents his solutions to this complicated practical matter in Romans chapter 14 and chapter 15:1-13, where we now direct our attention.

Now accept the one who is weak in faith, *but* not for *the purpose of* passing judgment on his opinions. [2]One person has faith that he may eat all things, but he who is weak eats vegetables *only*. [3]The one who eats is not to regard with contempt the one who does not eat, and the one who does not eat is not to judge the one who eats, for God has accepted him. [4]Who are you to judge the servant of another? To his own master he stands or falls; and he will stand, for the Lord is able to make him stand. (Romans 14:1-4)

Paul identifies those who are weak in faith (v. 1) and those who are strong (Rom 15:1). It is essential to grasp Paul's meaning of the "weak" and "strong" brothers' in Christ to make sense of his reasoning. The "weak in faith" is more literally "weak in *the* faith." This believer hasn't grown in his understanding that he is under no restrictions regarding the food he may eat, because Jesus has declared all foods to be clean (Mark 7:19). In the New Covenant era, in which we live, all the dietary regulations in the Law of Moses have been fulfilled by Christ and are no longer necessary to observe. One can enjoy eating any type of food he wants with thanksgiving (1 Tim 4:3). Those who understand this and eat all types of food are considered the stronger brothers, whereas those who don't are considered to be the weaker brothers. They are weak because they haven't grasped the full extent of their liberty in Christ, and feel bound to observe rules they don't need too. For this reason Paul considers them weak in faith.

The stronger brothers have *liberty* to eat anything because they grasp the teaching of Scripture on this matter. The weak brothers maintain a legalistic mindset regarding the food they eat. They feel they will be falling out of God's favor and sinning before God if they don't follow the dietary laws of the Old Testament. The weak in faith believe they may only eat vegetables, whereas the strong in faith feel they can eat all foods.

Paul considers himself to be one of the stronger brothers and speaks to them about how they should treat their weaker brothers. He commands the strong to "accept the one who is weak in faith" (v. 1). The strong are to accept their weaker brothers in Christ as equals, not as second-class citizens who are inferior Christians. The strong must not look down on the weak as if they are spiritually deficient and beneath them. In Romans 15:7 Paul uses the same word twice that he uses here in v. 1: "Therefore, *accept* one another, just as Christ also *accepted* us to the glory of God."

The rule of thumb for the strong is to consider how Jesus has accepted them in spite of all their faults, sinful behavior, shortcomings, and so forth. This is how they are to accept their weaker brothers. This means not looking down on them, judging them as immature Christians, withholding fellowship from them, but rather embracing them as fellow brothers and sisters in Christ, "not for *the purpose of* passing judgment on his opinions" (v. 1). The weaker brother, who in this case only eats vegetables, holds sincere and very deep convictions about the food he eats. He feels he is doing the right thing before God by observing these dietary regulations, even though he doesn't understand the Scriptures regarding the issue of food, and therefore places himself under restrictions that are unnecessary.

The stronger brother isn't to judge him on his deeply held convictions and opinions about food. The word *dialogismós* is translated "opinions." The range of meaning of the word includes: reasoning, calculation, plotting, back-and-forth reasoning, and disputable matters. The stronger brothers are to accept their weaker counterparts without judging or arguing with them about their *opinions* regarding the food they may or may not eat. Arguing about these things will prove to be fruitless, cause division in the church, and damage the weaker brother.

In the church at Rome there were those who had the liberty to eat all kinds of food, and there were those who were weak and only ate vegetables (v. 2). Paul commands the strong: "The one who eats is not to regard with contempt the one who does not eat" (v. 3a). The word contempt is a translation of the Greek word *eksoutheneō*, which is a very derogatory term. It means to look down on someone as if they are totally worthless, of no value, to despise, or view someone as abhorrent. This term goes way beyond the idea of disrespecting someone—it is much worse than that. Paul commands the stronger Christians to do an attitude check by making sure they don't develop a derogatory posture toward their weaker brothers, and stand in judgment over them as if they were inferior believers. This would be prideful, judgmental, divisive, and hurtful to those whom Jesus has accepted (Ro 15:7).

On the other hand, Paul addresses the weak Christians: "and the one who does not eat is not to judge the one who eats, for God has accepted him" (v. 3b). Paul commands the weak not to "judge" their stronger counterparts. In this verse "regard with contempt" and "not to judge" are virtually synonymous. The strong may tend to view their weaker brothers as though they are inferior, legalistic, and have a bad attitude toward them. The weak may be prone to view the strong as though they are ungodly, against the law, and taking way too much liberty in their walk with the Lord. In fact, they might not regard them as even being true Christians!

If these attitudes are maintained, by the weak and strong, they will destroy the church. The seed of destruction has been sown and it must be killed at the root in order for the church to thrive, have healthy fellowship, and demonstrate love toward one another. The last phrase of v. 3: "for God has accepted him," refers to both the weak and strong. God has accepted both, thus the weak and strong must accept each other, and not get wrapped up in squabbles over food. How can a believer, whether strong or weak, not accept one whom the Lord has accepted?

In v. 4 Paul sets forth another reason why believers must accept each other: "Who are you to judge the servant of another? To his own master he stands or falls; and he will stand, for the Lord is able to make him stand." This is addressed to both the weak and strong—they must not judge each other. Both the strong and weak serve the Lord, and Christians aren't to be judging their fellow believers. The word "servant" is the Greek word *oikétēs*, which comes from *oíkos*, meaning house. Therefore, the word more literally means a "household servant." One who is working for a family in the context of a household implies that the work is done with much care and devotion. Both the weak and strong are "household servants" working for the same Master—the Lord Jesus, in the household of God. We must not judge each other over issues that are not in the doctrinal core of the Christian belief system.

Each believer stands or falls before his own master. Whether weak or strong each believer will stand before his master, because the Lord Jesus will enable him to stand on judgment day. Jesus has accepted both the weak and strong, so on judgment day both will enter the portals of glory. The fact that the Lord accepts both groups makes it all the more ridiculous to pass judgment on those who differ with you about disputable matters.

Paul has been talking about different views on the types of food that can be eaten. Now he shifts gears and introduces the viewpoints that people have about observing various days of spiritual significance. People have differing positions on how these days should be observed as well. It is another disputable matter that people maintain a variety of opinions on.

One person regards one day above another, another regards every day *alike*. Each person must be fully convinced in his own mind. [6]He who observes the day, observes it for the Lord, and he who eats, does so for the Lord, for he gives thanks to God; and he who eats not, for the Lord he does not eat, and gives thanks to God. [7]For not one of us lives for himself, and not one dies for himself; [8]for if we live, we live for the Lord, or if we die, we die for the Lord; therefore whether we live or die, we are the Lord's. [9]For to this end Christ died

and lived again, that He might be Lord both of the dead and of the living. (Romans 14:5-9)

There were certain days that the Jews held in high regard, such as the Sabbath, and the different festivals like Passover, the feast of booths, the first fruits, and so forth. Some Jewish Christians felt compelled to continue observing them just as they did before becoming believers in Christ. He is the weaker brother because he doesn't have faith developed enough to suspend the observance of these days for they have been fulfilled in Christ. He has such deep-rooted convictions about observing these days that he feels it is necessary to please God by doing so.

The stronger Christian regards every day alike. He understands the teaching of Scripture in that it isn't necessary to continue observing these days. He is liberated from these strict observances that were mandatory under the Old Covenant, such that "he regards every day alike." He doesn't place himself under regulations that he isn't required to. The key point regarding how one views various days is found at the end of v. 5: "Each person must be fully convinced in his own mind." This means one must follow his heart. The one who continues to observe days must do so if in the depths of his heart he is persuaded that he must do this to please God. He is observing the Sabbath and other festivals to honor the Lord. The one who regards every day alike also does so to honor the Lord, and is fully persuaded that he has the liberty to be freed from the strict observance of these days. Both must be true to their deepest heart-felt convictions. Paul brings this out in the next verse:

He who observes the day, observes it for the Lord, and he who eats, does so for the Lord, for he gives thanks to God; and he who eats not, for the Lord he does not eat, and gives thanks to God. (Romans 14:6)

In matters such as these, that are not specifically forbidden or commanded in Scripture, the believer must search his heart and understand his motives that drive his spiritual practices. The one who observes a certain day does so to honor God. The one who eats everything does so to honor God and gives thanks for his provision of

222

food. The one who doesn't eat everything also does so to honor God, and he gives thanks as well.

There is an important principle to highlight from this passage. Every believer must follow his convictions and pay attention to his conscience. Whatever his conscience tells him to do he should do, and not violate his inner voice. The conscience is a moral guide that tells us what is right and what is wrong. This doesn't mean that one's conscience can't ever be wrong. For instance, one may have guilt lingering in his conscience when it doesn't need to because Jesus has forgiven him for the sin(s) he feels guilt over. One's conscience can become so desensitized to sin that a person may be in open rebellion against God, but his conscience is virtually inoperative to the point where he feels no guilt whatsoever over his behavior. Paul places a high premium on listening to the inner voice of one's conscience, which should be the person's guide in his daily behavior (1 Cor 8:7-13).

Paul made it clear that a person's conscience can be wounded, weak, defiled, and the stronger brothers in Christ must never do anything to influence someone to go against the dictates of their conscience. The issue becomes more complex because now believers at Rome have different views of what is proper to eat and how various religious days should be observed. The rule of thumb is to follow your conscience. If you don't, you will feel guilty because your conscience tells you that you did something wrong before God. The stronger brothers must be careful not to do anything that causes the weaker brothers to go against the dictates of their conscience. They must not try to impose their liberties on the weaker brothers because that can damage their conscience and cause them spiritual trauma.   Both the weak and strong must respect each other's differences for reasons that unfold in the following verses:

For not one of us lives for himself, and not one dies for himself; [8]for if we live, we live for the Lord, or if we die, we die for the Lord; therefore whether we live or die, we are the Lord's. [9]For to this end Christ died and lived again, that He might be Lord both of the dead and of the living. (Romans 14:7-9)

223

This may seem somewhat confusing, but it is actually very simple. No believer lives or dies for himself (v. 7). He lives or dies for the Lord, so whether the believer is alive or dead he belongs to the Lord (v. 8). All the believer does is to be done to the glory and honor of God, regarding the food he eats, the days he observes, and if the Lord calls him to martyrdom, or it is simply time to depart from this world, he dies for the Lord. Everything done by believers is for the higher glory of God.

The Lordship of Christ comes out loud and clear in v. 9, that in Jesus' death and resurrection he is the Lord of both the living and the dead. Each believer lives to please the Lord, but as this passage points out, there are different ways that believers choose to please the Lord that conflict with other brothers in Christ. We have to cut each other some slack because the way one honors the Lord may differ from how other believers honor the same Lord. We must suspend all judgment, stop holding each other in contempt, and accept each other's differences as though they are being done to honor God. This will bring harmony in the body of Christ. Paul again brings out the futility of standing in judgment of each other in the following verses.

But you, why do you judge your brother? Or you again, why do you regard your brother with contempt? For we will all stand before the judgment seat of God. ¹¹For it is written, "As I LIVE, SAYS THE LORD, EVERY KNEE SHALL BOW TO ME, AND EVERY TONGUE SHALL GIVE PRAISE TO GOD." ¹²So then each one of us will give an account of himself to God. (Romans 14:10-12)

Paul reiterates what he said in v. 3. The weak should not judge their brothers who eat everything and regard every day alike, while the strong shouldn't hold in contempt those who observe food restrictions and special days. All judging of how believers practice their faith needs to cease and desist because "we all stand before the judgment seat of God" (v. 10b). The Lord is the ultimate judge so it is only his role to play, not believers. When we judge each other we are actually usurping the role of God. All believers stand before the judgment seat of God, at which time the believer's works will be evaluated by the Lord and he will either be rewarded for his faithfulness, or suffer loss of reward because of his poor stewardship (1 Cor 3:13-15; 2 Cor 5:10).

Paul quotes Isaiah 45:23 that makes the point that all will answer to God and will bow to his Lordship (cf. Phil 2:10-11). All believers will do this; even nonbelievers will acknowledge the Lordship of Christ. Believers out of love, nonbelievers out of disdain, but all will acknowledge the Lordship of Jesus.

When the believer stands before God at the judgment seat (cf. 2 Cor 5:10) he will give an account of himself for the way he has lived his life—for the good works he has produced in the power of the Holy Spirit, and the overall stewardship of his life. The believer doesn't give an account to God for his fellow brothers and sisters that he disapproved of because of what they ate and how they observed various days. We stand before God one-on-one and give an account of our self—nobody else. Therefore, don't judge other believers for the way they practice their faith, leave that to God.

A Passover Supper

Ben Smith is a Christian who would have a Passover supper every year. This became a family tradition, which was done for the purpose of gathering the entire family and honoring God. They perfectly understood that they weren't under constraint to observe this special day—for they understood that Christ fulfilled this and believers were under no obligation have a Passover meal. This doesn't mean they are to be considered weaker Christians or legalistic. They were practicing their faith in this manner simply because they wanted to do this, not because they felt they had to do this—as if the Bible commanded it.

There is nothing in Scripture that says believers in Christ should or shouldn't celebrate the Passover in this fashion. This is something that Ben started as a family tradition, and he isn't trying to impose this practice on other people, this is done between him and God. The point of this story is that believers can use their freedom in Christ in creative and meaningful ways to practice their faith and honor God. Nobody should judge them as being weaker brothers, or legalistic because of how they are choosing to worship God.

Conclusion

One thing that everybody needs to grasp from the passage under consideration is that no two people are alike. We all have different views on things including the way we worship God. If Christians demand uniformity in the way they practice their faith, their church will be in a state of divisive chaos. People will be judging those who see things differently than they do, looking down on them, and viewing them with contempt. This action will kill the unity of the body that should be a characteristic of a healthy church.

The bottom line is this: *we must all learn to cut each other some slack when it comes to the way we express our faith.* I must suspend passing judgment on those who worship differently than I do, with the understanding that Jesus has accepted those people in the same way that he has accepted me. It's not my place to judge somebody else about disputable matters. On judgment day each person meets God one-on-one, face-to-face, at which time he answers for himself, not other people in church that he may have disapproved of.

Believers should learn to appreciate diversity in their church, rather then expecting everybody to practice their faith the same way they do. Perhaps those who want uniformity of practice in their church have a prideful motivation that can't tolerate anybody being different than they are. If this is the case that sinful attitude must be repented of.

Chapter 23 ~ Use Your Liberty Responsibly

Rather than nitpicking everybody in your church because they do things differently than you do, it is imperative for believers to pursue a course of action that builds up the people around them. In fact, edifying other people in one's church should be a way of life for Christians—this is part of loving one another (John 13:34-35). Paul is continuing his discussion about the weaker and stronger brothers regarding how they should relate to one another. The onus of the passage is clearly on the stronger brothers not to flaunt their liberty before their weaker counterparts, such that they influence them to do things they don't feel comfortable with.   This would be an irresponsible use of their liberty and would violate the love ethic of Jesus. Paul describes how the strong can navigate a course of love in the use of their liberty without being divisive and harmful to their weaker brothers in Christ.

Therefore let us not judge one another anymore, but rather determine this—not to put an obstacle or a stumbling block in a brother's way. ¹⁴I know and am convinced in the Lord Jesus that nothing is unclean in itself; but to him who thinks anything to be unclean, to him it is unclean. ¹⁵For if because of food your brother is hurt, you are no longer walking according to love. Do not destroy with your food him for whom Christ died. ¹⁶Therefore do not let what is for you a good thing be spoken of as evil; ¹⁷for the kingdom of God is not eating and drinking, but righteousness and peace and joy in the Holy Spirit. ¹⁸For he who in this *way* serves Christ is acceptable to God and approved by men. ¹⁹So then we pursue the things which make for peace and the building up of one another. ²⁰Do not tear down the work of God for the sake of food. All things indeed are clean, but they are evil for the man who eats and gives offense. ²¹It is good not to eat meat or to drink wine, or *to do anything* by which your brother stumbles. ²²The faith which you have, have as your own conviction before God. Happy is he who does not condemn himself in what he approves. ²³But he who doubts is

condemned if he eats, because *his eating is* not from faith; and whatever is not from faith is sin. (Romans 14:13-23)

The word "therefore," refers back to vv. 10-12 where Paul prohibits believers from judging each other because each one stands before God at the judgment seat, at which time he gives an account of his actions, not those of his fellow worshipers. What each believer should determine and focus on is "not to put an obstacle or a stumbling block in a brother's way" (v. 13). The word "to put" is a translation of the word *tithémi*, which is a present infinitive denoting nonstop continuous action. The word means to set before, place, establish, or fix. The significance of this is that the believer must continuously determine how the use of his liberty influences other people. He must continuously be sensitive to those around him, and make sure he doesn't "set before" other believers behavior that serves as an "obstacle" or "stumbling block" as he expresses his liberty.

An "obstacle" is the translation of the Greek word *proskomma,* which includes the idea of a stumbling block, a falling over something, and refers to a spiritual falling, or stumbling. The word was used to identify Jesus as the stumbling block (Ro 9:32, 33, 14:13; 20; 1 Pet 2:8) that people would trip over because they reject him. The "stumbling block" is the translation of *skándalon,* from which our English word scandalize is derived. The meaning of the word is to snare, trap, bring offense, or hindrance. Paul encourages the strong believers to be sensitive to their weaker brothers (1 Cor 8:9) and not do anything that causes them spiritual damage.

One example of this could be the consumption of alcohol. The Bible doesn't prohibit drinking alcohol it forbids drunkenness (Eph 5:18). If I'm at a restaurant with a friend of mine that I know is a recovering alcoholic, I'm not going to order a martini or any other alcoholic beverage because it could cause him to stumble in one of two ways. He might be tempted to order a drink, go against his conscience, and fall back into his addiction. The second way he might stumble is judging me as less than spiritual because I drank an alcoholic beverage, which he regarded as sinful. It would be totally inappropriate for me to flaunt my liberty before my brother in Christ in this fashion, for I would be bringing him into harms way spiritually.

228

Any practice that is somewhat of a gray area, because it isn't identified as sinful in Scripture, must be practiced with great care and sensitivity before other people who are weak. We are to suspend the use of our liberty for the greater good of our brothers and sisters in Christ, and to preserve unity in our church. The more we have concern for our fellow Christians who are weak in faith, the more willing we will be to give up our rights and liberty for their sake, and for the sake of the gospel. The issue for the strong believer isn't whether or not he has freedom; it is to exercise his freedom responsibly. When that happens unity can be promoted, the body of Christ is strengthened, and fellowship is enhanced.

We get a sense of how liberated Paul was in v. 14. His knowledge and convictions about nothing being unclean in itself was made known to him by revelation. The apostle Paul was a Pharisee who followed all the ancestral traditions scrupulously, which included food regulations and the observance of all the special days. He knew the Lord Jesus had declared all food clean, such that with the inauguration of the New Covenant the dietary regulations of the Mosaic Law have been abrogated. Paul was no longer compelled to keep these dietary regulations.

We have to appreciate how emancipated Paul was to forego all the food restrictions. Paul walked in liberty because he understood that God created all things good (food) so they can be enjoyed with thanksgiving (1 Tim 4:3-5; Titus 1:15). When a believer walks in liberty it is like having shackles taken off his wrists, for he is free to enjoy the things God created for him. Peter had a terrible time understanding this, as Acts 10 points out. The Lord explained to Peter three times that all foods could be consumed because God had cleansed them. "What God has cleansed, no longer consider unholy" (Acts 10:15).

Paul was an emancipated believer who had the freedom to enjoy all foods, but he understood that not all people have this knowledge: "but to him who thinks anything to be unclean, to him it is unclean." He is referring to the weaker brothers that don't have the knowledge and same convictions that he has to eat all kinds of food. The weaker brother's conscience is unduly sensitive in this area so he should follow the dictates of his inner voice. He isn't sinning in the sense of

229

having a moral failure, or being a heretic. He's lacking the Scriptural knowledge that will inform his conscience that he is free to eat all foods (1 Cor 8:7). The conclusion is that to him who thinks some foods are unclean, they are unclean.

For if because of food your brother is hurt, you are no longer walking according to love. Do not destroy with your food him for whom Christ died. (Romans 14:15)

The stronger brother must respect the weaker brother and not do anything to cause him to go against his conscience. When someone ignores what their conscience tells them they can become desensitized to sin, to the point where their conscience becomes virtually inoperative. Paul mentioned that the conscience can become seared as if burned by a hot branding iron, and put out of commission (1 Tim 4:2). When we influence someone to go against the inner voice of conscience by what we eat in front of him it can hurt our weak brother, because he may be emboldened to eat food his conscience tells him not to eat. The Greek word for hurt is *lupeó,* which has the meaning of being grieved, feeling deep emotional pain, and sorrow.

If a Christian is led by a brother in Christ to do something against his convictions he can suffer much spiritual grief. He may be overwhelmed with guilt that he has done wrong before God. He losses peace of mind, his joy is lost, he is filled with remorse, and feels he has gone backward spiritually. Mostly he went against the dictates of his conscience, which Paul considers to be very serious business.

When the strong influence the weak in this way Paul says: "you are no longer walking according to love." The strong must not give up loving their weaker brothers as they assert their liberty! This would be irresponsible. When the believer is filled with the love of Jesus, he will gladly give up his rights for the sake of the weaker brothers, be sensitive to them, and cautious to not put a stumbling block in anyone's path. Love has to guide the use of one's liberty. Love keeps liberty in check so that it isn't used recklessly to the detriment of those for whom Jesus died.

230

Paul's command to the strong is "do not destroy with your food him for whom Christ died" (v. 15b). The word destroy is *apóllumi*, which means utter destruction, to perish, to be lost. The word is used for nonbelievers that suffer eternal punishment in hell (Mat 10:28; Luke 13:3; John 3:16; Rom 2:12). Paul is pointing out to the strong how important it is to be respectful of the weaker brother's convictions and not do anything to harm them. This is strong language that Paul uses because the weak can suffer much spiritual trauma by the loveless influence of the strong.

Paul isn't saying that the weak brother could end up in hell, because their stronger brothers are influencing them to do things that their conscience tells them not to do. Rather he is saying their spiritual development will be seriously impaired. Their spiritual health will greatly suffer. That Christ died for the weaker brother should cause the strong to be careful not to flaunt their liberty in front of their weaker comrades in the faith. They must not do anything to corrupt their spiritual life.

Therefore do not let what is for you a good thing be spoken of as evil; ¹⁷for the kingdom of God is not eating and drinking, but righteousness and peace and joy in the Holy Spirit. ¹⁸For he who in this *way* serves Christ is acceptable to God and approved by men. ¹⁹So then we pursue the things which make for peace and the building up of one another. ²⁰Do not tear down the work of God for the sake of food. All things indeed are clean, but they are evil for the man who eats and gives offense. ²¹It is good not to eat meat or to drink wine, or *to do anything* by which your brother stumbles. ²²The faith which you have, have as your own conviction before God. Happy is he who does not condemn himself in what he approves. ²³But he who doubts is condemned if he eats, because *his eating is* not from faith; and whatever is not from faith is sin. (Romans 14:16-23)

Paul makes another conclusion in v. 16. The way the strong believers don't let the weak speak evil of what is for them a good thing (their liberty), is to do what it says in v. 15. They are not to flaunt their liberty before their weaker brothers and bring any harm to them because of the food they eat. If their love isn't operative, which leads them to become insensitive enough to eat food in front of their weaker brothers and brings them harm, their liberty will be criticized and spoken against in a negative fashion. The way the strong don't let what is good for them be spoken of as evil, is to make sure their love keeps the expression of their liberty in check so that it isn't used recklessly. In this way their liberty won't be spoken of as evil. On the other hand, if the strong aren't acting in love and eat meat in front of the weak brother, that brother may "speak evil" of the stronger brother's liberty. In this way, the offended weaker brother speaks negatively about the strong brother's liberty, which, in reality, is actually a "good thing."

The New Living Translation (NLT) does a superb job in bringing out the meaning of v. 16: "Then you will not be criticized for doing something you believe is good." It isn't that the strong don't have valid liberty; it is the expression of his liberty that Paul is encouraging to be used with great caution and care. Otherwise their valid liberty will be cast in a very bad light.

"Spoken of as evil" translates the Greek word *blasphēméō*, which is mostly translated blasphemy in English. The word means to speak against, slander, and use negative language against God. The term is also applied to a man who claims to be equal to God, or to be able to do things that only God could do.

The strong should realize that the careless expression of their liberty will bring a bad report from their weaker brothers in Christ. They will be regarded as lacking concern for godly living and taking huge leaps in liberty that go against God's word. They might even be regarded as non-Christians by the weak. The point is to use one's liberty with restraint and caution, always having regard for the weaker brother— not to bring spiritual harm to him.

The strong have valid liberty, but must safeguard that liberty by walking in love and keeping the use of his liberty under control. The uncontrolled expression of liberty could cause someone to appear like a bull in a china shop. He could bring multiple offenses to his weak brothers, cause them much harm, influence them to do things that their conscience doesn't agree with, and bring his valid liberty under harsh criticism.

The church picnic

Many years ago, I was having a discussion with a District Superintendent who told me about a problem he was having with one of the churches in his region. He said there was a newer church that was in search of a pastor, but an issue they had in their fellowship was that many of the people would drink beer and wine at social gatherings, church picnics, etc. He said it was causing a problem for those who don't drink. He said that many people go to church because they want to get away from alcohol, which is what they see in the world. They didn't want their kids exposed to that type of thing at church.

At the annual church picnic there were cases of beer and many bottles of wine made available to those who wished to partake. Those who were drinking alcohol openly in front of everybody claimed they had the liberty to do so. They felt there was nothing sinful about drinking as long as they didn't get drunk, although I was told some had way too much to drink. Other people in the church were deeply offended by the reckless expression of their liberty, especially in front of their children, and it was causing a divide in the church.

He asked me how I would resolve this issue if I was the pastor. I told him that I would do an extensive teaching on Christian liberty, and explain how all things must be guided by love, and concern for people in church that have differing opinions. The issue here is the loveless expression of valid liberty. The District Superintendent said he liked my answer.

The reason believers shouldn't get wrapped up in squabbles about food, observance of days, and other disputable matters is stated in v. 17:

for the kingdom of God is not eating and drinking, but righteousness and peace and joy in the Holy Spirit. [18]For he who in this *way* serves Christ is acceptable to God and approved by men.

Paul sets forth the focal point of life in the Kingdom of God, which is life in the Holy Spirit. When believers are Spirit filled they will express righteousness, peace, and joy. Righteousness refers to the believer's conduct. When he uses his liberty properly showing concern for the weaker brothers in his church, his righteousness is enhanced. He is pleasing God and expressing his liberty in a way that promotes unity of the body and does nothing to impede the Spirit's work of building up the church.

Peace refers to relationships that exist in the church. When liberty is used properly good fellowship will naturally follow. The relationships that exist will be tranquil in that the weak aren't judging the strong, and the strong aren't holding the weak in contempt. They are accepting each other's differences and respecting each other's convictions, which results in developing harmonious relationships.

Paul mentions joy, as another quality of life in the Spirit. Both peace and joy are mentioned as the fruit of the Spirit (Gal 5:22), which means these are supernatural characteristics that the Spirit of God develops in believers. Joy isn't based on circumstances for believers in Christ. Joy is rooted in one's relationship with Christ that goes well beyond external circumstances. In this context the joy one experiences is the joy of good fellowship with one's fellow worshipers. Going to church and mingling with the people you worship with becomes a joyous event that is fulfilling and enriching.

Righteousness, peace, and joy, are "in the Holy Spirit." The primary concern of the believer in experiencing Kingdom life is walking in the Spirit. If the weak and strong are arguing with each other about what is acceptable to eat and drink, and which days are to be observed they will grieve the work of the Holy Spirit in their church. The body will not be strengthened, believers will not be established in the faith, fellowship becomes dreadful, and righteousness, peace and joy in the Holy Spirit will be greatly inhibited.

The conclusion to be drawn from this is: don't get side-tracked on matters that aren't primary (eating and drinking), and focus on what is essential, such as life in the Spirit, and the unity of the gathering of believers. The one who keeps his focus on life in the Spirit: "For he who in this *way* serves Christ is acceptable to God and approved by men" (v. 18). When the weak and strong respect each other's convictions, and let love guide the expression of their liberty they are acceptable to God. In other words, God is pleased with them, and they will be in good standing with men—the people they worship with will approve them. The Greek word *dókimos* is translated "approved." It is used of testing the authenticity of metals, and coins through a process of careful examination. Once they passed the test they were labeled genuine and authentic.

When believers serve Christ by focusing on life in the Spirit, not arguing about disputable matters, the people in their church will have high regard for them. In other words, they will view this type of believer as the real deal—a genuine and authentic believer in Christ. Paul makes a conclusion about how believers should conduct themselves in v. 19:

So then we pursue the things which make for peace and the building up of one another.

Mature Christians always do things that promote peaceful relationships in the body of Christ and serve to build up their brothers and sisters in the Lord. The mature believer's behavior is governed by what is best for the welfare of the body. Arguing about food and the observance of days causes friction between believers and works against building a healthy community. The word "pursue" is written in Greek in the present tense, which means believers are to *continuously pursue* a course of action in their church that promotes peace and building one another up.

Do not tear down the work of God for the sake of food. All things indeed are clean, but they are evil for the man who eats and gives offense. ²¹It is good not to eat meat or to drink wine, or *to do anything* by which your brother stumbles. (Romans 14:20-21)

After stating the positive course of action for believers in verse 19, Paul states the negative. Arguing about what people eat and drink "tears down" the work of the Holy Spirit in one's church. This is to be avoided by all Christians. Paul asserts his conviction that all food is clean, but for the believer who flaunts his liberty before a weaker brother in the faith and brings an offense this is considered evil. Believers must have an awareness of how their actions affect other people. The rule of thumb is not to do anything that causes a brother in the Lord to stumble. The mature believer will suspend the use of his liberty for the sake of his weaker brothers.

The faith which you have, have as your own conviction before God. Happy is he who does not condemn himself in what he approves. ²³But he who doubts is condemned if he eats, because *his eating is not from faith; and whatever is not from faith is sin.* (Romans 14:22-23)

Paul addresses both the weak and strong in v. 22a. Each person should act on the basis of his own convictions before God. Every believer must determine for himself what is right and wrong regarding disputable matters such as: social drinking, movies, music, style of dress, and so forth. This will take time, study, prayer, and discussion with other believers to gain insights and discernment on these disputable matters.

In v. 22b Paul pronounces a blessing on the strong. "Happy (or blessed) is the one who doesn't condemn himself by doing something that he knows is right." His conscience is clear so when he eats all kinds of food he doesn't experience guilt. He can eat whatever he wants with no misgivings, because he is convinced that what he is doing is honoring to God. This man is blessed because his convictions are firmly established such that when he exercises his liberty he does so with a clear conscience—he is guilt free.

On the other hand, the weak one whom Paul addresses in v. 23 eats without having firmly established convictions about food and is not doing so from faith. This results in having a guilty conscience before God. Whatever is not done from one's faith is sinful and is to be avoided. Paul has pronounced a blessing on the strong who understand the liberty they have through their faith, while warning the weak not to act against their convictions, "for whatever is not from faith is sin."

In what sense does Paul mean sin in v. 23? Sin here refers to any act that does not conform to our most deeply held convictions about what our faith allows us to do, or prohibits us from doing. All decisions believers make and actions they commit must be justifiable on the grounds of their convictions, that they have the liberty in the Lord to do so. When a believer violates his inner voice, even when the conscience doesn't perfectly conform to the word of God, it is still sin for that person.

The strong must not force or influence the weak to eat meat, drink wine, or ignore holy days when their faith isn't strong enough to understand that they have the liberty to do so before God. The weak must first be taught from the word of God so that Scripture informs their consciences about what is right and wrong before God. Only when the weak believer's conscience gives him permission should he eat meat or suspend the observance of special days as the strong do.

Conclusion

My life isn't just about me! Church isn't all about me! People can be very selfish and view life as revolving around them. "It's all about me and what I want" seems to be the philosophy that many people employ these days. If everybody could put into practice what Paul has advocated in this passage of Scripture the world would be a kinder and gentler place. As we consider all the people we have in our life, not just in our church, and plot a course of action to deliberately build them up, seek a harmoniously existence with them, and do everything in our power to make their lives better we would be an amazing blessing to them.

In navigating through some turbulent waters with people it may be necessary to give up some of the freedoms we have for their benefit. When we gather at church we have to understand that many people may not agree with all the things we have liberty to do, and that has to be OK. This requires sensitivity training in the way people express their liberty. The over-riding concern of mature Christians, regarding their church involvement, is to build up their fellow worshipers, promote the unity of the body, and not do anything that could cause a brother or sister to stumble.

It is essential for all worshipers in a church to keep in mind that the primary focus of Kingdom living is "righteousness, peace, and joy in the Holy Spirit" (Rom 14:17). Getting sidetracked by arguing about what people eat and drink, and other disputable matters, can rob people of joy in the Spirit, and tear down the work of the Holy Spirit in their church.

In the next chapter Paul will point to the example of Jesus and demonstrate how the Messiah put into practice the principles that he has set forth in chapter 14 of Romans.

Chapter 24 ~ Follow the Example of Jesus

Chapter 15 of Romans is a continuation of Paul's discussion that he began in chapter 14. Of course, in the original manuscripts there were no chapter divisions, so Paul's presentation is one unit of thought. Unity is essential to the welfare of the body of Christ. Believers in Christ are unified by the Holy Spirit living within them, share a common faith in the Lord Jesus, are recipients of eternal life, and are called to worship the Lord in the context of a fellowship of other believers.

At times unity in practice may be sorely lacking. Paul addressed divisions in the church at Corinth (1 Cor 1:10), he encouraged the Ephesian believers to preserve the unity of the Spirit (Eph 4:2-6), he encouraged the Philippians to stand firm in one spirit (Phil 1:27), and he exhorted the Colossians to love one another which is the perfect bond of unity (Col 3:14). Lack of unity is a common problem in many churches, including the Roman church. If people couldn't get over their differences regarding disputable matters their very existence was tentative. How could they survive if they continue arguing with each other over nonessential matters, offending one another, tearing down the work of the Spirit, and not showing concern for their fellow worshipers? Their future was not very promising if they didn't take to heart Paul's correction offered in this passage.

When being called upon to do some difficult things Christians often ask the question: "What would Jesus do?" Paul directs the Roman's attention to Jesus as incentive to make the necessary adjustments that he is calling for. Jesus is the ultimate example of one who gave up his liberties for the welfare of other people, and didn't live a selfish life where he was concerned only with pleasing himself. His agenda was to please his heavenly Father, and offer himself as the one-time sacrifice to atone for sin. Believers should walk in his footsteps and follow his example of serving others (Mark 10:45), being concerned with the welfare of other people (Phil 2:3-5), and promote practical unity in their church.

Now we who are strong ought to bear the weaknesses of those without strength and not *just* please ourselves. ²Each of us is to please his neighbor for his good, to his edification. ³For even Christ did not please Himself; but as it is written, "THE REPROACHES OF THOSE WHO REPROACHED YOU FELL ON ME." ⁴For whatever was written in earlier times was written for our instruction, so that through perseverance and the encouragement of the Scriptures we might have hope. ⁵Now may the God who gives perseverance and encouragement grant you to be of the same mind with one another according to Christ Jesus, ⁶so that with one accord you may with one voice glorify the God and Father of our Lord Jesus Christ. (Romans 15:1-6)

Paul begins by addressing the strong and includes himself in that group. They "ought to bear" the weaknesses of those without strength. "To bear" is a translation of the Greek word *bastazo*, which means to carry a burden. The way the strong believers bear the weaknesses of their fellow Christians is to refrain from casting judgment on them, stop treating them as if they are inferior believers, and cease having a condescending attitude toward them. Rather, the strong should show love and respect to their brothers who are overly sensitive about a religious practice such that they continue to observe it, when it isn't required of them. The strong must voluntarily suspend the use of their liberty for the sake of the weaker brothers and sisters in Christ, so they don't bring an offense to them.

In this way the strong don't use their liberty to just "please themselves." "To please" is also written as a present infinitive, thus in v. 1 "to bear" and "to please" are actions that the strong are to continuously practice in their relationships with the weak. If believers were to use their God-given liberty focusing only on themselves the result would be mass chaos. The strong are to be sensitive to the spiritual convictions of the weak and give up the use of their rights for their benefit. In other words, they should not focus on pleasing themselves; they should have a focus on the greater good of the body and the weaker brothers with whom they worship. This perspective will promote unity, loving relationships, and health in the body of Christ.

Worshiping in the body of Christ isn't about the individual, it is about the welfare of the body, which is why Paul says: "Each of us is to please his neighbor for his good, to his edification" (v. 2). Being part of the church will at times require one to make sacrifices for the good of the body. The perspective to have is "pleasing one's neighbor." Jesus said the second greatest commandment is to "love your neighbor as yourself" (Matt 22:39). He also said in the Sermon on the Mount: "In everything, therefore, treat people the same way you want them to treat you, for this is the Law and the Prophets" (Matt 7:12). As the strong believer considers how he would want to be treated by someone else, that becomes the way he will treat his weaker brothers. The guiding principle is for the strong to make sure that all their actions are for the good and edification of their weaker brothers.

Paul now points to the example of Jesus, which believers are to emulate: For even Christ did not please Himself; but as it is written, "THE REPROACHES OF THOSE WHO REPROACHED YOU FELL ON ME" (v.3). Jesus wasn't selfish, he was selfless. He gave up his liberty out of obedience to the will of his Father and came to earth to be crucified to atone for the sins of the world. As a result of that he accomplished what was good and edifying for mankind (v. 2).

Paul quotes Psalm 69:9, which is a Psalm of David. The reproaches directed at God fell upon David, but Jesus as the Messiah—the Davidic King—fulfills this passage of Scripture in a far more significant way than King David. All the reproaches of sinful humanity were directed at Jesus as he had the sin of the world imputed to him when he hung on the cross. The perfectly righteous, sinless man, bore in himself the punishment for the sin of the world so that those who believe in him can be forgiven and have eternal life. This proves that Jesus is the ultimate example of doing what is good, edifying, and pleasing to his neighbors (vv. 1-2). Believers are called to walk in his footsteps, especially the strong. The use of one's liberty is always to be other-centered, rather than self-centered.

In Paul's lengthy discussion of liberty he certainly doesn't want to give the impression that he doesn't have a high regard for the Old Testament Scriptures. Even though the law has been fulfilled in Christ such that ceremonial observances like the sacrificial system, the Sabbath regulations, dietary laws, and so forth are no longer necessary to practice, Paul wants to point out the high place Scripture plays in the life of believers in v. 4: "For whatever was written in earlier times was written for our instruction, so that through perseverance and the encouragement of the Scriptures we might have hope."

Because Christ fulfilled the law, and has freed believers from many of the practices the Hebrew Bible called for, doesn't mean that the Old Testament has no value, for all Scripture is God-breathed (2 Tim 3:16). The Old Testament provides today's Christian with a goldmine of wisdom and instruction that is beneficial for his spiritual development. To conclude that because Christ fulfilled the law, that the Old Testament no longer occupies a place in the Christian's life would be totally inappropriate.

Through perseverance, which is closely related to patience, and the encouragement that comes from studying Scripture, the believer will be provided with hope. This verse might not seem to fit tightly into Paul's argument, but the church in Rome was in a hostile environment being persecuted from the outside. In addition to that, they had internal problems dealing with the weak and strong that threatened to derail them. They needed hope: so Paul points to the example of Jesus (v. 3), and the Scriptures to encourage them and offer them hope for the future.

He pronounces a benediction in vv. 5-6:

Now may the God who gives perseverance and encouragement grant you to be of the same mind with one another according to Christ Jesus, [6]so that with one accord you may with one voice glorify the God and Father of our Lord Jesus Christ.

God will supply the believer with perseverance and encouragement, for all the Christian life is lived through God's resources that are graciously given. Paul wants to see unity established in the fragile church at Rome, so his prayer is that God would grant them "to be of the same mind with one another according to Christ." In disputable matters, where believers have differing opinions about things that are not in the doctrinal core, they need to respect each other's views and not argue about them to the point where polarization occurs in their church.

All things should be done to the glory of God in the community of faith. When a church is fractured because people are arguing over disputable matters that detract from the purposes for which the church exists, this brings no glory to God whatsoever. Minor issues, which believers can have different opinions about, take center stage and become the focal point of the church. The main thing, doing all for the glory of God, no longer becomes the main thing. The mission of the church is placed on the bench, and the primary concern of people becomes arguing about disputable matters and promoting individual agendas.

Conclusion

God will always supply the grace to accomplish whatever he calls us to do. Paul asks that God may grant them the ability to be of the same mind with one another as they glorify God (v. 6). Believers should pray that God would enable their church to be unified so that the higher purpose of glorifying God can be accomplished. A simple rule of thumb for everything people do in their church, and individual lives, should be this: is God glorified in what we are doing?

Each Christian must consider how Jesus lived for the welfare of others and seek to follow his example. The Lord's focus wasn't on his personal needs, but the needs of others and pleasing his heavenly Father. If every believer can emulate the example of Jesus the world would be a much nicer place, and churches would have a greater degree of unity in glorifying God.

In a culture like ours where there is so much emphasis on the individual, living one's life focused on the welfare of other people is

243

difficult to do. It goes against the grain of our culture. Each believer must take to heart how his actions affect those with whom he worships and the overall unity of the church.

Chapter 25 ~ The Big Picture of God's Plan of Redemption

Paul comes to the conclusion of his discussion of the weak and strong (vv. 7-13). He makes his final appeal to accept one another because of Christ's acceptance of all believers. Then he states the goal of the gospel of having Jews and Gentiles worshiping Christ together. The state of affairs at Rome must have been very fragile between weak Jewish Christians and their strong Gentile counterparts. Jewish and Gentile unity in Christ is one of the major themes in Romans and throughout Paul's other letters (Gal 3:28-29; Eph 2:11-22; 3:6).

There are many nations in the world, different languages that people speak, cultural differences that exist, which tend to divide people. In God's plan for world redemption these differences will be overcome as people around the globe worship the Lord Jesus. Consider what John said in Revelation 7:9-12:

> After these things I looked, and behold, a great multitude which no one could count, from every nation and *all* tribes and peoples and tongues, standing before the throne and before the Lamb, clothed in white robes, and palm branches *were* in their hands; ¹⁰and they cry out with a loud voice, saying, "Salvation to our God who sits on the throne, and to the Lamb." ¹¹And all the angels were standing around the throne and *around* the elders and the four living creatures; and they fell on their faces before the throne and worshiped God, ¹²saying, "Amen, blessing and glory and wisdom and thanksgiving and honor and power and might, *be* to our God forever and ever. Amen."

This is an amazing picture of what heaven is like. A multitude that no man can count, consisting of a diverse group of people from different nations, tribes, peoples, and languages are worshiping the Lord. Additionally, the angels are joining in the chorus of praise directed to God and the Lamb. Obviously in heaven there won't be any divisions among people that impede the worship of God, for there will be perfect unity. That is the direction that God is taking us for the future. It is necessary for believers to grasp the nature of diversity that will exist in the heavenly state, but there will be no divisions. There will be no arguing about disputable matters between the weak and strong. All those things that were threatening the church at Rome will not exist in the heavenly state, for there will be perfect unity among God's people as they worship him. If only we could capture this state on earth! However, we won't until we are fully redeemed from our sinful condition at the return of Christ.

Paul addresses how the two biggest people groups of his day, Jews and Gentiles, will come together in God's plan for the redemption of the world and worship together.

Therefore, accept one another, just as Christ also accepted us to the glory of God. ⁸For I say that Christ has become a servant to the circumcision on behalf of the truth of God to confirm the promises *given* to the fathers, ⁹and for the Gentiles to glorify God for His mercy; as it iswritten, "THEREFORE I WILL GIVE PRAISE TO YOU AMONG THE GENTILES, AND I WILL SING TO YOUR NAME." ¹⁰Again he says, "REJOICE, O GENTILES, WITH HIS PEOPLE." ¹¹And again, "PRAISE THE LORD ALL YOU GENTILES, AND LET ALL THE PEOPLES PRAISE HIM." ¹²Again Isaiah says, "THERE SHALL COME THE ROOT OF JESSE, AND HE WHO ARISES TO RULE OVER THE GENTILES, IN HIM SHALL THE GENTILES HOPE." ¹³Now may the God of hope fill you with all joy and peace in believing, so that you will abound in hope by the power of the Holy Spirit. (Romans 15:7-13)

Paul had previously appealed to the Roman believers "to accept one another" (Rom 14:1; 3) and he brings this up again (v. 7). Since Christ has accepted all believers, Jew and Gentile alike, there is no basis for not accepting a fellow believer. How can a Christian not accept a fellow believer that Jesus died for and has accepted? The weak and strong, Jews and Gentiles, must warmly embrace their fellow worshipers and put aside their differences on disputable matters.

This is "to the glory of God." God had an eternal plan for the redemption of the world in Christ (Eph 1:5-6). This plan involved people from all nations coming together in one body—the church (Ro 1:17, Gal 3:8; 28; Eph 2:14-15; 3:6-12). Gentile inclusion into the community of faith wasn't an afterthought in the mind of God. It was part of his agenda from the very beginning. When people of different nationalities, cultures, languages, and so forth, come together sharing a common faith in Christ, this is glorifying to God.

Paul doesn't highlight the differences between the Christians at Rome he emphasizes the common bond that they all share in Christ. This is the family of God, consisting of diverse peoples accepted by Christ and adopted into his family. He wants the people in the church at Rome not to view themselves as distinct from their culturally different worshipers, but as being of the same spiritual bloodline. The believer's identity isn't defined by his nationality, cultural distinctives, or language he speaks, but by his incorporation into the community of believers. He now has a community identity that transcends all the markers that tend to divide people, such as race, language, culture, etc.

In v. 8 Paul says "Christ has become a servant to the circumcision" meaning the Jews. He wants to bring any thoughts of anti-Semitism to a screeching halt. Additionally, since Christ was a servant to the Jews, and was a Jew himself, the Gentile worshipers should adopt the same mindset and be willing to serve their circumcised brothers. Gentiles shouldn't be looking down on their Jewish brothers in the Lord, because their very salvation came from the Jews. Instead, Gentiles should owe them a debt of gratitude expressed by accepting and loving them.

Paul states the reason why Christ became a servant to the Jews: "on behalf of the truth of God to confirm the promises *given* to the fathers, ⁹and for the Gentiles to glorify God for His mercy." God's promises were proven to be truthful through Jesus' ministry. Many of the promises God made to the fathers (patriarchs) are yet to be fulfilled (Ro 11:25-32). Through Christ's first and second coming all God's promises will be fulfilled for the Jews and the Gentiles. This is a reminder that the Gentiles must not forget that the gospel is for the Jew first then everyone else who believes (Ro 1:17). Gentiles must see God's mercy extended to them and offer praise to him, because they are grafted into the olive tree (Ro 11:17), thus Christ isn't just a servant of the Jews, he is also a servant to the Gentiles (Mark 10:45).

Paul anchors this fact into the ocean of truth by quoting four Old Testament passages from the law (v. 10), the writings (vv. 9b, 11) and the prophets. His purpose is to show that Gentile inclusion was always part of God's plan. The first quote is from Psalm 18:49 (also quoted in 2 Sam 22:50 by King David). David has scored a victory in battle and thanks God by saying: "THEREFORE I WILL GIVE PRAISE TO YOU AMONG THE GENTILES, AND I WILL SING TO YOUR NAME." It is the defeated nations that hear God's name praised, and are invited to join in the praise. In Romans 15 it is the Gentiles that praise God. The Jewish believers are invited to praise God's name along with their Gentile converts.

The second quote is from Deuteronomy 32:43, which is the last verse in the Song of Moses: "Again he says, "REJOICE, O GENTILES, WITH HIS PEOPLE (V. 10)." This is a victory celebration where the nations are to rejoice with Israel over God's miraculous deliverance from Egypt. Paul pictures the nations rejoicing with God's people as being fulfilled in the New Testament as Gentiles and Jews worship together.

The third quote is from Psalm 117:1: And again, "PRAISE THE LORD ALL YOU GENTILES, AND LET ALL THE PEOPLES PRAISE HIM (V. 11)." In this passage the Gentiles are praising God by themselves, not with their Jewish counterparts, as in the previous two quotes. All the peoples are praising God, with no group being excluded. This is a picture of universal worship (Rev 7:9).

The fourth quotation is taken from Isaiah 11:10: Again Isaiah says, "THERE SHALL COME THE ROOT OF JESSE, AND HE WHO ARISES TO RULE OVER THE GENTILES, IN HIM SHALL THE GENTILES HOPE" (V. 12). The root of Jesse is the Davidic King—the Messiah—who would deliver his people. The Messiah will also rule over the Gentiles, such that they will put their hope in him. Thus, both Jews and Gentiles place their hope in the Messiah, which should bring unity in the body of Christ.

These four quotes demonstrate that Gentile inclusion was part of God's plan from the beginning. God's plan for redemption was always global, not specific to the nation of Israel. Israel was called upon to be a light to the nations surrounding them, which was something they failed to do. The Jews must rid themselves of any thoughts of exclusivity thinking that God is for them only. They must embrace Gentile worshipers.

Now may the God of hope fill you with all joy and peace in believing, so that you will abound in hope by the power of the Holy Spirit. (Romans 15:13)

Paul concludes his discussion with a benediction or a short prayer. He identifies God as the "God of hope" for both Jews and Gentiles. They share the same hope in Messiah. His request is that God would fill them with all joy and peace in believing. Joy and peace would result in harmonious relationships through the Holy Spirit (Ro 14:17) in the church at Rome. This will only come about through their faith / believing. Through faith believers experience all of God's blessings. Paul wishes to see the believers abound in hope through the power of the Holy Spirit. As the believers at Rome tap into the power supply of the Holy Spirit they can achieve a deeper level of unity, such that they can truly accept one another, just as Christ has accepted each of them.

Conclusion

Jews and Gentiles may seem like archaic terms in today's vernacular, but in the ancient world it was commonplace. It was Jews and Gentiles, slaves and freemen. In today's world we may think in terms of black and white people, Republicans and Democrats, liberals and conservatives, middle and upper class, and many other ways in which people divide. It wasn't that long ago where six million Jews were systematically exterminated in the holocaust. Hate, prejudice, and bigotry run deep in sinful human beings. We need to be mindful that all people are made in the image of God and are valuable to him.

Jesus died for people of all nationalities, colors, ethnicities, languages, and so on. It is imperative for Christians to see people as image-bearers of God who have infinite worth in his eyes, and repent of any prejudicial attitudes toward other peoples.

One day in the future all God's people stand before the throne and worship the Lord in one voice. This fact makes arguing over disputable matters seem ridiculous. Unity is hard to attain in a church setting. People argue over the most trivial things such as: what color to paint the sanctuary, what color the new carpet should be in the classrooms, whether or not to start a second service, hymns or praise choruses, and so on. We all should keep in mind God's big picture for world redemption, when everybody praises the Lord with one unified voice. *Disputable matters will be a thing of the past!*

In the next chapter there will be a number of principles extracted from the discussion of Romans 14:1-15:13, that are pertinent to the contemporary reader. Everybody can greatly profit from understanding Paul's teaching on liberty, not just legalists.

Chapter 26 ~ Bridging the Horizon

Reading through the previous chapters on Romans 14:1-15:13 may leave the reader concluding: "this has nothing to do with me, or anything even remotely close to the world I live in." Drawing that conclusion would be unfortunate because there is much to learn from that portion of Scripture about Christian liberty and legalism. The previous discussion has a multitude of applications and thought provoking ideas for the reader to mull over. However, in order to bring these applications to the surface we need to cross over a bridge from the First Century that takes us into today's world.

In the churches I've pastored I've never encountered a situation that comes even remotely close to what Paul had to deal with at Rome. The type of food people eat at potlucks was never an issue that divided the church, nor were the observance of special days. Where I live in Sacramento there are no temples where animals are sacrificed to idols, then the meat is cooked up, served to patrons, and some of the meat is sold in local markets and grocery stores. This situation doesn't exist today in America, as it did in the First Century, so we have to cross the bridge into our modern world, taking with us the principles that Paul developed and apply them to our own cultural situation. The purpose of this chapter is to identify the principles Paul taught that are transcultural, and can be utilized to effectively deal with disputable matters that appear in the body of Christ today.

Disputable Matters

In Romans 14:1 Paul informed his readers not to argue about disputable matters. He was speaking to the strong and telling them to accept their weaker brothers in Christ. In the specific context he was talking about food preferences, and the observance of special days. There are many things that Christians can have differing opinions about. Disputable matters are not items in the doctrinal core of the

Christian belief system. These are peripheral items that people can have different views on. Everybody has an opinion about various practices, but when people who worship together have conflicting views and ways of expressing their faith, how can they have unity as brothers and sisters in Christ?

Adding to this situation at Rome were people of drastically different cultures. Jews and Gentiles were miles apart culturally, and Jews avoided Gentiles before they became believers in Christ. They wouldn't enter the home of a Gentile because they would become ritually unclean. There were slaves and freemen, Jews and Gentiles, which made the church at Rome a very interesting mixture of people. This blend of people creates a situation that can beautifully display the love of Jesus as people accept each other's differences, while focusing on the higher call of serving God together. Or this mixture of people can be a toxic environment that is like a powder keg waiting to explode at any moment. Paul never called for uniformity of practices, and certainly allowed for each person to have their own convictions and scruples, but how do you enable believers to retain their own cultural identity, traditions, and spiritual practices, while fostering the unity of the body and vibrant fellowship? How can believers have different opinions about spiritual issues than their fellow worshipers, and not have massive divisions in their church?

This is the issue Paul had to deal with, and this is the same issue that pastor's are confronted with as they shepherd their congregations today. Individual believers will come across people in their church that have deep rooted convictions about various things. What might be a critical issue for one believer might be meaningless to another. How can believers avoid bringing offenses to each other when their ideas, convictions, and practices conflict with those with whom they worship?

It is important to understand that disputable matters, or opinions on issues outside of the doctrinal core, are valid; there is no sin in having an opinion on a matter that is on the periphery. It becomes sinful when people begin to argue about the correctness of their view, because this causes hurt feelings, fosters division in the church, and

252

tears people down. Most importantly, this kind of bickering impedes the work of the Holy Spirit in building up the congregation.

When two believers are having a heated disagreement on an issue it is important to identify the nature of the matter under discussion. Is this a debate over something in the doctrinal core, a secondary matter of importance, or something that is a disputable matter on the periphery (cf. Chapter 12)? If the issue under discussion is a disputable matter both parties must ask themselves if this is a mountain they want to fortify and die on. Is it worth severing a relationship by arguing about opinions on matters that are farthest away from the doctrinal core? If a disputable matter is being debated, each party must let the other person have their own opinion and be OK with it.

When Scripture doesn't give clear guidance on an issue in that it isn't commanded to do, or prohibited from doing, you have a disputable matter. There are some things in the Bible that are black and white, crystal clear with no ambiguity whatsoever such as: do not steal, do not lie, do not commit adultery, and so on. These are black and white prohibitions with no room for debate about their meaning. However, there are some things in the Bible that aren't black and white, they are gray, cloudy, and unclear because Scripture doesn't specifically command or prohibit the action. In cases like these where the Bible is silent, the best one can do is search for Biblical principles and try to apply them to any given practice. When this is done believers will inevitably see things differently, develop different viewpoints, and express their faith in ways that other's don't. At times believers may even take such drastically different views on an issue they may have a rift over it, which is unfortunate.

Disputable matters take much careful deliberation, prayer, Scripture reading, and discussion with other believers to determine what is right and wrong. Believers must be open and accepting of the fact that not everybody will come to the same conclusions about disputable matters as they do. There will be those who strongly disagree with some of their opinions, there will be those who see issues the same way, and there will be those who don't really care.

Making things more complicated, today's culture is much different than the First Century. Movie theaters, the Internet, cable TV, and many other technological innovations didn't exist in Bible days, so the Scripture has nothing directly to say about the use of these things. However, there are principles given in Scripture that can shed some light on the proper use of these technologies. Following are some examples of things about which Christians have differing opinions.

Movies

One disputable matter is the type of movies believers can watch, and what should be avoided. There are those believers who feel any movies rated above G are sinful to watch, and have deep convictions about that. Other believers may have no problem watching an R rated movie. Given the fact that movies didn't exist in Bible days Scripture offers us no direct guidance on the issue of what types of movies are permissible to watch.

The best one can do is look at principles the Scripture sets forth and apply them as best they can to this situation. Certainly viewing pornographic material should be avoided because of the guidance provided by Matthew 5:28. However, if a movie is rated R because of violence, language, or other mature content, is this inherently sinful and to be avoided? One of my all time favorite movies is "Saving Private Ryan." It was rated R because of the violent graphic images, and there was language that could be offensive to people, but it was a great movie. This is where the issue becomes cloudy, grey, and lacks clarity. In cases like this each believer needs to decide for himself what his conscience permits him to do. This is between him and the Lord. Believers will come up with different opinions on this issue as they search their hearts and do what they feel is right before God. It is essential to respect the views of those who see this issue differently than you.

Politics

In roughly the last ten years I've noticed that some believers measure one's spirituality by which candidate they will vote for, or which political party they affiliate with. If one votes for a certain candidate they are considered either less than spiritual, or their choice verifies their loyalty to Christ and testifies to their spiritual depth. One's political orientation should not be viewed as a marker of spiritual maturity. There is no justification for claiming true Christians will vote for so-and-so, but that is what some people do.

If a candidate has some views that don't line up with what some people think is Christian, or in line with the Bible, is it wrong to vote for that person? Some would say it's outright sinful to support a candidate like that. I've heard some heated discussions between Christians about their political views. Believers can worship together that support different candidates for public office. Republicans and Democrats can worship Christ in the same church without being at each other's throats. This is a disputable matter, and each believer needs to decide for himself what is right without casting judgment on those who support a candidate they don't.

Education

Another issue that Christians debate is the education parents provide for their children. Some parents feel the public schools will corrupt their children, so they enroll them in a Christian school. They have very strong convictions about protecting their children from what they consider to be an essentially anti-god education provided by the public schools, so they prefer to have them in a Christian educational environment. They want their children exposed to the Bible, and the Christian worldview, along with the influence of godly teachers.

Those Christians who send their children to public schools will often take the position that their children have to live in the real world, learn to resist temptations that come, and develop skills at relating to nonbelievers. They feel that Christian schools are an artificial environment, and that their kids need to live out their Christian faith in the real world. Going to a public school is a mission field that their children can participate in. For these reasons they send their children to public schools.

Other parent's feel that homeschooling is the best approach to education because they can be directly involved in their children's education, both academically and spiritually. Homeschooling is thought to protect children from the evil influences of the world that kids in the public schools are exposed to, and parents can choose curriculum that is Christian based.

All these approaches to education are valid and Scriptural support can be found for each of these views. I've personally witnessed heated debates among Christians about the issue of education. Where it becomes sinful is when believers argue that their view is correct, judge those who take a different approach than they do as less than spiritual, and establish one's approach to education as a marker of spiritual maturity. This is a disputable matter that should not be viewed as a marker of one's spiritual depth. Believers must allow others to have their own opinion on this matter without judging them, and having a rift over it.

Social Drinking

One of the more toxic issues that Christians have differing opinions on is the consumption of alcoholic beverages. Heck, wars have been fought over this issue. Some believers take the position that it is best to abstain from all alcoholic beverages for several reasons: First, purchasing alcohol supports an ungodly industry. They feel their money can be better spent in other areas. Secondly, if nonbelievers see them drinking alcohol it may damage their testimony. Thirdly, some feel that it is not worth risking the chance of developing a dependence on alcohol, so they choose to abstain altogether. Fourthly, some parents feel strongly that if they drink alcohol in front of their children it will encourage them to do the same, so they choose not to drink altogether.

These are some valid points. There are many alcoholics in the world who have suffered greatly because they couldn't control their consumption of alcohol. The cost to our society that alcoholism levies on industry, and health care is very high. Additionally, the cost in personal trauma, and family disruption is very extreme and painful.

256

For these reasons many believers consider the industry ungodly, and choose not to support it.

To the first point about the production of alcoholic beverages being an ungodly industry, it must be noted that the production of alcoholic beverages has been taking place almost forever. Wine was tithed (Deu 12:17; 18:4), used in various sacrifices (Num 28:14), considered a blessing from God (Deu 7:13), and Solomon tells us to drink wine with a joyful heart with God's approval (Ecc 9:7). Jesus turned water into wine at the wedding feast of Cana (John 2:9), it was used in love feasts (1 Cor 11:21), and Paul recommended Timothy drink a little wine for his stomach and frequent illnesses (1 Tim 5:23). Wine was a commonly consumed beverage throughout the Bible. There is no Scriptural justification to say that the production of alcoholic beverage is sinful and should be prohibited. If it were Jesus wouldn't have turned the water into wine at the wedding feast of Cana.

It is the misuse of alcoholic beverage that is to be safeguarded against. The Bible doesn't forbid the drinking of alcohol it forbids drunkenness (Eph 5:18). Church leaders must not be addicted to wine (1 Tim 3:3; 3:8), but Paul told Timothy to drink a little wine for the sake of his stomach and frequent ailments (1 Tim 5:23). Jesus turned the water into wine at the wedding feast of Cana (John 2:9), the people drank wine at their love feasts at Corinth and got drunk (1 Cor 11:21), which Paul condemned. Scripture does offer prohibitions about the irresponsible use of alcohol (Pro 20:21; 21:17; 23:20), which everyone should take seriously.

The second point, about damaging a believer's testimony to a nonbeliever needs some consideration. In many conversations I've had with nonbelievers I've found just the opposite to be true. In other words, there are nonbelievers who have been told by over zealous Christians that drinking is wrong and is prohibited if one becomes a follower of Christ. Their reaction is often: "Why?" "For what reason?" It doesn't make any sense to them that to become a Christian they can't drink any alcohol. It portrays the gospel to them in a very negative legalistic way. They often ask if there are other things that they can't do if they become a Christian. In some cultures drinking wine with lunch or dinner is a common cultural practice. People might view the one who abstains from alcohol as the odd man out, in which case that doesn't help the gospel.

The third point is well taken. Some people may have a family history of alcoholism in which case they would be wise to consider being very cautious about drinking. Alcoholism is a serious malady that many people become victim to. The pain and trauma that children can experience when their mother or father becomes an alcoholic is severe. The last point about the example parents provide their children is valid. If children grow up watching mom and dad sloshing down beer and other drinks they may be influenced to do the same.

When it comes to drinking alcohol this can be a very divisive issue among believers. Each one must do what he feels is right before God, which means that he may arrive at a different conclusion than someone with whom he worships.

In practice we need to be very sensitive regarding the issue of drinking alcohol around our fellow worshipers. One never knows who is a recovering alcoholic. If I know that somebody has a history with alcoholism it would be totally insensitive to order a beer when having lunch with him. If I invite him over to the house and offer him an alcoholic beverage I would be violating every principle that Paul set forth in Romans 14 and 15. If my influence caused him to drink and he went back into his addiction then I bear some responsibility for that.

Often times people who are recovering alcoholics, or those recovering from other addictions, may come across as very legalistic. They may take the position that all drinking is wrong and is to be avoided, but they have to be that way. Because of their addiction they have to put walls around themselves because they can't afford to have a relapse, thus they need to be in a very structured tight environment and may appear very legalistic to others.

Smoking

Is it wrong to smoke a cigar if I'm celebrating some monumental accomplishment? Often cigars are passed out when someone gives birth to a child. Is this wrong before God? Is it wrong to smoke a pipe? Is it wrong to smoke cigarettes? These days a lot of people are vaping. Electronic cigarettes are becoming popular. I'm not aware of any Scripture that forbids smoking. However, the body is the temple of the Holy Spirit and smoking can have serious effects on one's health. As a steward of the body that God gave each of us, we should be mindful of those things that can detract from the quality of our health. To become *addicted* to smoking is a sinful habit, just as is becoming addicted to alcohol, gambling, comfort eating, and so on. Many of the same arguments against drinking alcohol can be applied to smoking. Therefore the use of liberty with tobacco should be exercised very cautiously.

Baseball players will often put a big chaw in their mouth and chew away. Is chewing tobacco sinful? The same can be said about this use of tobacco. Don't let it master you. This is the key to any practice. People can develop bad habits and find themselves out of control with just about anything including: eating, gambling, compulsive shopping, pornography, smoking, drinking, watching TV, social media, and more. The key is don't let any practice master you to the point where you are out of control and can't stop. Each individual must exercise the use of his liberty responsibly and make sure that he retains control over the practice, and not let the practice control him. The principle the apostle Paul set forth regarding the use of one's liberty must be taken very seriously: "All things are lawful, but not all things are profitable. All things are lawful, but not all things edify" (1 Cor 10:23).

The bottom line with disputable matters is to *agree to disagree agreeably* with those who see things differently than you. It is often the result of human pride and arrogance that we have to be right and everybody else should see things our way. The person that disagrees with us is still accepted by Jesus, so we have no basis for breaking fellowship with someone over a disputable matter. Uniformity isn't required in one's church so each believer needs to accept those who have different opinions than they do.

The Role of Conscience

The role of one's conscience can't be underestimated in disputable matters. God has given each person a conscience to serve as a moral guide telling him what is right and wrong. Each person must be sensitive to his inner voice and never go against what his conscience is telling him. The conscience can be wounded causing much spiritual harm to those who violate their inner voice. For example, when someone goes against the dictates of his conscience this can result in being filled with guilt, he may experience the loss of joy and peace in his spirit, and feel that he has sinned against God. Let your inner voice guide you in disputable matters. If one violates their conscience over-and-over it can become desensitized and virtually inoperative. For Paul this is a very serious matter not to be taken lightly. This brings us to the first principle Paul sets forth:

Never go against what your conscience tells you regarding disputable matters.

Although one's conscience is a God-given moral guide the conscience isn't infallible. In other words, sometimes our conscience will tell us not to do something that the Bible says is acceptable. Other times our conscience may lead us to do something that the Bible informs us is unacceptable. After being educated in the Scripture on a certain matter one's conscience can change and permit him to do things he previously thought were sinful, or he may realize that some things he was doing should be avoided because Scripture says they are sinful. In this sense the conscience is moldable. This brings us to the second principle that Paul established:

Scripture, not our peers, political correctness, or the opinions of others, must always inform one's conscience about disputable matters.

The use of one's liberty must be exercised responsibly. Paul informed the Romans who had liberty to eat all kinds of food to be sensitive to those who did not have the same liberty and ate only vegetables. Under no circumstances are the strong believers to use their influence on their weaker veggie-eating-only brothers to go against the dictates of their conscience. They must never pressure those people to follow their own practices, for if they do they wound their brothers' conscience, and aren't demonstrating the love of Jesus.

Liberty is Rooted in Scripture

One's liberty to do certain things must always be conformed to the Scripture. *Liberty is defined as freedom from all man-made rules, regulations, codes, and religious systems that have no Scriptural foundation.* It may take someone a long time of study, prayer, and deliberation with other believers to recognize areas in his life where he was in shackles. After gaining a deeper understanding of what the Scripture teaches on a given issue, one's conscience may give them permission to change their behavior. In this way Scripture guides the expression of liberty and gives the conscience time to adjust.

Love Balances Liberty

Believers who have liberty are to be willing to give up their rights and suspend the use of their liberty for the sake of the weaker brother and the gospel. This is where love comes into the picture. When believers are walking in love they will gladly give up their liberty for the welfare of others with whom they worship. Liberty without love can lead to a reckless insensitive expression of personal freedom that can deeply offend others and cause friction in someone's church. This brings us to the third principle Paul establishes:

The expression of one's liberty must be guided by love.

The onus of the passage in Romans was placed on the ones with liberty (the strong) to be cautious of how they express their freedom. They are called to suspend their rights for the weaker brothers. This goes against the grain of popular culture, which seems to be a me-centered society where personal freedom, personal expression, personal choice, and personal rights are always at the foreground. This goes against the example of Jesus and the apostles who were willing to give up their rights to see the gospel advance. Giving up personal freedoms is part of dying to self and taking up our cross daily to follow Jesus (Luke 9:23; 14:27). This brings us to the fourth principle:

Believers must be willing to give up their liberty / rights for the welfare of other believers and the sake of the gospel.

Unity is Essential

Mature Christians always promote the unity of the body, peace, and edification of their peers. Unity can be destroyed when people argue about disputable matters, and use their liberty in such a way that they present stumbling blocks to their peers. Arguing about disputable matters and expressing your personal liberty without love can destroy the work of the Holy Spirit in the church. For the sake of the unity of the body believers must be willing to give up their liberty as needed.

Imagine what the church at Rome would look like if Paul didn't correct the situation. There would be a virtual rift between the strong Gentile Christians and the weaker Jewish believers over the issue of food and holy days. This is to be avoided at all costs by the strong being sensitive to their Jewish brothers and not eating meat in front of them so as to bring offense and possibly damage them by influencing them to do the same. What is of primary importance is stated in Romans 14:17: "for the kingdom of God is not eating and drinking, but righteousness and peace and joy in the Holy Spirit." This verse establishes what is primary and what is tertiary. Kingdom life is living in the fullness of the Holy Spirit, which shouldn't be minimized by people arguing about what they eat, and other disputable matters.

Believers can't be constantly judging each other on their opinions because it will have a negative effect on the body. They need to accept each other, just as they have been accepted by Jesus, and understand that it is OK to disagree on issues without breaking fellowship with someone. The fifth principle is:

The expression of one's liberty must be secondary to the welfare of their church.

262

Is the Strong Believer Held Captive by the Weak?

Reading through Romans 14 might lead one to conclude that the strong are held captive by the weak. They are constantly walking on pins and needles and have their valid liberty controlled by the weak. It is true that the onus of the passage is placed on the strong using their liberty responsibly. Paul isn't suggesting the strong are held captive by the weak. In private the strong may do as they please, but in the presence of the weaker brothers they must express their liberty in a way that doesn't cause the others to stumble. In this way their liberty won't be spoken of as evil (Ro 14:16).

The sixth principle that Paul develops is:

The strong must be wise and sensitive in the use of their liberty in the presence of their weaker brothers.

Unity not Uniformity

Paul had a difficult situation to smooth over at Rome. People of vastly different cultures—and social statuses are worshiping Christ together. The common denominator is the people's identity as believers in Christ and their community identity as the people of God. Believers must learn that diversity isn't something to be feared rather it should be appreciated. Being around people of different cultures can be an enriching experience.

The seventh principle to be gleaned from this discussion is:

Unity in the core doctrines of the faith must never be compromised, but uniformity over disputable matters, and things rooted in cultural differences isn't necessary in the body of Christ.

Liberty Facilitates Serving Christ

A believer's God-given liberty isn't to be expressed selfishly. When all the chains of legalism are removed from a believer and he is set free from all man-made rules and regulations that are without Biblical foundation he is in a blessed position. Paul said something in Galatians 5:13 that sheds light on the purpose of one's liberty: "For you were called to freedom, brethren; only *do* not *turn* your freedom into an opportunity for the flesh, but through love serve one another."

One's freedom in Christ isn't for the purpose of gratifying his sinful nature, it is granted for the purpose of enhancing his ability to serve one another in love. Jesus and the apostles utilized their liberty to spread the gospel and build up the body of Christ (Ro 15:3; Mark 10:45; 1 Cor 8-10). They were free to serve! The eighth principle Paul establishes is:

> *Liberty is given for the purpose of becoming a more effective servant of Christ.*

Liberty Enables People To Enjoy God's Creation

It is true that God-given liberty is also granted for the purpose of enjoying the things that God created for us, such as food. God is pleased to have us enjoy the things he gave us as we give thanks to him for his provisions. Abstaining from foods, marriage, and other things that God created for our benefit does nothing to put us in a better position with God. In fact, those who advocate ascetic views such as abstinence from marriage and food, and whatever else God created for people to enjoy, are promoting doctrines that have their origin in the demonic realm. Paul makes this clear in 1 Timothy 4:1-5:

> But the Spirit explicitly says that in later times some will fall away from the faith, paying attention to deceitful spirits and doctrines of demons, ²by means of the hypocrisy of liars seared in their own conscience as with a branding iron, ³*men* who forbid marriage *and advocate* abstaining from foods which God has created to be gratefully shared in by those who believe and know the truth. ⁴For everything created by God is good, and nothing is to be rejected if

it is received with gratitude; [5]for it is sanctified by means of the word of God and prayer.

God is not a joy-killer! Going back to the creation narrative in Genesis reveals that all God created was good. Everything created was a gift to man to be gratefully received and enjoyed. It is insulting to God to advocate abstinence from that which he created for people to enjoy. We can't label the things God created for our enjoyment as not good, when in point of fact God said they are all good. The ninth principle Paul lays down is:

Liberty is given to enjoy the things God created with thanksgiving.

Conclusion

When it comes to disputable matters every believer will be confronted with issues that they need to think through, ranging from social drinking to political matters. These are thought provoking issues to sort through, and on some matters there are no easy answers. Each believer must be willing to study the Scripture, pray, and discuss disputable matters with other believers to gain their insights on things of this nature. In the process of doing this it must be understood that you will arrive at conclusions that may differ from the people with whom you worship, but that has to be OK. You can agree to disagree agreeably! There must be unity in the core doctrines of the faith, but tolerance with the nonessentials, or peripheral matters.

People who are in legalistic churches most likely aren't getting a lot of teaching on liberty. This is unfortunate because understanding this topic is crucial to having healthy relationships and fellowship in one's church. No two Christians are the same, for God never intended things to be that way. Diversity is one of the characteristics of the church, which means that people will have different views, preferences, and ways of expressing their faith. Understanding the teaching on liberty will help us be able to accept those who are different than we are, and create a much more healthy and vibrant fellowship in one's church.

The best cure for the disease of legalism is to have two prescriptions filled: one is a strong dose of teaching on sanctification, the other is a strong does of instruction on liberty. Studying these two areas of Scripture can do wonders in breaking the chains of legalism.

If you are feeling spiritually oppressed because you are expected to adhere to a code that isn't founded on Scripture, and the leaders expect uniformity in the expression of people's faith, you are most likely in a very legalistic spiritual environment. Let your own study of Scripture inform you about the accuracy of the teaching you are receiving in your church.

It is difficult to break out of a legalistic church or legalistic patterns of behavior. Even the apostle Peter and Barnabas had a difficult time breaking out of legalism—it is difficult for everybody! In the next chapters we will be examining how Peter broke out of his legalistic roots.

Chapter 27 ~ Peter's Liberation From Legalism

The gospel was to spread to all the nations (Mat 28:19). The message of God's salvation through Jesus Christ was to be shared with everybody, barring none. No people groups, or nations were to be excluded from hearing the gospel message and being incorporated into the body of Christ. Thus, inherent in the churches' existence was a call to mission. Christians had to reach out beyond themselves and bring other people into the community of faith.

On the other hand, the nation of Israel was confined to the Promised Land (Gen 17:8). It was in the land that they would find rest and God's Shalom. They were a geographical entity with boarders, a political structure, and theocratic government. They were to be God's light, displaying his ways to the other unbelieving nations around them. Throughout their history they failed miserably at this task, and developed an exclusivity that mitigated against reaching out to the other nations. Gentiles were unclean and to be avoided, so the Israelites developed an isolationist attitude, and felt that God's grace was exclusively for them.

As we move into the New Testament, God poured out his Spirit on the day of Pentecost and the church was born (Acts 2). God's plan was to bring together people from all nations into one body—the church. This meant, unlike Israel, the church isn't a geopolitical entity it is transnational. It knows no borders, should not discriminate between people of different ethnicities, languages, colors, and so on. The church is intended to be global in nature. There are many prophesies in the Old Testament that foretold an ingathering of the Gentiles into the community of faith, so this isn't something entirely new for the people of Israel to hear (Isa 11:10; 42:1; 46:9).

Jesus equipped the disciples for a ministry tour with the instructions: "Do not go among the Gentiles or enter any towns of the Samaritans. Go rather to the lost sheep of Israel" (Mat 10:5-6). Since salvation begins with the Jews, Jesus focused his disciples first on Israel. However, he never turned away Gentiles that came to him, as is the case with the Syro-phonecian woman (Mark 7:26-30), and the Roman centurion (Mat 8:5-13). The mission parameters of the church expanded throughout the ministry of Jesus. Acts 1:8 is a critical passage for us to consider:

but you will receive power when the Holy Spirit has come upon you; and you shall be My witnesses both in Jerusalem, and in all Judea and Samaria, and even to the remotest part of the earth.

The disciples were in the Upper Room waiting to receive the gift of the Holy Spirit (Acts 1:4), which is tied to mission. The purpose for which they would receive the Spirit would be to empower them as Christ's witnesses. Through the power of the Spirit the disciples would testify about what they knew to be true about Jesus' death and resurrection. The Jesus movement began in Jerusalem on the day of Pentecost, but was to spread outward from the epicenter of the Spirit. I refer to this as the *outward expanding circle*: from Jerusalem, to Judea, Samaria, and the remotest parts of the globe.

The book of Revelation informs us that there will be people worshiping the Lord from every tribe, language, people, and nation (Rev 5:9). The apostle Paul spoke of how God was bringing together Jew and Gentile into one body, by reconciling them through the cross (Eph 2:14-16). He spoke of the mystery that has been revealed to him that the Gentiles are heirs along with Israel and share in the promises God made through Christ (Eph 3:6-11). He saw the body of Christ as a Temple of the Holy Spirit consisting of Jews and Gentiles (Eph 2:21-22).

Peter was the leader of the band of brothers. It was Peter who preached the first sermon in the history of the church (Acts 2:14-40), which resulted in 3,000 people becoming believers and being baptized. This occurred in Jerusalem within a Jewish context. However, the gospel couldn't be confined to Jerusalem, it had to spread outward to Judea, Samaria, and the remotest corners of the globe.

In order for this to happen there would have to be a radical liberation that each of the disciples needed to experience. All the anti-Gentile sentiments they entertained needed to go in order to accomplish the mission of spreading the gospel. They needed to be liberated from all the legalistic tendencies that had been instilled in them through their upbringing as Torah observing Jews. Failure to do this would have crippled the spread of the gospel. This was no easy task for Jews who had certain attitudes ingrained in them from their childhood regarding avoiding sinners, and Gentiles, as well as complying with food regulations, Sabbath restrictions, laws of being clean and unclean, and more.

Reinventing Themselves

Not only did each of the disciples need to have their lives transformed by God's grace through Jesus Christ, they needed to be liberated from the above things to be effective in spreading the gospel. In a sense, they needed to reinvent themselves as believers in Christ who have been freed from all the things that Jesus fulfilled by inaugurating the New Covenant. Jesus brought new wine that couldn't be placed in the old wine skins of the practices of the religious leaders of the day, and the current state of Judaism. Their attitudes about people of different color, ethnicity, and religion, all needed to change. This was radical for them and no easy task to accomplish.

On one occasion John and his brother James wanted to call down fire on a Samaritan village because they rejected Jesus (Luke 9:5f). Jews do not associate with Samaritans (John 4:9) because they were considered to be half-breeds to be avoided like the plague. Jews wouldn't enter the house of a Gentile because they would become unclean. Jesus had no problem befriending sinners and even called a tax collector to be one of his disciples, which no doubt was a controversial choice among the other disciples. Jesus wasn't trapped by the legalistic tendencies that were advocated by the religious leaders of the day, but the disciples needed to be set free from them. This must happen for their own personal benefit as believers in Christ, but also to be effective in spreading the gospel. All these prejudicial attitudes they had about other people groups, and their legalistic tendencies had to change in order to spread the gospel and interact with people of other ethnicities. Would the apostles be able to undergo this liberation and reinvent themselves?

Since Peter emerged as the leader of the early church we will evaluate how Peter went through his liberation of all man-made rules, regulations, and all those things that were no longer necessary to be observed as believers in Christ.

The Spread of the Gospel

The book of Acts reveals the story of how the gospel spread throughout the Mediterranean world. The initial chapters of Acts confine the spread of the gospel to Jerusalem in a Jewish context (Acts 1-7). In other words, many Jews, even priests, were becoming Christians (Acts 6:7). After the stoning of Stephen a great persecution broke out against the church instigated by Saul of Tarsus, causing all the believers except the apostles to flee through Judea and Samaria (Acts 8:1). God used this scattering of the believers for a divine church-planting program. Everywhere the believers went they preached the gospel (Acts 8:4). Philip went to Samaria and preached Jesus accompanied by miraculous signs, exorcisms, and healings as he confronted the powers of darkness. Many believed and were baptized.

When word of this got back to the leaders in Jerusalem they sent Peter and John to check it out (Acts 8:14). It is necessary to grasp the animosity that existed between the Jews in the Southern Kingdom, and the Samaritans in the North. At one time in their history there was civil war between the two Kingdoms, and Samaritans were considered half-breeds that were despised by Jews. It was shocking to the Jews that the Lord Jesus could accept the Samaritans into the Kingdom. As the gospel spread these prejudicial attitudes maintained by people for centuries had to be overcome in order for them to be incorporated into the church. The tendency to view the Samaritan believers as second-class citizens, lower than their counterparts in Judea, had to be done away with. The Jerusalem church needed to accept the Samaritan believers as equals. They couldn't view these people as unclean any longer, they had to extend the love of Jesus to them and embrace them as brothers in Christ.

Peter and John show up and notice that they haven't received the Holy Spirit; they had been baptized only into the name of Jesus. The apostles lay their hands on them and the Samaritans receive the Holy Spirit (Acts 8:17). This is important for several reasons. The apostles needed to see for themselves that the Spirit was given to the Samaritans so they could testify to this fact to the other leaders in Jerusalem. The presence of Peter and John also indicated that the new Samaritan church was subject to the authority of the apostles, such that Jewish and Samaritan believers were part of one body—the body of Christ. If the Samaritans received the Holy Spirit independent of the presence of apostles there could have been two separate churches—a Jewish Christian church and a Samaritan Christian church. This would totally go against God's divine plan of having one church (Gal 3:28).

It would have been shocking for the Jews to see that their hated rivals in Samaria had received the Spirit. This would be a hard pill for them to swallow, for the animosity ran deep. Peter and John return home to Jerusalem as they did some preaching on the way in Samaritan villages, which resulted in more converts (Acts 8:25). In John 4:1-42 the episode of Jesus' encounter with the Samaritan women is recorded as he stopped by Sychar to drink from Joseph's well. As he spoke to the Samaritan woman he was violating all the cultural norms of the day. It was taboo for a Jewish man to speak to a Samaritan woman, especially a rabbi, which is why the disciples were shocked that Jesus was talking to her (John 4:27).

It is necessary to understand how difficult it would have been for Jesus' disciples to be in Samaria because of the bad blood that existed between them. I believe that Jesus was using this preaching tour throughout Samaria as a teaching experience for his disciples. He was showing them that the gospel wasn't just for Jews—it was for everybody including their enemies. No doubt the disciples felt uncomfortable being in Samaria, but Jesus was showing them that many of the cultural norms that have been established over the generations needed to change as they transitioned into the New Covenant era.

The woman at the well became a believer, went back to her village and told the people about Jesus which resulted in many of them becoming believers (John 4:39). Jesus stayed with them for two days and more people became believers.

In this episode Jesus told his disciples in vv. 35-38:

> Do you not say, 'There are yet four months, and *then* comes the harvest'? Behold, I say to you, lift up your eyes and look on the fields, that they are white for harvest. [36]Already he who reaps is receiving wages and is gathering fruit for life eternal; so that he who sows and he who reaps may rejoice together. [37]For in this *case* the saying is true, 'One sows and another reaps.' [38]I sent you to reap that for which you have not labored; others have labored and you have entered into their labor."

Jesus is speaking metaphorically about a spiritual harvest that would take place in Samaria. The field of Samaria is ripe for a harvest of souls that would believe in Jesus. The disciples are experiencing a small taste of the harvest with Jesus in this episode. There is sowing and reaping in agriculture, just as there is sowing and reaping is God's Kingdom. For centuries people have been sowing seed in Samaria, but now the time of harvest has come. The disciples are reaping what others have sown. They are in a blessed position to be realizing this harvest of souls for the Kingdom of God.

How did the disciples process this? Samaritans are coming into the Kingdom of God. This must have been difficult for them to accept. No doubt when Peter and John came to Samaria (Acts 8) and laid their hands on them to receive the Holy Spirit they must have thought about what Jesus said regarding the Samaritan harvest. Perhaps, this was an insightful moment for Peter and John, when they saw the Holy Spirit come upon the Samaritan believers. Maybe they thought to themselves this is what Jesus meant by reaping a harvest? Did they overcome their prejudicial attitudes about the Samaritans even though they laid their hands on them to receive the Spirit? Were they really willing to accept them as brothers and sisters in Christ, as equals before God? It appears the barriers that divided Jews and Samaritans are disintegrating and the apostles are heading in the right direction.

Philip and the Ethiopian Eunuch

Luke records for his readers that Philip is instructed by an angel of the Lord to travel to the road that descends from Jerusalem to Gaza (Acts 8:26). It is there that he comes across an Ethiopian eunuch who was the treasurer for Candace—the queen of the Ethiopians. The eunuch just happens to be reading Isaiah 53 and Philip is instructed by the Spirit to go to his chariot. He explains to the eunuch the meaning of the passage and preaches Jesus to him, which results in the eunuch receiving Christ into his heart and is baptized. He doesn't stick around to have fellowship with Jewish believers, so he goes home to Ethiopia most likely spreading the gospel there.

We see how the gospel is moving into Gentile areas. It seems as though the barrier between Jews and Gentiles is coming down with the Samaritans becoming believer's in Christ and receiving the Spirit. Now a high-ranking court official of the Ethiopians becomes a believer in Christ. However, there is a huge barrier that needs to be breached if there is to be one body of Christ and unity with God's people. The apostle Paul said in Galatians 3:28: "There is neither Jew or Greek, there is neither slave or free man, there is neither male nor female; for you are all one in Christ Jesus." In order for unity to occur in the body of Christ the massive cultural divide between Jews and Gentiles had to be breached so they could worship the Lord Jesus together as equals. This brings us to the story of Peter reaching out to Cornelius marking the inclusion of Gentiles into the church of Jesus Christ.

Cornelius and Gentile Inclusion

A historic moment occurred when Peter met up with Cornelius, which is recorded in Acts 10. This meeting marks the beginning of the Gentiles coming into the church. If you put yourself in the shoes of

Peter and the other Jewish Christians, this is as radical as it gets. Jews avoided Gentiles and would have nothing to do with them. Even the dirt of a Gentile country was considered defiled, so Jews would shake the dust off their feet before they entered Israel. Jews wouldn't eat food that was prepared by Gentiles, and cooking utensils that were purchased from Gentiles had to be cleansed before using them. Rubbing shoulders with Gentiles would make one unclean and defiled by being in their presence. The thought of God extending his love and grace to Gentiles was repulsive to Jews, which was demonstrated by Jonah's anger over God saving the Assyrians—Israel's enemy (Jonah 3:10-4:4).

If the Great Commission was to be fulfilled the Jews couldn't avoid Gentiles and act as if they were less than human. All the legalistic tendencies that the Jews had instilled in them about Gentiles, from their childhood, had to go in order for the church to spread throughout the world. If they weren't able to rid themselves of their prejudicial attitudes and legalism the church would have remained a small sect within Judaism based primarily in Jerusalem. This would go against God's plan to make disciples of all nations. Peter and the other Jewish Christians needed to be reinvented so they could be effective in reaching out to Gentiles and fulfill God's plan for the church.

One of the biggest boundary markers between Jew and Gentile was the food they ate. God gave specific instructions to Israel about the food they could and couldn't eat which is recorded in Leviticus 20:25-26:

> You are therefore to make a distinction between the clean animal and the unclean, and between the unclean bird and the clean; and you shall not make yourselves detestable by animal or by bird or by anything that creeps on the ground, which I have separated for you as unclean. 26Thus you are to be holy to Me, for I the LORD am holy; and I have set you apart from the peoples to be Mine.

The dietary regulations God gave to Israel were designed to keep her separate from the other nations. Since Jews ate Kosher they wouldn't have table fellowship with Gentiles who would eat anything. God wanted his people to remain distinct and separate from the nations surrounding them, and food was one way to accomplish that. Jews would not sit down with Gentiles and share a meal.

Now that the New Covenant has arrived, the day of these restrictions, boundary markers, and cultural norms was over. Since God was incorporating the Gentiles in the church these restrictions about food being clean and unclean needed to go. Peter and the other Jews needed some divine help in overcoming these barriers. Their consciences were overly sensitive about eating food that was regarded as unclean, for they felt they would be defiled by eating unclean food, and unfit to worship the Lord in that state.

Acts 10 displays the sovereignty of God very clearly and boldly. He was preparing Cornelius, a Roman centurion, to hear the gospel and be saved, as well as Peter so that he could rid himself of his legalistic views of food and Gentiles, so that he could share the gospel with him. Peter needed to go through a transformation so that he could connect with the Gentiles and share the gospel. The inclusion of the Gentiles into the church would be effected through Peter sharing the gospel to a hated Roman officer. Cornelius was a God-fearer who prayed to the God of Israel, but wasn't a full convert to Judaism. God gave him a vision where an angel appeared to him and instructed him to send for Peter who was in Joppa. He dispatched three people to find Peter.

That Peter was staying in the house of Simon the tanner shows us that he was beginning to loosen up because Jews despised tanners. This was a big step for Peter. He gets hungry and goes up on the roof to pray. While the meal is being prepared he fell into a trance and had a vision, which is recorded in Acts 10:11-17:

> and he saw the sky opened up, and an object like a great sheet coming down, lowered by four corners to the ground, 12and there were in it all *kinds of* four-footed animals and crawling creatures of the earth and birds of the air. 13A voice came to him, "Get up,

Peter, kill and eat!" [14]But Peter said, "By no means, Lord, for I have never eaten anything unholy and unclean." [15]Again a voice *came* to him a second time, "What God has cleansed, no *longer* consider unholy." [16]This happened three times, and immediately the object was taken up into the sky. [17]Now while Peter was greatly perplexed in mind as to what the vision which he had seen might be, behold, the men who had been sent by Cornelius, having asked directions for Simon's house, appeared at the gate;

There are several things about the vision Peter had that are noteworthy. The four corners most likely represents the four corners of the globe. The animals mentioned in v. 12 are unclean and wouldn't be eaten by Jews. That the command to kill and eat was sternly rejected by Peter reveals how deeply ingrained in his conscience these dietary restricts were (v. 14). He didn't want to do what he felt would be wrong before God and put him in a state of ritual impurity. Peter hears a voice a second time saying: "what God has cleansed, no *longer* consider unholy" (v. 15). This not only refers to all food being declared clean, which Jesus already announced in Mark 7, but it refers to the Gentiles as well. Peter is being instructed not to view the Gentiles as unclean, and now that the food restrictions are done away with the boundary marker is removed so that he can have interaction with Gentiles. Jews can now go to the four corners of the globe and interact with Gentiles so they can hear the gospel and fulfill the Great Commission.

The vision is repeated three times, which reveals how difficult it was for Peter to grasp this—once wasn't enough, and he's still left wondering what this vision meant (v. 17). In God's sovereignty Cornelius' envoys arrive at the conclusion of Peter's vision. Peter is notified by the Holy Spirit of their presence, and is instructed to go with them. He invites the men to be guests in the house (v. 23), which is not the normal practice for a Jew, especially to a Roman soldier. This shows that Peter is loosening up and the barriers between Jew and Gentile are slowly deteriorating. That Peter agreed to go with the men and visit the Roman centurion shows us that Peter is going through a gradual transformation, he's being reinvented with God's help, which would enable him to accept the Gentiles.

The next day they leave for Caesarea, but Peter takes some brothers from Joppa with him, which will prove to be important in that more witnesses will see the Holy Spirit poured out on the Gentiles. Cornelius has invited his relatives and close friends to hear Peter, which is also important because more Gentiles are present. If only Cornelius was present and received the Holy Spirit this could be viewed as an anomaly, but with many Gentiles receiving the Spirit it proves that God has accepted the Gentiles into the household of the faith. There was a large gathering of people that Peter would share the gospel with (v. 27).

When Peter finally meets up with Cornelius he is given a most respectful greeting—Cornelius falls at his feet and worships him (vv. 25-26). Peter will have none of that so he instructs him to stand up and comes into his home, where he finds all the people assembled. What Peter says next reveals that he had an insightful moment with light bulbs going on in his head:

> And he said to them, "You yourselves know how unlawful it is for a man who is a Jew to associate with a foreigner or to visit him; and *yet* God has shown me that I should not call any man unholy or unclean. ²⁹That is why I came without even raising any objection when I was sent for. So I ask for what reason you have sent for me." (Acts 10:28-29)

Peter now gains clarity regarding the meaning of the vision God gave him three times. It must be common knowledge to Cornelius that Jews don't associate with foreigners (Gentiles) or even enter their homes, for he said, "you yourselves know" about this. It is considered unlawful to associate with Gentiles, but God taught Peter what he needed to learn in order to be effective at spreading the gospel. He should not call any man unholy or unclean.

This is a crucial moment for Peter because his whole worldview is being transformed. Peter is being reinvented with God's help.

Barriers came tumbling down in this insightful moment because he views the Gentiles as people, like himself, made in the image of God. If the church is going to reach out and bring people in, they can't consider people of other nationalities as unclean, unholy, and to be avoided. That is why Peter came to see Cornelius without raising objections.

I wonder what the Gentiles thought when they heard Peter's words. To have Jews call them unclean or unholy must have been insulting to the Gentiles. What kind of religion do these Jews, and Jewish Christians practice? What makes them think they're so holy and we're so terrible that they would be defiled if they come into my house?

This is a watershed moment for Peter and the history of the church. After Peter asks why he was sent for, Cornelius shares the vision God gave him, where he was instructed to send for him to hear what he has to say. This is the moment of truth. God has set up this encounter by preparing Cornelius to hear the gospel and Peter to be able to come into his home to share the gospel. Peter offers another insightful comment that reveals the depth of the transformation he is going through:

> Opening his mouth, Peter said: "I most certainly understand *now* that God is not one to show partiality, [35]but in every nation the man who fears Him and does what is right is welcome to Him. (Acts 10:34-35)

Finally, Peter is getting it! God is truly impartial. The playing field is level for all nations. God accepts all people who place their faith in Jesus Christ for the forgiveness of their sins. Peter was probably gaining insights as to what Jesus meant when he said I have other sheep that are not of this fold (John 10:16). God's impartiality was taught in the Old Testament (Lev 18:34; Deu 10:17; 2 Chron 19:7; Job 34:19), but the understanding of what this meant was clouded by the views of the religious leaders of the day. God is the God not just of Jews but of Gentiles—he is universal in scope or as Peter says in v. 36: "he is Lord of all."

Peter shares the gospel with Cornelius and his friends. When he is getting to the conclusion of his talk the Holy Spirit shows up and ends Peter's message:

> Of Him all the prophets bear witness that through His name everyone who believes in Him receives forgiveness of sins." [44]While Peter was still speaking these words, the Holy Spirit fell upon all those who were listening to the message. [45]All the circumcised believers who came with Peter were amazed, because the gift of the Holy Spirit had been poured out on the Gentiles also. [46]For they were hearing them speaking with tongues and exalting God. Then Peter answered, [47]"Surely no one can refuse the water for these to be baptized who have received the Holy Spirit just as we *did*, can he?" [48]And he ordered them to be baptized in the name of Jesus Christ. Then they asked him to stay on for a few days. (Acts 10:43-48)

When Peter said: "everyone who believes in Him receives forgiveness of sins" (v. 43), his Gentile audience must have all believed in Jesus at that moment for the Holy Spirit fell upon them and they were speaking with tongues and praising God. Peter must have thought, "this is just like what we experienced on the day of Pentecost." This manifestation of the Spirit would help convince the Jews that the Gentiles received the Spirit just like they did. This is a groundbreaking moment for this clearly displays that God gives the Spirit to Gentiles, which is an earth shattering thought to Jews. They were amazed that God gave the Spirit to those whom they had formerly thought to be unclean (v. 45). Peter went ahead and had them baptized, which further demonstrates that they fully accepted them into the church. Peter and his friends stayed with them for a few days, which further shows how Peter is being reinvented through God's grace, and the walls between Jews and Gentiles were tumbling down.

This was an epochal moment in church history, which marked the beginning of Gentile incorporation into the church. It is also epochal because it marks the beginning of Peter's transformation into liberty found in the gospel. Peter is being liberated from all the traditions that were ingrained in him since his childhood, so he can better serve the Lord and experience his grace.

Applications and Insights

Do we view people as equals? Do we maintain prejudicial attitudes like Peter and the Jews of the First Century about people who are unlike us? Do we avoid people of certain ethnic backgrounds because we don't like them and find them to be undignified and repulsive? We may think that God accepts them, but we don't want anything to do with them. In the gospel all people stand as equals before Christ. Peter went through a transformation with God's help. I contend that every believer needs to go through a similar transformation. When we are born again, through faith in Christ, we are transformed and brought to life in Christ, then begin our journey of sanctification. Part of this journey involves being liberated from man-made rules, and regulations that may impair our ability to be effective witnesses for Christ. God wants us to walk in liberty so we can better serve him. Every believer needs to evaluate their attitudes and practices so that they are truly free, thus, being more effective in serving him and experiencing the abundant life Christ offers.

Some believers in Christ don't go through the same degree of liberation that others do in their post-conversion state. I've known Christians who attend churches that preach from the King James Version of the Bible only, won't let divorced people serve in their church, don't believe in casually dressing for Sunday worship, any instruments beside the piano and organ are of the devil, and anything but hymns are anathema. I don't doubt that these people are genuinely saved and love the Lord with all their heart, but they never were transformed and liberated from their legalistic tendencies. *It is my contention that part of the sanctification process involves ridding oneself of all legalistic attitudes and practices so that he can walk in the freedom Christ provides, which facilitates his ability to serve the Lord.*

Conclusion

It wasn't easy for Peter to break out of his legalistic attitudes, for God gave him the vision three times and he still had a difficult time understanding what it meant. It was a process for him, and, no doubt, it is a process for everybody else as well. In the next chapter we will see that Peter wasn't fully liberated from his legalistic tendencies and took some backwards steps.

Chapter 28 ~ Peter's Fall Into Legalism

In the previous chapter we saw how the Lord assisted Peter in becoming liberated by deleting all kinds of legalistic attitudes that he had about Gentiles and food. He did this so that the church could flourish and be successful in its mission. Peter went through a radical transformation, which was life impacting for him, as it would be for any other Torah observing Jew. There was a time when Peter went to Antioch and took some backward steps behaving like the old Peter, not the Peter who visited Cornelius. This incident is recorded in Galatians 2:11-16:

But when Cephas came to Antioch, I opposed him to his face, because he stood condemned. ¹²For prior to the coming of certain men from James, he used to eat with the Gentiles; but when they came, he *began* to withdraw and hold himself aloof, fearing the party of the circumcision. ¹³The rest of the Jews joined him in hypocrisy, with the result that even Barnabas was carried away by their hypocrisy. ¹⁴But when I saw that they were not straightforward about the truth of the gospel, I said to Cephas in the presence of all, "If you, being a Jew, live like the Gentiles and not like the Jews, how *is it that* you compel the Gentiles to live like Jews?

Peter was one of the pillars of the early church that was instrumental in bringing the Gentiles into the body of Christ. When he was at Antioch Paul had a confrontation with Peter—two spiritual heavy weights that certainly left their mark on the Christian faith. Peter was eating with Gentiles, which shouldn't surprise us because of what is recorded in Acts 10. He has understood that God has declared all food to be clean and Gentiles are no longer to be viewed as unclean either, so Peter is having table fellowship with Gentiles, eating all kinds of food that he previously wouldn't come near. The boundary marker of food has been removed between Jew and Gentile, so that there can be one body of Christ.

Peter was hanging out with Gentiles, which is an expression of how free he was in Christ. He was eating their food, visiting them in their homes, drinking wine with them, so he was in a sense living like a Gentile. This is a beautiful picture of how Peter has been transformed through God's Spirit. For a Torah observing Jew, like Peter, to become a Christian and stop observing all the food regulations, Sabbath restrictions, no longer advocate circumcision, and mingle with Gentiles is as radical as it gets. To the average Jew Peter's behavior would be repulsive and heretical.

Something happened to Peter that caused a reversal. "Certain men from James" showed up and Peter became intimidated and fearful of them, so he withdrew from the Gentiles and would no longer eat with them. The result of Peter's actions has severe consequences. Paul rebuked him publically because his sin was publically displayed. Before these men came from James (the Lord's brother) it appears that Jews and Gentiles ate together, and shared all kinds of food, even what was forbidden in the Old Testament. However, for some reason Peter became fearful when James' entourage came so he separated himself from the Gentiles. It appears that Peter digressed back to the Peter of old and only ate Kosher with his fellow Jewish believers. His behavior influenced even Barnabas, another spiritual heavy weight, to join in his hypocrisy along with the rest of the Jews.

Now it appears that the dividing line between Jew and Gentile has been re-established, which goes against the truth of the gospel. By doing this Peter was in essence advocating the position that to become a believer in Christ one had to follow the food regulations in the Old Testament and basically become Jewish. Peter was in effect compelling the Gentiles to live like Jews to be part of the body of Christ. This goes against everything that was revealed to Peter in Acts 10, and is to be considered a false gospel.

Paul said that Peter stood condemned, that is condemned before God! This is serious business for Paul. Peter had so compromised the truth of the gospel that he butchered it, by his behavior. Peter's behavior wasn't driven by theological conviction; rather it was driven by intimidation and fear that he felt from the men who came from James and the party of the circumcision. The pressure Peter felt from these people must have been so intense it caused him to compromise his position on the gospel. Sadly, everybody else followed Peter's lead— even Barnabas.

There are many issues scholars debate over the identity of the "men from James" and the "party of the circumcision." Because of lack of information in the text itself it is difficult to know with exactitude why Peter was afraid and took backward steps into legalism. It seems unlikely that James would advocate Gentiles having to become Jewish to become Christians, so possibly the men claimed to be from James but were not. Perhaps, they were sent by James, but misrepresented James' position. We simply don't know all the facts.

It is possible that the men from James informed Peter that persecution at the hand of Jewish nationalists was increasing against the Jewish believers in Christ because they were departing from food laws and were eating with Gentiles. It could be that Peter separated himself from the Gentiles to protect the Jewish believers from persecution, and to avoid a schism between Jewish Christians who ate Kosher and those who didn't. At the end of the day we just don't know all the details, and much speculation is involved, but we do know that, for whatever reason, Peter acted inappropriately.

Motivated by fear he compromised the truth, and presented a false gospel. I don't believe that Peter actually acted on his theological convictions, in other words, I don't think he reversed his position theologically that to become a Christian one has to be circumcised, and become Jewish. I believe he acted out of fear and peer pressure, but by his actions he led many astray.

Peter really messed up on this one. It makes me think of some of the times that Peter messed up in the gospels. This wasn't about an incidental issue somewhere out there on the periphery; this was an issue that hit right at the core of the gospel. That Peter was afraid and succumbed to the pressure he felt from others shows how easy it is to slip back into legalistic tendencies that had been ingrained in him since his childhood days. Old attitudes often die hard. Peter should have held his ground and fortified his position so the gospel would remain pure, but he didn't. It is equally amazing to me that Barnabas didn't say something to Peter, nor did the other Jews to correct his error. Why didn't Barnabas point out Peter's error? Peter must have been held in very high regard by the other people to follow him in this blatant hypocrisy. Leaders have a lot of clout and others are easily influenced by their example.

'Fear of criticism, loss of friendships, loss of reputation, persecution, loss of social standing, and so on, can cause believers to compromise their convictions. Believers who have liberty will always be criticized by others who don't. God expects us to be courageous and live by our convictions regardless of what other people may think.

It isn't just a matter of what a person believes; it is a matter of how he applies the truth in his life. Peter's behavior didn't match his belief system, and unfortunately made him a hypocrite. He wasn't true to his convictions, and presented himself as something that he wasn't. When the gospel is compromised openly it must be corrected before all. Paul acted boldly by rebuking Peter and straightening him out, and it appears that Peter took Paul's correction to heart. It must have been an embarrassing moment for Peter.

Conclusion

This chapter leaves us wondering if we act differently when we feel pressure from the people we worship with. Are there any behavior patterns that we tend to fall back into when we are around certain individuals? Do legalistic tendencies reappear in us depending on whom we hang out with? There are times when believers have to hold their ground and not compromise the gospel. On this occasion Peter failed. Peter's slip into legalism shows us those old patterns of behavior that go all the way back to one's childhood don't die easily. We need to have the courage to stick up for the truth of the gospel, regardless of whom we feel pressure from or who opposes us.

Peter's slip back into legalism shows how difficult it is to break free. If the great apostle Peter struggled with this, don't be surprised if you struggle with breaking free as well. In the next chapter we direct our attention to Saul of Tarsus, and examine his trek to freedom in Christ.

Chapter 29 ~ Paul's Liberation From Legalism

In the previous chapters we've seen how Peter, the apostle to the Jews, had to reinvent himself, with God's help, enabling him to reach out to the Gentiles. Peter went through a transformation by which he was able to overcome his legalistic tendencies in reaching out to Cornelius. Now Paul (Saul of Tarsus) needed to go through a similar transformation so that he could be effective in the Gentile world.

The transformation Paul went through is nothing short of amazing. He went from being a hyper-legalistic Pharisee to a hyper-liberated Christian. He was called by the Lord Jesus to be the apostle to the Gentiles, but how could Paul possibly travel throughout the Gentile world and reach out to them without ridding himself of his legalistic ways? If he considered the Gentiles unclean, wouldn't eat with them, or go into their homes how could he possibly plant Gentile churches throughout the Mediterranean world? Once Paul became a believer in Christ he needed to go through a transformation where he came to grips with his Pharisee-ism and reinvent himself through God's assistance. If he continued to observe the law and the traditions that were so close to his heart he would be a failure as an apostle to the Gentiles. He couldn't impose the law and Jewish scruples on Gentiles, so with God's help he would have to change and reinvent himself.

First, we will take a look at how Saul of Tarsus appears in the book of Acts so we can see what he was like prior to becoming a disciple of Christ.

Saul of Tarsus

When the stoning of Stephen occurred that was a decisive moment for the church in Jerusalem (Acts 7). There was a great persecution that came upon the church, which caused everybody except the apostles to scatter throughout Judea and Samaria (Acts 8:1). The Christians were now refugees that had to flee from their homes, which no doubt brought them into crisis mode. The hardship that came upon these believers in Christ was, no doubt, severe, but God used this situation as a divine church-planting program. Wherever people were scattered they preached the word (Acts 8:4). God used this terrible situation to further his plan to spread the gospel throughout the world.

Who was the instigator of the persecution that broke out against the church that day? It was Saul of Tarsus. He is introduced for the first time in the book of Acts when Stephen is stoned to death. Stephen was chosen as one of the deacons and was doing ministry, which included great wonders and miraculous signs (Acts 7:8). Some of the Jews began to oppose him and brought false witnesses to accuse Stephen of speaking blasphemy against the Law of Moses and God, so they stirred up the people and brought Stephen before the Sanhedrin to answer these charges. Stephen went into a long speech where he recounted much of Israel's history, then came to the conclusion of his talk and dropped a bomb on the Sanhedrin:

"You men who are stiff-necked and uncircumcised in heart and ears are always resisting the Holy Spirit; you are doing just as your fathers did. [52]Which one of the prophets did your fathers not persecute? They killed those who had previously announced the coming of the Righteous One, whose betrayers and murderers you have now become; [53]you who received the law as ordained by angels, and yet did not keep it." [54]Now when they heard this, they were cut to the quick, and they began gnashing their teeth at him. [55]But being full of the Holy Spirit, he gazed intently into heaven and saw the glory of God, and Jesus standing at the right hand of God; [56]and he said, "Behold, I see the heavens opened up and the Son of Man standing at the right hand of God." [57]But they cried out with a loud voice, and covered their ears and rushed at him with one impulse. [58]When they had driven him out of the city, they began stoning him; and the witnesses laid aside their robes at the feet of a young man named Saul. [59]They went on stoning Stephen as he called on the Lord and said, "Lord Jesus, receive my spirit!" [60]Then falling on his knees, he

cried out with a loud voice, "Lord, do not hold this sin against them!" Having said this, he fell asleep. (Acts 7:51-60)

Stephen pulled no punches and let the Sanhedrin have it. Talk about brutal honesty, Stephen indicted them for behaving just like their fathers did in being stiff-necked, hard-hearted, resisting the Holy Spirit, persecuting the prophets, murdering Jesus, and not keeping the law. Perhaps Stephen needed some sensitivity training in closing his sermon and calling for a kinder and gentler response, but that isn't the way it happened. When Stephen said he saw the heavens opened and the Son of Man standing at the right hand of God, the Sanhedrin went over the top and lost it. They reacted like a bloodthirsty mob by dragging him out of the city and began to stone him to death, making Stephen a martyr for the cause of Christ.

Luke informs his readers that: "the witnesses laid aside their robes at the feet of a young man named Saul" (v. 58). This is the first mention of Saul and indicates that he had a key role in the proceedings regarding Stephen. He was most likely a member of the Sanhedrin, or affiliated with them such that he was given authority to initiate a persecution against the church in Jerusalem.

There are many uncanny similarities between Stephen and Jesus that are worthy of consideration:

- Both were Spirit-filled
- Both boldly confronted the religious authorities
- Both were convicted by lying witnesses
- Both were innocent of any wrongdoing
- Both were accused of blasphemy
- Both were savagely killed
- Both were killed outside the city
- Both were buried by their sympathizers
- Both committed their spirit to God at their death
- Both prayed for their executioners

It is the last point that is of special interest. It is safe to assume that Saul was there listening to Stephen's talk, so Stephen knew who Saul of Tarsus was. Stephen saw the witnesses were laying their robes at

288

Saul's feet. Did Stephen look right into Saul's eyes as he was being stoned and pray for him as he cried out in a loud voice: "Lord, do not hold this sin against them" (Acts 7:60)? Perhaps, their eyes met and they had a brief eye-to-eye moment, and Stephen's prayer was not just for the crowd in general, but for Saul as his chief executioner. Stephen, like Jesus, prayed that this sin wouldn't be held against them. It is very possible that this prayer played a key role in Saul's conversion to Christ. Augustine's comment: "If Stephen had not prayed, the church would not have had Paul" has some merit.

Later in Saul's life he made mention of Stephen's death when he was speaking to the crowd in Jerusalem: "And when the blood of Your witness Stephen was being shed, I also was standing by approving, and watching out for the coats of those who were slaying him" (Acts 22:20). No doubt his participation in Stephen's death had an impact on him. There may have been people in the crowd, that Paul was addressing, that hurled some stones at Stephen as well, and were part of the mob that began the great persecution against the Christians the day of his death. Perhaps this is one of several things that haunted Paul throughout his life.

After Stephen's death there was more violence to follow. At the hands of Saul a great persecution broke out against the church that day, which is recorded in Acts 8:1-4:

Saul was in hearty agreement with putting him to death. And on that day a great persecution began against the church in Jerusalem, and they were all scattered throughout the regions of Judea and Samaria, except the apostles. ²Some devout men buried Stephen, and made loud lamentation over him. ³But Saul began ravaging the church, entering house after house, and dragging off men and women, he would put them in prison. ⁴Therefore, those who had been scattered went about preaching the word.

People were scattered, which suggests that they had to run for their lives because Saul began to "ravage the church." The word "ravage" is a translation of the Greek word *lumainomai*, which has a range of meaning: to destroy, ruin, damage, or devastate. This indicates that the great persecution instigated by Saul was serious business. He

289

literally wanted to destroy the church, so he entered people's homes and dragged believers away to be incarcerated.

Several other places in Acts provide more information about Saul's passionate hateful persecution against the church. For instance, Acts 22:3-5 informs the reader:

"I am a Jew, born in Tarsus of Cilicia, but brought up in this city, educated under Gamaliel, strictly according to the law of our fathers, being zealous for God just as you all are today. ⁴I persecuted this Way to the death, binding and putting both men and women into prisons, ⁵as also the high priest and all the Council of the elders can testify. From them I also received letters to the brethren, and started off for Damascus in order to bring even those who were there to Jerusalem as prisoners to be punished.

This is Paul reflecting back on his persecution of the church as he is speaking to the crowd in Jerusalem. He describes himself as an axeman, as if his mission was to purge the planet from believers in Christ. He persecuted the Way (Christians) to their death. He would have them bound in chains and brought to prison. He received permission from the authorities to go to other cities on a search and destroy mission, and bring the believers back to Jerusalem. Saul was a man with a mission and wouldn't be stopped.

When Paul was speaking before King Agrippa he shared some other information about his persecution of the church:

So then, I thought to myself that I had to do many things hostile to the name of Jesus of Nazareth. ¹⁰And this is just what I did in Jerusalem; not only did I lock up many of the saints in prisons, having received authority from the chief priests, but also when they were being put to death I cast my vote against them. ¹¹And as I punished them often in all the synagogues, I tried to force them to blaspheme; and being furiously enraged at them, I kept pursuing them even to foreign cities. (Acts 26:9-11)

Paul was responsible for the death of many Christians. He would go to the synagogues, which would be a natural place for a Jewish believer

290

to go, and force them to blaspheme. He would give them a chance to retract their faith in Christ as the Messiah. If they didn't he would escort them off to prison. Paul describes himself as "being furiously enraged at them." Why the bad attitude toward the Jewish believers in Christ? Why was Saul filled with venom and anger toward these people? His anger almost seems irrational, and he appears to be a bloodthirsty, intolerant religious fanatic! Saul isn't presented in a very positive light, to say it mildly. If you were a Christian you didn't want to come anywhere near Saul of Tarsus—it could cost you your life!

Misguided Zeal

One thing about Saul of Tarsus that I think everybody would agree with is that he was a "no nonsense" kind of guy. There was no half-heartedness in Saul. What he set his mind to do he got it done. He was a passionate individual who was driven by his deeply rooted convictions. Saul was zealous for God, however his zeal was misguided and way off course.

Of all the Jews in the First Century who strictly observed the Torah and all the ancestral traditions, Saul would be on top of the list. You couldn't be more Jewish than Saul of Tarsus. His strict observance to the traditions of the elders far exceeded that of your average Jew. In other words, Saul was hardcore! The Pharisees may have believed that stricter observance to the Torah and the traditions could hasten the coming of Messiah. When Jews began turning to Christ, people like Saul regarded them as Jewish heretics. Since the church initially existed within a Jewish context in Jerusalem, the Christians were viewed as a heretical sect within Judaism, which threatened to poison their religion. All the talk of Jesus fulfilling the law, the Temple sacrifices, the Sabbath restrictions, etc. was more than people like Saul, and the other religious authorities could tolerate. Something had to be done about this.

Saul and the authorities felt they had to purge Judaism from these Jewish Christian heretics to preserve the purity of Judaism. Saul, and company, felt they were doing a noble thing before God, after all, there seems to be a precedent for this type of purging in Israel's history. In the day of Moses when the Israelite men began to intermingle with the Moabite women they started worshiping their gods, and committed sexual immorality with them. The Lord instructed Moses to have the transgressors killed in broad daylight to curb the Lord's fierce anger (Num 25:1-5). The community of God's people couldn't be corrupted by a false religion that could have poisoned future generations of Israelites.

The golden calf incident is another time in Israel's history when the Lord called Moses to take drastic measures to weed out the heretics that worshiped the calf—a god of Egypt. The Levites rose to the occasion and by the Lord's instruction, given through Moses, put to the sword 3,000 people who worshiped the calf (Ex 32:25-28). The community of the faithful needed to remain pure and couldn't be infected by those who wanted to worship the gods of Egypt.

Saul and the religious leaders of the day probably looked at their situation as potentially damaging to Judaism as the golden calf incident, and the intermingling of the Israelites with the Moabite women mentioned above. What was at stake here was the future of Judaism! From Saul's perspective, would future generations of Jews be infected by believing in a false Messiah named Jesus Christ, who had no regard for their ancestral traditions, and was viewed as having a low opinion of the Mosaic Law? This was unacceptable to the religious hierarchy of the day, so drastic measures had to be taken and Saul was just the man for the job. He had the courage to stand up for his convictions, do what he felt was right before God, and preserve the future of Judaism. This was Saul's motivation. He was a fierce, passionate, zealous (albeit misguided) man of conviction.

In Jesus' last talk with his disciples in the Upper Room he made a prediction: "but an hour is coming for everyone who kills you to think that he is offering service to God" (John 16:2b). This prediction is fulfilled in Saul of Tarsus, and others like him. Their misguided zeal caused them to do the unthinkable: kill Christians as if they were doing a great service to God.

Conclusion

People like Saul of Tarsus, who are filled with zeal, are very talented, well educated, highly intelligent, with a type A personality would make great Christians. Imagine the impact a guy like Saul could have if he harnessed all his energy and skills for good purposes in serving Jesus. Think of what he could accomplish for the Lord. As we all know, the Lord did get hold of Saul and reversed the course of his life when he was on the road to Damascus. Saul of Tarsus did make more than a significant contribution to the Christian faith after he became a believer in Christ. In the next chapter we will take a look at how this antagonist toward the Christian faith became one of the most devoted followers of Jesus the church has ever known.

Chapter 30 - Saul's Conversion to Christ

Saul was an interesting character to say the least. He was born into a family that appears to be well off that lived in Tarsus, which Saul described as no ordinary city (Acts 21:39). It was located in the Roman province of Cilicia, near the intersection of Asia Minor and Syria. Its university was highly rated and famous in the Roman world. He was a Roman citizen by birth, so his father must have been a citizen of Rome. He was educated in Jerusalem by Gamaliel, who was one of the top-level scholars of the day. He was of the strictest sect of the Pharisees, holding the ancestral traditions near his heart. Saul was fluent in several languages including Greek, Hebrew, and Aramaic. He had established himself as an upcoming star in Judaism, who was on the fast track to success.

Saul is a man who had everything going for him in his career in Judaism: He was born into a family of means, he was a world-class scholar, he had clout with the Sanhedrin, he was a passionate Jew, and was a visionary with a type A personality who got things done. He was in every respect a no nonsense kind of guy. His persecution of Jesus' followers was something he was doing based on his deep-seated convictions that he was doing right before God, by protecting Judaism, by agreeing with his colleagues on the Sanhedrin that Jesus wasn't the true Messiah.

When he was on the road to Damascus the Lord Jesus got hold of him and he experienced a great reversal regarding the direction of his life, and more importantly his view of Jesus Christ. Paul's conversion experience is not your typical conversion. When I listen to people share their testimony about how they came to know Christ, I've never heard anybody come up with anything even remotely close to Saul's experience, which is recorded in Acts 9:1-9:

Now Saul, still breathing threats and murder against the disciples of the Lord, went to the high priest, ²and asked for letters from him to

the synagogues at Damascus, so that if he found any belonging to the Way, both men and women, he might bring them bound to Jerusalem. ³As he was traveling, it happened that he was approaching Damascus, and suddenly a light from heaven flashed around him; ⁴and he fell to the ground and heard a voice saying to him, "Saul, Saul, why are you persecuting Me?" ⁵And he said, "Who are You, Lord?" And He *said*, "I am Jesus whom you are persecuting, ⁶but get up and enter the city, and it will be told you what you must do." ⁷The men who traveled with him stood speechless, hearing the voice but seeing no one. ⁸Saul got up from the ground, and though his eyes were open, he could see nothing; and leading him by the hand, they brought him into Damascus. ⁹And he was three days without sight, and neither ate nor drank.

By the authority of the high priest Saul was on the way to Damascus to weed out any of the Jewish heretics that believed in Jesus as the Messiah. There was a substantial Jewish population there, and through the ministry of Philip, Peter, and John some Jews may have become followers of Christ, which may have given Saul more incentive to go there and bring the heretics to justice. He would visit the synagogues in search of any disciples' of Christ and would bind them in chains then escort them back to Jerusalem. Saul isn't confining his persecution to Jerusalem, he's going to other places on his search and destroy mission. This gives the reader an indication of how zealous Saul is in his crusade to ravage the church and rid the earth from Jesus' disciples. Then it happened. As he is nearing Damascus Saul's life would be forever changed.

Most people become Christians when somebody sits down with them over coffee and tells them about Jesus, and may even lead them in prayer to receive Jesus into their heart. Nobody would approach Saul of Tarsus and try to convince him that Jesus is the Messiah because everybody was scared to death of him. It would take a direct intervention from God to get Saul's attention, which is exactly what happened.

As he was traveling, it happened that he was approaching Damascus, and suddenly a light from heaven flashed around him; ⁴and he fell to the ground and heard a voice saying to him, "Saul, Saul, why are you

persecuting Me?" ⁵And he said, "Who are You, Lord?" And He *said*, "I am Jesus whom you are persecuting," (Acts 9:3-5)

It isn't clear whether or not Saul was on horseback when the light flashed around him at high noon, knocking him and his companions down so they hit the deck (Acts 26:14). The voice was none other then the Lord Jesus who asked him a question: "Saul, Saul, why are you persecuting me?" Persecuting the church is the same as persecuting Jesus. When Christians suffer on earth at the hands of their persecutors the Lord Jesus feels the pain. There is an inseparable link between the Lord and his body on earth. To persecute the church is to persecute its Lord. Naturally Saul would want to know who the speaker was, so he said, "who are you, Lord?" Then the moment of truth came that would rock Saul's world: "I am Jesus whom you are persecuting." With those words Saul came to the shocking realization that he was wrong. The other men heard the sound, but were unable to distinguish the words because they were for Saul's ears only.

The light wasn't bright sunlight; it was Jesus displaying his glory to Saul, which he mentioned several times after the event (Acts 9:17; 27; 22:14; 26:16; 1 Cor 9:1; 15:8). The other men just saw a bright light, but Saul saw the risen glorified Jesus. How interesting it is that the last person recorded to have seen Jesus was Stephen, as he was being stoned to death under the guiding hand of Saul (Acts 7:55-56). Now Saul sees Jesus, which establishes another link between the two.

One can only imagine what was going through his mind at that moment. Saul was convinced Jesus was just one of many false Messiahs that showed up periodically in Palestine, but now he can no longer occupy that view. He must come to grips with his grave error about Jesus and think things through.

but get up and enter the city, and it will be told you what you must do." ⁷The men who traveled with him stood speechless, hearing the voice but seeing no one. ⁸Saul got up from the ground, and though his eyes were open, he could see nothing; and leading him by the hand, they brought him into Damascus. ⁹And he was three days without sight, and neither ate nor drank. (Acts 9:6-9)

The only instruction that the Lord gave him was to get up and proceed into the city and wait for further instructions. Saul is blind, so the other men, who were speechless, must guide him by the hand into Damascus. Saul is totally humbled. He was knocked down, is blind, and at the mercy of those who are guiding him to his destination. Saul goes without food or water for three days. The Lord put him in a place where he could do some inner reflecting and think things over. The dominant thought that must have occupied his mind was I WAS WRONG! WHAT HAVE I DONE? Perhaps he's thinking that Jesus is going to get even with him and let him have it, after all he was persecuting his people. Saul realized that Jesus isn't dead, he's quite alive and well, and he is God. He is completely humbled and helpless for three days.

Conclusion

Saul's salvation was totally engineered by God. Who would have ever thought that Saul would have become a believer in Christ? Nobody is outside of God's saving grace, even one, like Saul, who hated Jesus' followers, put many to death, and rejected Jesus as the Messiah. The Lord got hold of Saul—now he is a believer. Saul is undergoing a transformation through divine grace. He will never be the same. A great reversal will now take place in the direction of his life. If you know someone who is a God-mocker that is going down the wrong path in life don't give up on him. Keep praying because if God could save Saul of Tarsus and transform him into one of the most committed followers of Christ ever, God can get hold of anybody's heart. Saul's transformation is a picture of God's grace and mercy that he willingly extends to those who believe.

Chapter 31 - Saul Sees Things Differently

I wonder what the three days were like for Saul being blind and fasting from food and water. This was a time of serious reflection for Saul as he considered his grave error in rejecting Jesus as the Messiah and persecuting his people. Of the many thoughts that occupied his mind I'm sure he thought: WHAT HAVE I DONE? HOW COULD I HAVE BEEN SO WRONG? HOW CAN I MAKE UP FOR THIS? WHAT DO I DO NOW? In the Acts narrative Luke focuses his readers' attention away from Saul to a disciple named Ananias.

Now there was a disciple at Damascus named Ananias; and the Lord said to him in a vision, "Ananias." And he said, "Here I am, Lord." [11]And the Lord *said* to him, "Get up and go to the street called Straight, and inquire at the house of Judas for a man from Tarsus named Saul, for he is praying, [12]and he has seen in a vision a man named Ananias come in and lay his hands on him, so that he might regain his sight." [13]But Ananias answered, "Lord, I have heard from many about this man, how much harm he did to Your saints at Jerusalem; [14]and here he has authority from the chief priests to bind all who call on Your name." (Acts 9:10-14)

Ananias was a believer in Christ who was a devout man that was held in high regard by the Jews in Damascus (Acts 22:12). He was probably one of the leaders of the church there. The Lord Jesus spoke to him in a vision instructing him to go to Judas' house located on Straight Street, and ask for a man named Saul from Tarsus. While Saul was praying the Lord spoke to him in a vision informing him that a man named Ananias would come to him and lay hands on him so that he would regain his sight. The Lord Jesus has engineered this meeting between the two of them.

What else could Saul do but pray? Perhaps, Saul thought his punishment for persecuting the church was to be blind for the rest of his life. Maybe he was continuously praying for forgiveness and

298

restoration of his sight. The Lord spoke to Saul in a vision and reassured him that he would see again.

Ananias is filled with reservation about going to Saul because he heard the reports of Saul's persecution of the church and was naturally afraid to go near him. He didn't want to end up like many of his friends who felt Saul's wrath and were incarcerated.

But the Lord said to him, "Go, for he is a chosen instrument of Mine, to bear My name before the Gentiles and kings and the sons of Israel; [16]for I will show him how much he must suffer for My name's sake." [17]So Ananias departed and entered the house, and after laying his hands on him said, "Brother Saul, the Lord Jesus, who appeared to you on the road by which you were coming, has sent me so that you may regain your sight and be filled with the Holy Spirit." [18]And immediately there fell from his eyes something like scales, and he regained his sight, and he got up and was baptized; [19]and he took food and was strengthened. (Acts 9:15-19)

The Lord gave Ananias assurance that his life wouldn't be in danger by going to Saul because there was a special plan that Jesus had for him. Saul is now a chosen instrument of the Lord's to declare the name of Jesus to the Gentiles, to their kings, and to the people of Israel. Saul would become the apostle to the Gentiles, while Peter is the apostle to the Jews. In this new role that the Lord has for Saul, there will be a lot of suffering that he will have to endure for Jesus' sake. Certainly, Saul's life of privilege is now over.

When Ananias shows up he addresses Saul as "brother Saul" which means he is welcoming Saul as a member of the family of God. He informs Saul of the purpose for which the Lord sent him (cf Acts 22:14-15). He lays hands on Saul and scales drop out of his eyes. He can see again, but he sees things from a completely different perspective. He is now a believer in Christ, not a Christ hater. He receives the Holy Spirit and his commissioning directly from the Lord Jesus Christ. Saul is now a Spirit-filled believer in Jesus. Armed with the Holy Spirit to empower Saul in his calling as an apostle to the Gentiles, the Spirit will begin his work of transforming Saul into the image of Christ.

The Spirit will utilize Saul's natural talents, his intellect, his work ethic, and so forth, while imparting spiritual gifts to him so that he is equipped to fulfill his mission. Additionally, the Spirit will begin his work of sanctification where Saul will go through a transformation of his character where his Pharisaic pride will be drained from him, his hatred will be replaced with love, and his aggressive toughness will be replaced with a gentle sensitivity for people. Saul will undergo a transformation at the core of his being through the Holy Spirit, who now resides in him.

Saul is baptized into the body of Christ—the very body he was trying to eliminate from the face of the earth. He is now a member of Christ's church in fellowship with other believers that he used to hate. He strengthens himself with food and water.

Now for several days he was with the disciples who were at Damascus, [20]and immediately he *began* to proclaim Jesus in the synagogues, saying, "He is the Son of God." [21]All those hearing him continued to be amazed, and were saying, "Is this not he who in Jerusalem destroyed those who called on this name, and *who* had come here for the purpose of bringing them bound before the chief priests?" [22]But Saul kept increasing in strength and confounding the Jews who lived at Damascus by proving that this *Jesus* is the Christ. (Acts 9:19-22)

After being baptized into the body of Christ Saul spent several days with his fellow believers at Damascus. No doubt, the Christians there would have had reservations about the genuineness of Saul's conversion to Christ and would have been afraid of him. Perhaps, he was just putting on a front to trap them and hall them off to prison. I'm sure they questioned him as Saul related his story, as did Ananias of how the Lord saved him and called him into service. Saul is seeing things differently now. The people he wanted to exterminate are embracing him as a member of Christ's body, and he is having good fellowship with them. Saul, no doubt, informed them about how wrong he was about Jesus, his persecution of the church, and it appears that the believers in Damascus praised God for the transformation that Saul went through. This must have been a great source of encouragement for the believers there to hear that the man who was used of Satan to destroy the church of Christ, was now a believer and was called into service by the Lord himself. It appears that they welcomed Saul as a brother and praised God for saving him.

We get an indication of Saul's no nonsense personality. Jesus has called him to declare his name so Saul gets right at it and begins to preach Jesus in the Damascus synagogues, to the amazement of all who heard him. They were skeptical about his conversion and very cautious of him because they knew he came to Damascus under the authority of the chief priests to haul the believers in Christ back to Jerusalem. Saul didn't waste any time before beginning to preach Jesus. He was proving to the Jews that Jesus was the Messiah and baffling them with his wisdom.

During the time that Saul was blind he must have done some thinking and reflecting about the Scriptures that pointed to Jesus as the Messiah, and was able to astonish the Jews by proving that Jesus is the Christ. With his new understanding about Jesus being the Messiah he had the key that unlocked the vast wealth of Scripture that he had stored in his mind. He was utilizing his knowledge of Scripture and keen intellect to promote Jesus. Saul's preaching must have shocked the Jews, because they were expecting him to continue his persecution of the Jewish Christians. In their minds something wasn't right with this picture of Saul being an advocate of Jesus.

When many days had elapsed, the Jews plotted together to do away with him, ²⁴but their plot became known to Saul. They were also watching the gates day and night so that they might put him to death; ²⁵but his disciples took him by night and let him down through *an opening in* **the wall, lowering him in a large basket. (Acts 9:23-25)**

Luke tells his readers that "when many days had elapsed" they plotted to kill him. How long is many days? By looking at other passages of Scripture it is possible to construct a timeline of Saul's activities. In Galatians 1:17-18 we are given an indication of the period of time that elapsed:

> "nor did I go up to Jerusalem to those who were apostles before me; but I went away to Arabia, and

returned once more to Damascus. [18]Then three years later I went up to Jerusalem to become acquainted with Cephas, and stayed with him fifteen days."

Saul went from Damascus to Arabia. Perhaps Saul was experiencing opposition in Damascus such that he felt it was best to get away from the action and go to Arabia where he could think things over. This may have been a long spiritual retreat for Saul to study the Scriptures and, of course, continue to preach Jesus. He was in the Kingdom of the Nabatean Arabs but may have worn out his welcome there, which prompted his return to Damascus. It appears that Saul has upset everybody as an overbearing preacher of Jesus. Upon his return to Damascus the Jews plotted to kill Saul, but their plot became known to him. The ethnarch under King Aretas in Damascus was trying to seize Saul, so he is now a hunted man (2 Cor 11:32). The walled city is under surveillance in an attempt to locate Saul, but the believers figure out a way to get Saul out of Damascus. He is lowered down the wall in a basket at night, perhaps from a believer's house that was on the wall. Saul has escaped and now goes off to Jerusalem.

When he came to Jerusalem, he was trying to associate with the disciples; but they were all afraid of him, not believing that he was a disciple. [27]But Barnabas took hold of him and brought him to the apostles and described to them how he had seen the Lord on the road, and that He had talked to him, and how at Damascus he had spoken out boldly in the name of Jesus. [28]And he was with them, moving about freely in Jerusalem, speaking out boldly in the name of the Lord. [29]And he was talking and arguing with the Hellenistic *Jews*; but they were attempting to put him to death. [30]But when the brethren learned *of it*, they brought him down to Caesarea and sent him away to Tarsus. (Acts 9:26-30)

When Saul went to Jerusalem he had to expect to get a cold shoulder from the disciples. They didn't believe that he was a follower of Christ and were afraid of him. After all, he was the chief instigator of the persecution that occurred when Stephen was stoned. They didn't believe or trust him. His appearance in Jerusalem is like having Hitler showing up at Auschwitz telling the Jews he's on their side. Saul is having a rough go of it because nobody wants anything to do with him. All the believers are rejecting him so he needs some help gaining acceptance with the Christians. A decisive moment in Saul's life occurred when he met Barnabas, who introduced Saul to the apostles and vouched for him. Barnabas was known as the Son of Encouragement (Acts 4:36), which gives us an indication of his personality type. He was a people person—an encourager! The Jews and the apostles held him in high regard, so his word on Saul's behalf meant a lot. He informed the apostles about Saul's conversion, his preaching in Damascus, and apparently Barnabas' recommendation of Saul was enough to cause them to accept Saul as a genuine believer.

Now he can move about freely in Jerusalem so he continued to boldly tell people about Jesus. However, he began to debate with the Hellenistic Jews about Jesus and they plotted to kill him. When the believers heard about this they felt it was best to get Saul out of Jerusalem so they sent him off to Tarsus by way of Caesarea. He stayed in Jerusalem for only fifteen days (Gal 1:18), which indicates that it didn't take long for him to stir things up before people wanted him dead. Saul received instructions from the Lord himself to leave Jerusalem which are recorded in Acts 22:17-21:

"It happened when I returned to Jerusalem and was praying in the temple, that I fell into a trance, 18and I saw Him saying to me, 'Make haste, and get out of Jerusalem quickly, because they will not accept your testimony about Me.' 19And I said, 'Lord, they themselves understand that in one synagogue after another I used to imprison and beat those who believed in You. 20And when the blood of Your witness Stephen was being shed, I also was standing by approving, and watching out for the coats of those who were slaying him.' 21And He said to me, 'Go! For I will send you far away to the Gentiles.'"

Saul is having a time of prayer in the Temple, falls into a trance and saw Jesus saying to him that it's time to get out of Jerusalem, and do so quickly. Saul must have been filled with a high degree of anxiety because everywhere he goes people are rejecting him and want to kill him. He is a marked man and was probably wondering if he would survive, which may have been what Saul was praying about in the Temple. Perhaps the one place that he felt safe was in the Temple, and, of course, what better place for a Jew to go than the Temple to commune with God. The Lord Jesus' appearance to Saul must have been an encouragement to him such that he could take comfort that Jesus was aware of his circumstances and was guiding his steps.

For Saul to do ministry in Jerusalem was an attempt in futility. Jesus told him to give it up because the people wouldn't accept your (Saul's) testimony about me. Saul is agreeing with Jesus by recounting how the people remembered his persecution of believers and how he led the mob against Stephen. The next words Jesus spoke are critical for our understanding of Saul's ministry: "Go! For I will send you far away to the Gentiles." It seems that everywhere Saul goes he stirs up the hornets' nest, so by divine decree he needs to get out of the Jewish world, where his reputation is trashed, and get into the Gentile world.

The problem is how can Saul be effective in taking the gospel to Gentiles if he is doesn't step out of his Pharisaic box of legalism? Remember, there was nobody who observed the Torah, and the traditions of the elders, more strictly than Saul. He would have to undergo another transformation that would enable him to break free of his legalism so he could interact with the Gentiles. He's been transformed by the grace of God, is a Spirit-filled believer called as an apostle to the Gentiles, but he needs to go through another transformation with the help of the Spirit, so he could reinvent himself. He would be a miserable failure in the Gentile world if he tried to impose all the legalistic regulations on them, to which he been committed. Peter went through that same transformation as recorded in Acts chapter ten.

Saul is now back in his hometown of Tarsus. During this time he went to Syria and Cilicia preaching the gospel (Gal 1:21), and must have founded some churches in that area (Acts 15:23). It was Barnabas who went to Tarsus to find Saul and bring him to Antioch (Acts 11:25-26).

Paul's Educational Background

We can assume that Paul started his education at or around the age of five, studying the Pentateuch. At the age of ten, he would have advanced to the Mishnah, which dealt with detailed tradition. At the age of thirteen he would have completed his study of the Mishnah, and would have been ready for formal rabbinical school training. It was more than likely at this age that Paul left Tarsus to live in Jerusalem, probably with his married sister (Acts 23:16) to begin his formal training at the Hillel rabbinical school in Jerusalem. Paul studied under the renown rabbi Gamaliel I, who was one of the greatest rabbinical teachers of the first century (Acts 22:3).

In addition to his studies, Paul had to memorize the ancient Hebrew language Targums, and be able to translate it into Aramaic. Paul, when he had finished rabbinical school, had received the best education that his religion had to offer. The Hillel school could only be attended by the best Jewish minds of Paul's day. When analyzing the cultural and educational influences upon the amazing life and theological intellect of the Apostle Paul, one can only step back and marvel at the tremendous accomplishments made in his life, utilizing all of the broad exposure to the world and learning that life afforded him.

Paul was not averse to using any tool in his broad arsenal to the fullest extent for the cause of Christ. Paul's early life in his hometown of Tarsus exposed him to Hellenistic Judaism, which allowed for Grecian learning and influence, even though his parents were devout Jews. Without doubt in those early formative years in Tarsus, Paul became exposed to different cultures and teaching as well as Orthodox Pharisaic Judaism, which allowed him to learn "Classic Greek," Greek philosophy, *Koine* Greek (This form of Greek was spoken by everyone in Tarsus, even Orthodox Pharisaic Jews) and other disciplines. By his family being wealthy tentmakers and Roman citizens, he was, no doubt exposed to high-ranking Roman officials, and Roman practices, law, and customs.

Paul's rabbinic education was first class, as he learned his craft from one of the most noted rabbis in history. Along with his rabbinic education, the Hillel school was noted for giving their students a balanced education, giving Paul broad exposure to classical literature, philosophy, and ethics. Paul, in his letters, borrowed heavily from his knowledge of Stoic philosophy, using Stoic terms and metaphors to assist his new Gentile converts in their understanding of the revealed word of God.

Paul also relied heavily upon his training concerning the law and the prophets, utilizing this knowledge to convince his Jewish countrymen of the unity of past Old Testament prophecy and covenants with the fulfilling of these in Jesus Christ. Paul, as the evangelist, is without peer. God, in his divine wisdom and grace, exposed Paul to a wide spectrum of experiences and education, giving the Apostle to the Gentiles the tools to effectively spread the Gospel and establish the church solidly in all parts of the Roman Empire. Paul's education, keen intellect, and no nonsense personality establish him as much more than an average person. His background qualifies him to be the perfect fit for the position of apostle to the Gentiles. (biblicaltheology.com/Research/WallaceQ01.html)

Paul's Transcultural Adaptability

People came from all over the Roman Empire to study at the university in Tarsus, which was one of the top-level schools of its day. The city was very prosperous—excelling at trade and commerce. Paul was exposed to Greco-Roman culture in his formative years so he was accustomed to being around Gentiles. Because of this, Saul was uniquely suited to travel around the Gentile world and interact with them. Being a Hellenistic Jew who was familiar with Greek thought and culture would make it easier for Saul to travel and mingle with Gentiles. The other disciples of Jesus like Peter and John who weren't raised with the same Hellenistic influence, weren't equipped to travel in the Gentile world and sit around the table with them. Saul most likely was. Even though he was Hellenized he still adhered to the ancestral traditions being of the strictest sect of the Pharisees.

He had a unique cultural adaptability such that he could flip back and forth between the Jewish and Gentile world, and appears to be very comfortable doing that. He was amazingly flexible and adaptable to different cultural situations. In 1 Corinthians 9:19-23, Paul talks about his ability to be like the Jews, Gentiles, and the weak to win them for Christ. He demonstrated an uncanny ability in his ministry to be flexible in different cultural situations for the sake of sharing the gospel and making converts to Christ.

I'm suggesting that Paul's upbringing, education, and all the above-mentioned factors made him well suited for the task of being the apostle to the Gentiles. God choose just the right man for the job, but, of course, Paul would have to go through a radical change of heart regarding Jesus, and sift through all the Scriptures embedded in his mind about the Messiah and make sense of them. With his razor-sharp intellect that wouldn't prove to be a difficult task. One can see how God had his hand on Paul and formed his unique personality before his calling and conversion.

Conclusion

Paul's life is a picture of an amazing before and after. He was trying to destroy the church, and then he became the major builder of the church. He was a hyper-legalist then he became a hyper-liberated believer. He felt he was doing a good deed before God in persecuting the church, and then discovered how wrong he was after his conversion. He was a picture of violence, and then he became a picture of God's grace.

One has to appreciate the transformation that Paul went through. He didn't delay preaching the gospel, he got right at telling people the Jesus story. This gives you an indication of his no nonsense personality. He has a job to do and he gets right to it. However, because his reputation is smeared in the Jewish world he has to get out of that context and begin his trek into Gentile territory beginning to plant churches around the Mediterranean world.

One also has to see the sovereignty of God in appointing Paul to be the apostle to the Gentiles. There was probably not a man on the planet that was better suited to occupy this role than Paul. He never dreamed he would end up serving Christ in this way. I can only imagine what Paul must have thought in his times of reflection regarding his persecution of Christians. He must have dealt with feelings of guilt, shame, and remorse. How would he cope with these feelings? It is to a discussion of this issue that we now direct our attention.

Chapter 32 ~ Coming to Grips With His Past

Everybody needs to reconcile with their past. When someone becomes a follower of Christ they must understand all their sins are forgiven, and that they have a new beginning in life (2 Cor 5:17). Nothing they've done before they received Jesus into their heart is held against them, for the slate is wiped clean. This was the case with Saul of Tarsus. Even though he persecuted Christ's church and was responsible for the death of many Christians his sin was completely forgiven. Saul is a new creation in Christ, called into service as an apostle to the Gentiles. He is now a man with a mission working for the Lord Jesus. For the duration of his life he will travel around the Mediterranean world and establish new churches. He will experience much hardship and suffering, just as Jesus told him he would, but he pursued his calling with reckless abandon. He is totally committed to spreading the gospel and fulfilling his mission that the Lord assigned to him.

There is one thing that Saul needs to do, namely be reconciled with his past. The sheer gravity of his sin lingered in his conscience for the duration of his life, and it was something that haunted him at times. Saul had a guilty conscience because of his persecution of the church, which he had to reconcile. He offers us an insight into how he came to grips with his past in 1 Timothy 1:13-17:

I thank Christ Jesus our Lord, who has strengthened me, because He considered me faithful, putting me into service, ¹³even though I was formerly a blasphemer and a persecutor and a violent aggressor. Yet I was shown mercy because I acted ignorantly in unbelief; ¹⁴and the grace of our Lord was more than abundant, with the faith and love which are *found* in Christ Jesus. ¹⁵It is a trustworthy statement, deserving full acceptance, that Christ Jesus came into the world to save sinners, among whom I am foremost *of all*. ¹⁶Yet for this reason I found mercy, so that in me as the foremost, Jesus Christ might demonstrate His perfect patience as an example for those who

would believe in Him for eternal life. ¹⁷Now to the King eternal, immortal, invisible, the only God, *be* honor and glory forever and ever. Amen.

Saul understands what he was, without any reservations whatsoever, for he identifies himself as a blasphemer, a persecutor, and a violent aggressor. He is brutally honest about himself. He isn't displaying any degree of denial about his sinful past, he acknowledges it, and owns it. When someone becomes a believer in Christ they can feel good about their sins being forgiven. Saul's list of sins ran very deep, and he knew that, but what that did is magnify God's mercy and grace in his life. He knew he didn't deserve to be saved and forgiven—nobody does. His actions were born out of his ignorance and unbelief, but he received God's mercy, which means he didn't get what he deserved to get from God—punishment. He received the grace of the Lord Jesus Christ, which is unmerited favor—a gift. The grace of the Lord was his salvation, and being called into his service as an apostle to the Gentiles. He was amazed that Christ would commission him as an apostle, for he considered himself to be the least of the apostles because of the fact that he persecuted the church (1 Cor 15:9).

When you contrast Saul's sins with the grace and mercy of God they are polar opposites. What stood out in Saul's mind was that he was an undeserving object of God's mercy and grace. He recognizes that Christ's mission in coming to the earth was to save sinners, and he identifies himself as the foremost of sinners because of his persecution of the church. The gravity of his sin points out the gravity of God's mercy and forgiveness, except God's mercy always runs deeper than our sins. The Lord used Saul's life as an example to others of his patience, mercy, and forgiveness.

When people consider Saul's life they see the depth of God's love and mercy to even the worst of sinners. Saul understood that his life can be a source of encouragement to those who need forgiveness. People will often view themselves in a negative way and think that God would never forgive them, thinking that they are beyond hope, even with God. Perhaps, they have gone through a painful divorce and it was their fault. Maybe they're in the death grip of a serious addiction and can't break free from it. Perhaps, they've had a failed business adventure and lost everything. Maybe they're in jail doing hard time for a serious crime they've committed. Whatever the sin(s) may be, if God can forgive Saul for putting Christians to death he can forgive anybody for their sins.

Saul understood that his life was a picture of God's mercy that he willingly extends to all people who will place their faith in Jesus for the forgiveness of their sins. As Saul considers the depth of love and mercy the Lord Jesus extended to him, he ends this section of Scripture by breaking out into a doxology of praise:

Now to the King eternal, immortal, invisible, the only God, *be* honor and glory forever and ever. Amen. (1 Timothy 1:17)

Saul speaks of the transcendent qualities of God rather than the immanent qualities that describe Jesus in coming to earth to save sinners (vv. 12-16). That contrast is what makes this doxology so meaningful. In God's transcendence he is the eternally existing King who governs the universe. He is immortal which means that he isn't subject to destruction, or corruption. He exists in the invisible realm of the spiritual dimension. He alone is the only God, which affirms monotheism as one of the basic tenants of the Christian faith. As the only God he alone is worthy of honor and glory to be given him by those whom he created for all eternity. Saul presents God in high and lofty terms, which brings to the surface God's transcendent attributes.

Saul is grateful to God, the high and lofty one, for sending his son to become one with humanity and offer himself as the sacrifice for the sins of mankind. It was through Jesus' death and resurrection that Saul received grace, mercy, patience, forgiveness, faith and love. Thus we see Saul contrasting the transcendence of God with the immanent ministry of his Son in coming into the world to save sinners, of which Paul considers himself to be the foremost because he persecuted the church. In summary, Saul praises God for sending his only begotten Son to die for the sins of mankind and offer forgiveness to those who believe.

Cleansing a Guilty Conscience

When Saul thinks about his past, yes, there were times when guilt lingered in his conscience, but accompanying his guilt was a heightened sense of God's mercy and grace. These are the things that believers' in Christ should be thinking about in coming to grips with their past. Own your sins, confess them before God and others (if necessary), and bask in the knowledge of God's forgiveness and grace. Think about God's mercy and let your conscience be cleansed from guilt (1 John 1:9).

Part of walking in the freedom that Christ offers is being freed from guilt. Christ's sacrifice was sufficient to atone for all our sins, not just a few of them. Whatever guilt you may be carrying in your conscience, understand that when you become a believer in Christ all your sins are forgiven. Jesus died for the sins that may be infecting your conscience, and he doesn't want you to be carrying that burden of guilt.

We know that guilt can be a powerful tool of Satan, who constantly accuses God's people (Rev 12:10). Satan doesn't want believers to walk in God's grace and be freed from a guilty conscience. Guilt can also be the product of the human mind as well, as we fail to appreciate God's forgiveness in our lives. We don't believe that God will forgive us, or that Christ wants us to be free from guilt, so we don't appropriate the forgiveness that Christ died to give us.

The Holy Spirit convicts people of their sins, not to lay a guilt trip on them and make them feel miserable. Rather, he brings conviction of sin to people so that they will confess their sins and receive God's forgiveness and a cleansed conscience. Guilt trips are of the enemy, not from God.

Conclusion

Saul wrestled with his past throughout his life, just as many of us do, but at the end of the day he always stood on God's love and mercy that was displayed to him. That is where each of us should end up as well. We all have some skeletons in our closets. There are things each person has done that they wish they could take back, but can't. Whatever things you've done that you regret, remember, Jesus died for those mistakes and wants you to walk in freedom from guilt.

Chapter 33 ~ Into the Gentile World

As Saul of Tarsus began his travels in the Gentile world he is identified by his Greek name Paul. Christ commissioned him as an apostle to the Gentiles so he would naturally travel extensively outside of Jerusalem and Judea, and mingle with Gentiles. In order for Paul to interact with Gentiles he would have to divest himself of his strict Pharisaic legalism. If he didn't, how could he interact with Gentiles—the very people he is trying to reach with the gospel? As a Pharisee he wouldn't be caught dead in the house of a Gentile. He couldn't try to impose on the Gentiles the ancestral traditions that the Pharisees and scribes advocated. Paul needed to reinvent himself so he could function as the apostle to the Gentiles.

It doesn't seem that Paul had much difficulty doing this. The issue that the early church had to deal with was what to do with the Gentiles that are becoming disciples' of Christ regarding the Law. Do they have to be circumcised, observe the Sabbath, and the dietary codes in the Law of Moses? In other words, do Gentiles have to become Jewish to be saved? Is it faith in Christ plus keeping the law that is required for one's salvation? The Jewish believers were amazed that God gave the Holy Spirit to Gentiles when they believed in Jesus as the Messiah (e.g., Acts 10).

As Paul spread the gospel he did battle against false teachers that took the position that Gentiles had to become Jewish in order to be saved. Paul took exception to that position and made it clear throughout his entire ministry that the only thing required for one's salvation is faith and repentance in Jesus Christ, and that's it. Many of the Jews who became Christians remained in their Jewish context and continued to practice many of the Jewish traditions they had all their lives. Many of them couldn't break free of those practices, even though they believed in Christ. Other Jews who became Christians seem to have been able to break free from the limitations imposed upon them by

Jewish traditions, which enabled them to mingle with Gentiles with relative ease.

For example, Acts 11 records for us how the word of God was spreading to the Gentiles and they were becoming believers in Christ. The apostles and others in Judea heard reports coming back to them about this. Peter returned to Jerusalem after visiting with Cornelius and was confronted by the circumcised believers in Christ. Their objection to Peter's visit to Cornelius was: "You went to uncircumcised men and ate with them" (Acts 11:3). Peter violated a cultural taboo because Jews didn't go into the home of a Gentile and eat with them, which is why they objected to Peter's visit to Cornelius. They couldn't bear the thought of the Gentiles coming into the church, or imagine themselves mingling with unclean Gentiles. Torah observing Jews just didn't go into the home of a Gentile and eat with them! This shows us how great the barrier was between Jews and Gentiles in the First Century.

Peter recounted the vision that God game him to show that all food and people are clean. The Spirit instructed him to go with the men Cornelius dispatched without any misgivings (Acts 11:12). When Peter arrived at Cornelius' house he shared the gospel with them, but before he finished his sermon the Holy Spirit fell upon them in the same way the Spirit fell upon the Jews on the day of Pentecost. Peter concluded that God was giving the same gift of the Spirit to the Gentiles as he gave to the believing Jews, so he wouldn't stand in the way of what God was doing with the Gentiles. After Peter shared his experience with the people Luke records for us the following: "When they heard this, they quieted down and glorified God, saying, "Well then, God has granted to the Gentiles also the repentance *that leads* to life" (Acts 11:18).

The circumcised believers seem to have changed their position about the Gentiles after hearing Peter relate to them how the Spirit was given to the Gentiles, so they glorify God because of it. It was extremely difficult for the Jews to break out of their legalistic mold and be OK with the Gentiles coming into the church on the same terms as they were. In other words, they had to understand that the playing field is now leveled, and God accepts all people through their faith in Christ, regardless of one's race, color, ethnicity, nationality, language, and so on. It was earth shattering for the Jews to understand that God was giving the Spirit to the Gentiles, and they were no longer to be viewed as unclean second-class citizens.

The Church at Antioch

The church at Antioch goes down in history as being the first cross-cultural church where Jews and Gentiles worship the Lord Jesus together. How did this happen? During the stoning of Stephen and the great persecution that broke out against the church the Christians had to leave Jerusalem. They were scattered, which resulted in a divine church-planting program. Luke records how the gospel spread in Acts 11:19-26:

So then those who were scattered because of the persecution that occurred in connection with Stephen made their way to Phoenicia and Cyprus and Antioch, speaking the word to no one except to Jews alone. [20]But there were some of them, men of Cyprus and Cyrene, who came to Antioch and *began* speaking to the Greeks also, preaching the Lord Jesus. [21]And the hand of the Lord was with them, and a large number who believed turned to the Lord. [22]The news about them reached the ears of the church at Jerusalem, and they sent Barnabas off to Antioch. [23]Then when he arrived and witnessed the grace of God, he rejoiced and *began* to encourage them all with resolute heart to remain *true* to the Lord; [24]for he was a good man, and full of the Holy Spirit and of faith. And considerable numbers were brought to the Lord. [25]And he left for Tarsus to look for Saul; [26]and when he had found him, he brought him to Antioch. And for an entire year they met with the church and taught considerable numbers; and the disciples were first called Christians in Antioch.

As the believers were scattered due to the persecution some went to Phoenicia, Cyprus, and Antioch, but shared the gospel with Jews only. This should not surprise anybody because of the negative attitudes Jews employed toward Gentiles. However, there were some believers that began to share the gospel with Greeks—Gentiles—and the results were astounding! Great numbers of Gentiles were turning to Christ such that it was obvious the Lord's hand was with them. How was it that some had the liberty to share the gospel with Gentiles, and others did not? Those who shared the gospel with Gentiles had the liberty to step out of the box of their legalist cultural traditions, and go against the grain of what their religion and culture told them not to do. This took tremendous courage and enlightenment for these Jews to share the gospel with Gentiles. This is a watershed moment for these Jews to evangelize Gentiles, worship with them, visit them in their homes, and eat with them.

Some of the Jewish Christians couldn't step out of their legalistic box and continued to observe all the traditions they did before they became followers of Christ. Others had the understanding that God was doing something totally new, and had little or no problem at all stepping away from the legalistic practices they were indoctrinated with since childhood. That they were Jews living outside of Jerusalem, and more familiar with Gentile culture, probably made it easier for them to speak to the Gentiles, but nonetheless it was a monumental step for them to reach out to the Gentiles.

When news of what God was doing in Antioch reached the apostles in Jerusalem they sent Barnabas, who was a Jew from Cyprus of the tribe of Levi, to examine the situation and report back to them. Barnabas was known as the Son of Encouragement, and was held in high regard by all the people. He saw evidence of the grace of God in the Antiochian church as people were getting saved, Gentiles and Jews were worshiping together, and lives were being transformed so he encouraged them to remain true to the Lord. However, with all the new converts that were coming into the church he realized that he was in over his head. He needed some help and he knew just the man who could help the church be established and lay a foundation for the new believers there. He went off to Tarsus to find Paul and brought him back to Antioch, so together they taught the disciples for one year. They made a great team with Barnabas as an encourager, and Paul as a teacher. They seem to have complimentary gifts and personalities, so God continued to bless their work and more people are coming into the church.

Paul and Barnabas appear to have had no difficulty mingling with Gentiles. Saul being a Pharisee, who strictly observed the law and the traditions, doesn't appear to be conflicted about being with Gentiles in Antioch in any way shape or form. It seems as though Paul is liberated! The church in Antioch was founded about seven years after the day of Pentecost. That Paul is able to do this is amazing! Paul never seemed to struggle with stepping outside the box of his legalistic Pharisaic past. The reason for this must be that he had a great teacher.

Paul's Gospel

Paul made it clear to the Galatians that the gospel he preached wasn't something he or somebody else invented. It wasn't of human origin. He stated this in Galatians 1:11-12:

For I would have you know, brethren, that the gospel which was preached by me is not according to man. ¹²For I neither received it from man, nor was I taught it, but *I received it* through a revelation of Jesus Christ.

Paul received the gospel directly from the Lord Jesus. We have to assume the Lord imparted to him one of the primary aspects of his teaching: by the works of the law no one will be justified (Gal 2:16). The Lord must have made it clear to him that the Gentiles don't have to be placed under the burden of the law, which the Jews themselves couldn't keep. Righteousness would not be found in one's ability to keep the law, but through faith in Christ. The Lord made it clear to him that if he was going into the Gentile world he would have to be freed from his Jewish scruples and live like a Gentile.

I never see a place in Scripture where Paul struggled with this. He seems to have gone through an immediate emancipation from his Pharisaic roots, which ran pretty deep. Peter went backwards and dragged Barnabas along with him in Antioch, but Paul seems to have straightened out the situation there (Gal 2:11-14). It appears that the Lord Jesus thoroughly taught Paul about the freedom that is inherent in the gospel that he preached. If Paul hadn't understood this about

318

the gospel he would have been a monumental failure as an apostle to the Gentiles. The Lord taught him well! Paul's transformation away from legalism is nothing short of amazing.

Paul would do battle against those who advocated the false gospel of faith in Christ plus adherence to the Law of Moses. Paul never backed down from the false teachers, which gives you an idea of how firm in his convictions he was. Given his Pharisaic background one would think it would have been easy for Paul to adopt the position, along with the Judaizers, that one needs to become Jewish along with faith in Christ to be saved, but he didn't go there. He never caved in because of peer pressure like Peter and Barnabas did, instead he always held his ground and never gave an inch to those who opposed him and his gospel.

The Jerusalem Council

A critical moment in the church came about when the leaders in Jerusalem had to figure out what to do about the large numbers of Gentiles that were becoming believers in Christ. Some people took the position that they had to be circumcised according to the Law of Moses to be saved (Acts 15:1). In other words, they had to become Jewish proselytes first. Jews who had devoted themselves to keeping God's law and the ancestral traditions found it disturbing that Gentiles were becoming Christians and were on equal footing with them. Perhaps, they felt it wasn't fair that Gentiles could bypass stepping over the threshold of Judaism, fearing that with increasing numbers of Gentiles coming into the church that they would loose their culture, traditions, and influence.

Paul and Barnabas went to Jerusalem to confer with the apostles and elders about this issue. This meeting came be known as the Jerusalem Council, which occurred around 50 A.D. Its importance can't be minimized, for the decision that was made would have severe consequences for future generations of Christians. The apostles, elders, Pharisees who had believed in Christ, Paul, Barnabas, Peter, and James were in attendance. I wish I could have witnessed the

319

debate that took place among these spiritual heavy weights, for there was much at stake here.

The Pharisees wanted the Gentiles to keep the law, but Peter chimed in and said the Gentiles are receiving the Spirit in the same way that we Jews did, thus making no distinction between Jews and Gentiles (Acts 15:8-9). What Peter says next is an amazing statement:

Now therefore why do you put God to the test by placing upon the neck of the disciples a yoke which neither our fathers nor we have been able to bear? (Acts 15:10)

Peter seems to have won the day with his statement. Why place Gentile believers under the oppressive yoke of the law when neither we, nor our ancestors were able to keep it. What right do we have to place Gentiles under the law when God does not require that of them? No doubt, Peter thought of his meeting with Cornelius and his household when they received the Spirit without being circumcised, or performing any other ritual (Acts 10:44-48). It isn't necessary because people are saved solely by the grace of the Lord Jesus (Acts 15:10). Paul and Barnabas told the council stories of how God was doing signs and wonders among the Gentiles.

It seems as though James (the Lord's brother) had the final word, and was the recognized leader of the early church. The issue of Gentile inclusion in the church had been settled. They were under no obligation to keep the Law of Moses, get circumcised, or obey any other ritual to be saved, for salvation was entirely of grace. However, James was concerned about how Jews and Gentiles could have fellowship if Gentiles were doing things that were terribly offensive to Jews. They wrote a letter and had it delivered by Paul, Barnabas, Judas, and Silas to the churches in Antioch, Syria, and Cilicia. The decision of the council presented four things that Gentiles were to abstain from, which are found in vv. 28-29:

"For it seemed good to the Holy Spirit and to us to lay upon you no greater burden than these essentials: 29that you abstain from things sacrificed to idols and from blood and from things strangled and

from fornication; if you keep yourselves free from such things, you will do well. Farewell."

The first is "abstaining from things sacrificed to idols." This is a reference to meat sacrificed to a pagan god, then sold in local markets. Idolatry was highly offensive to Jews and considered to be blasphemous. There are many prohibitions in Scripture against idolatry (Ex 20:3; 34:17; Deu 5:7), and the practice of idolatry was one of the contributing factors to the destruction of the nation (2 Kings 17:7-8; 2 Chron 36:14-16). For Jews to eat meat that was sacrificed to idols would be repulsive. There is no way that Jews would sit at the table and eat meat sacrificed to idols with Gentile believers. Nor would they sit at the table with their Gentile brothers and watch them eat meat that was sacrificed to idols. Later, Paul would deal with this issue in more detail in his letter to the Corinthians (1 Cor 8:1-13). If the Gentile believers would continue this practice it would be a barrier to fellowship and keep Jews and Gentiles divided.

The second and third practices that Gentiles should abstain from are: "blood and from things strangled." These prohibitions refer to the way animals are killed and meat was cooked. In the dietary laws of the Old Testament, it was prohibited to eat any animal unless the blood was completely drained. If the animal was strangled the blood had to be completely drained before it could be consumed (Lev 17:13-14; 18:6-30). If Gentiles ate meat without having the blood drained, there is no way that Jews would join them in table fellowship, for that, too, is a repulsive sinful practice to them.

The fourth prohibition was from fornication, which, no doubt, refers to pagan worship practices. It was common practice to visit temple prostitutes and have ritual sex, and participate in orgies. This practice was to cease, as Gentiles became believers in Christ. This was a moral issue as well, for sexual relations are only to occur between a husband and wife.

James put forth these four things required of Gentiles that became Christians, so that barriers could be removed between Jew and Gentile believers paving the way for them to have good fellowship. He realized that if the Gentiles would not be sensitive to Jewish scruples there would be massive offensives they would bear against Gentiles that would fracture and divide the two groups. For these reasons he wanted the Gentiles to be sensitive to their Jewish brothers regarding the preparation of food for the sake of unity in the church.

This wasn't a matter of how one gets saved; it was a practical matter of removing offensives so that two culturally distinct groups, Jews and Gentiles, can have fellowship together. The amazing thing is that Paul, and the others, didn't want to place the burden of the law on Gentiles. If ever they had a chance to do so it would have been in the Jerusalem Council, but they didn't go there.

The decision of the Council is utterly amazing to me because when considering the 613 commandments in the Old Testament, and the host of ancestral traditions, there are only four things the Gentiles are to do in coming into the body of Christ. Three of them regarding the preparation of food are concessions to their Jewish brothers. The only moral issue is abstaining from fornication, although that was also attached to the worship of pagan gods.

It is fair to conclude the Jerusalem Council made it easy for the Gentiles to become part of the church. The decision of the leaders reflects their own experience regarding their inability to comply with the Law of Moses and the ancestral traditions, as well as understanding that righteousness is found through faith in Christ not keeping the Law. This is an epochal moment in the life of the church, for they could have easily decided to impose the Law on Gentile converts, in which case it would have been disastrous.

Conclusion

When I consider the hoops to jump through in joining a local church in my neighborhood, there are usually far more requirements than what the Jerusalem Council placed on the Gentiles. Some of the requirements to join a church may include: filling out a membership application, having references checked, having a background check, sharing your testimony, being baptized, agreeing with the churches' statement of faith, agreeing to support the church financially, agreeing to serve in some capacity, agreeing to not be divisive, agreeing to participate in church meetings, agreeing to regular attendance, attend for a minimum period of time before becoming a member, and in some churches even more things may be required. The decision of the council shows how emancipated the leaders were from the Law and their ancestral traditions, which is utterly amazing.

Paul's emancipation from his Pharisaic roots is incredible. It may be difficult for the modern reader to appreciate how deeply ingrained the ancestral traditions were in people like Paul. With God's help he was able to strip the layers of legalism off himself, so that he could be effective ministering to the Gentiles. Additionally, he discovered what true righteousness was all about, which was the path of his liberation. Righteousness isn't found in keeping the law, it is found apart from the law in the gospel of Christ. It isn't a righteousness of his own doing; it is a righteousness that is given to all who believe. Paul wrote about this glorious truth in Romans 3:21-24:

But now apart from the law the righteousness of God has been made known, to which the Law and the Prophets testify. [22]This righteousness is given through faith in Jesus Christ to all who believe. There is no difference between Jew and Gentile, [23]for all have sinned and fall short of the glory of God, [24]and all are justified freely by his grace through the redemption that came by Christ Jesus.

This amazing discovery that Paul made about righteousness being apart from the law was a watershed moment for the apostle. This understanding of righteousness led to Paul's renunciation of the things that he cherished as a Pharisaic Jew, which will be discussed in the next chapter.

Chapter 34 ~ Paul's Renunciation

In the Philippians passage about to be evaluated, Paul writes his resume about his life as a Pharisee, which gives us some insights into how his worldview changed when he became a Christian. He is warning the Philippians to be cautious of those who advocate a false gospel of faith in Christ plus circumcision for salvation. There may be those who would show up in the Philippian church and teach the Gentiles that they needed to be circumcised to be truly saved. For Paul that was a false gospel, and he would have none of that.

To show the Philippians the futility of that viewpoint he directs their attention to his life before he became a Christian, living as a strict Torah observant Pharisee. Nobody was more zealous in keeping the law then Paul, but he discovered that Pharisaic Judaism was a failed system. Righteousness derived from keeping the law was inadequate for one's salvation. In essence, Paul is saying don't let false teachers con you with a false gospel that says you have to become Jewish to be saved. Paul's word to them is: "I've been there done that, and it doesn't work." Thus Paul is presenting himself as exhibit A to the Philippians to show them the futility of adhering to that theological system.

Paul discusses his life as a strict Torah observing Pharisee and renounces all the things that were badges of honor for him before he became a believer in Christ. In doing this Paul gives his readers an insight into how he was able to break out of the legalistic box he grew up in. He saw Pharisee-ism as an ineffective religious system that didn't accomplish the objective of making one right with God. Following is an evaluation of Philippians 3:1-11:

Finally, my brethren, rejoice in the Lord. To write the same things *again* is no trouble to me, and it is a safeguard for you. [2]Beware of the dogs, beware of the evil workers, beware of the false circumcision; [3]for we are the *true* circumcision, who worship in the

Spirit of God and glory in Christ Jesus and put no confidence in the flesh, [4]although I myself might have confidence even in the flesh. If anyone else has a mind to put confidence in the flesh, I far more: [5]circumcised the eighth day, of the nation of Israel, of the tribe of Benjamin, a Hebrew of Hebrews; as to the Law, a Pharisee; [6]as to zeal, a persecutor of the church; as to the righteousness which is in the Law, found blameless.

[7]But whatever things were gain to me, those things I have counted as loss for the sake of Christ. [8]More than that, I count all things to be loss in view of the surpassing value of knowing Christ Jesus my Lord, for whom I have suffered the loss of all things, and count them but rubbish so that I may gain Christ, [9]and may be found in Him, not having a righteousness of my own derived from *the* Law, but that which is through faith in Christ, the righteousness which *comes* from God on the basis of faith, [10]that I may know Him and the power of His resurrection and the fellowship of His sufferings, being conformed to His death; [11]in order that I may attain to the resurrection from the dead.

Rejoicing in the Lord is one of the dominant themes in Philippians (v. 1). Joy for a believer in Christ isn't based on circumstances. It is based on the relationship that he has with Jesus. Therefore, even in the most dire circumstances of life believers can have joy filling their hearts because they know Christ. The joy believers have is a spiritual, inner type of satisfaction rooted in knowing that they are right with God through Jesus, and will be with him for all eternity. The joy believers have is a fruit of the Spirit (Gal 5:22) and a precious gift that is imparted to all Christians.

One of the things that can threaten the joy that is inherent in the gospel is false teaching. If a believer is derailed because he embraces a false gospel, like that of the Judaizers, that can rob him of joy and pose a threat to his spiritual life. Paul doesn't want that to happen to the Philippians so he offers a warning:

To write the same things *again* is no trouble to me, and it is a safeguard for you. [2]Beware of the dogs, beware of the evil workers, beware of the false circumcision; (Phil 3:1b-2)

Paul has been battling false teachers for over a decade, so he is diligent in making sure he protects his churches from being infected with a diseased gospel. He must have mentioned this to them previously but, like any good pastor he wants to make sure they get it, so he reminds them once again of the threat false teachers pose. His language to describe them is not complimentary, to say the least.

He warns the Philippians to "beware of the dogs." This is a highly pejorative term because dogs were considered to be unclean, Gentiles were often referred to as dogs, and few people had dogs that were household pets in Bible days. Dogs were used in herding sheep, but most dogs were scavengers that roamed the streets looking for food, were mean, and often diseased. Perhaps, the Judaizers were trying to make the Gentile dogs clean through circumcision, but Paul, using a twist of irony, says the Judaizers are the unclean dogs to be avoided, not the Gentiles.

Paul issues another command to "beware of the evil workers." By urging the Gentiles to practice the works of the law the false teachers prove themselves to be "evil workers." They are advocating a religious system that is ineffective and they present themselves as those who are of the flesh rather than the Spirit. They are not spiritually minded, they are earthly minded. Steering people away from the true gospel is the work of evildoers.

The third command Paul issues is to "beware of the false circumcision." The Greek word *katatomé* is translated by the NASB "false circumcision," but a more literal translation of the word is "mutilation." A great source of pride to Jews was circumcision because it was a sign of being incorporated into the covenant community. Every male child was circumcised on the eighth day. When this Jewish practice contradicts the gospel it becomes nothing more than a worthless ritual similar to the rituals that the Gentiles practice in their pagan religions. The false teachers presented circumcision as a requirement for salvation, which is a view that Paul adamantly opposes. The fact that the Judaizers take this position is an indication that they aren't part of God's people. It's as if they are the new Gentiles, while the Christians, whether of Jewish or Gentile backgrounds, are the true Jews (Ro 2:28-29). If the Gentile Christians were to adopt Jewish rituals as a requirement for salvation it would be no different than practicing their pre-Christian pagan rituals, and being enslaved by them (Gal 4:9). By using the term mutilation Paul may be alluding to some of the Gentile pagan religious practices, but it is better to see Paul indicating that when circumcision is practiced with the intention of gaining God's favor it is nothing more than a meaningless ritual, like mutilating the flesh.

Paul has issued three warnings to the Philippians to keep their spiritual guard up and not be directed off course by any teaching offered by the Judaizers that contradicts the true gospel.

for we are the *true* circumcision, who worship in the Spirit of God and glory in Christ Jesus and put no confidence in the flesh. (Philippians 3:3)

In contrast to the false teachers Paul says, "we are the true circumcision." In the New Testament circumcision isn't regarded as an external physical ritual, rather it is a spiritual event that occurs when someone becomes a believer in Christ (Rom 2:28-29; Col 2:11). Circumcision is of the heart, done by the Spirit (Rom 2:29), and circumcision is described as something that happens not by human hands: "and in Him you were also circumcised with a circumcision made without hands, in the removal of the body of the flesh by the circumcision of Christ" (Col 2:11).

Even in the Pentateuch circumcision is referred to as something much more than a mere ritual. Moses describes circumcision as a spiritual quality in the following passages in Deuteronomy:

> So circumcise your heart, and stiffen your neck no longer. (Deu 10:16)

> Moreover the LORD your God will circumcise your heart and the heart of your descendants, to love the LORD your God with all your heart and with all your soul, so that you may live. (Deu 30:6)

One can't help seeing an allusion to the future outpouring of the Spirit in the New Covenant era in the above passages. The teaching of spiritual circumcision was in seed form in the Old Covenant. Today's believer has experienced a spiritual circumcision not made by human hands, but is of the heart; hence Paul describes Christians as "the true circumcision."

One characteristic of the true circumcision is that they are those "who worship in the Spirit of God." Christians have the Holy Spirit living inside them. One can't be a Christian without the Spirit of God resident in their hearts (Rom 8:8-9; 1 Cor 6:19). Christians worship God in the realm of the Holy Spirit, which enables them to offer worship that is pleasing to him (Rom 12:1).

Another characteristic of the Christian is they: "glory in Christ Jesus." The Christian's boast or glory is in all that Jesus has done for him. Paul boasted only about Christ's work on the cross (Gal 6:14). Christians give all glory to God and are to avoid any self-boasting, self-exaltation, or pride in one's self-righteousness. Such boasting goes against the humility that believers are to display.

Paul gives more meaning to what it means to "glory in Christ Jesus" when it is viewed in contrast with the next phrase: "and put no confidence in the flesh." There are two spiritual realms of existence that one can be part of. One is being "in the Spirit" which is the realm of existence that all Christians live in. The other is "in the flesh" which is the spiritual realm that all nonbelievers exist in. These two realms are mutually exclusive, for one can't live in both places at the same time, and they are totally incompatible. Those who live in the Spirit glory in Christ Jesus, while those who live in the flesh do not glory in Christ. Those in the flesh, like the Judaizers, place their confidence in everything outside of Christ, which leaves only their own human achievements, accomplishments, rituals like circumcision, and their own self-righteousness to boast about.

Christians "put no confidence in the flesh" because it gives them no spiritual advantage with God whatsoever. Silva observes that:

The circumcision of the flesh, as preached by the Judaizers, became for Paul the symbol of a total mindset that is opposed to the Spirit and leads to death (Rom 8:5-8; Gal 5:16-21). (Silva, p. 149)

Paul's Renunciation of his Spiritual Achievements

How was it that Paul was able to breakout of his Pharisaic box of legalism so that he could interact with Gentiles and tell them about Jesus? Paul will now share from his own life about how he was able to make a monumental shift in his theological thinking such that he began his journey to complete liberty in Christ.

If ever there was a person who put confidence in the flesh it was Saul of Tarsus. He has an impressive spiritual resume with plenty to boast about. He lists his achievements then renounces them because he came to see that, as a believer in Christ, they gave him no spiritual advantage before God. It was this realization that enabled Paul to go through such a radical transformation to being a liberated believer.

It may be that Judaizers appeared in Philippi and were boasting in their spiritual credentials as Jews, to sway the people to their false gospel. Paul's spiritual credentials will blow the Judaizers away, for Paul's resume of spiritual achievements are far more impressive than his opponents'.

although I myself might have confidence even in the flesh. If anyone else has a mind to put confidence in the flesh, I far more: ⁵circumcised the eighth day, of the nation of Israel, of the tribe of Benjamin, a Hebrew of Hebrews; as to the Law, a Pharisee; ⁶as to zeal, a persecutor of the church; as to the righteousness which is in the Law, found blameless. (Phil 3:4-6)

Paul has a lot to brag about, that is, if he wants to. Few people could come even remotely close to matching Paul's credentials, so he begins his list of spiritual trophies that he could take pride in.

Trophy #1: Paul Was Circumcised

He was circumcised on the eighth day. He was a born into a Jewish family and was circumcised long before he or the Judaizers ever heard about Jesus. The Judaizers advocated that the Gentile believers in Christ should be circumcised so they can be identified with God's people in keeping with the Abrahamic covenant (Gen 17:13-14). Circumcision was the primary issue with the false teachers, so Paul begins his list with this item.

Trophy #2: Paul Was An Israelite

Paul is an Israelite by birth, which distinguishes him from proselytes—converts to Judaism—that are often viewed as second-class citizens. The Judaizers were hoping that the Gentile believers would share in the blessing of becoming part of God's covenant people by being circumcised. Paul was part of God's covenant people from birth.

Trophy #3: Paul Was of the Tribe of Benjamin

Paul could trace his family origins to the tribe of Benjamin. Gentile converts could just become Israelites, but couldn't identify with a specific tribe. It was the tribe of Benjamin that bears the distinction of setting forth Saul who served as Israel's first King. This tribe is referred to as, "beloved by the Lord" (Deu 33:12) as Moses was blessing the tribes before his death. Benjamin alone remained loyal to the Davidic covenant by siding with Judah, which constituted the Southern Kingdom. Paul could have pride in being part of this tribe for they had an illustrious history.

During the years of exile many Jews of different tribes intermarried, which made it difficult to trace one's tribal origin. By Paul's day many Jews didn't know which tribe they descended from, but Paul's family remained pure Benjamites. In all probability some of the Judaizers didn't know what tribe they were part of, which elevated Paul above them.

The first three trophies were Paul's by way of birth, for he did nothing to receive these honors.   The last four reflect Paul's personal achievements.

Trophy #4: Paul is a Hebrew of Hebrews

Paul couldn't be any more Jewish than he was.   He was of pure Hebrew stock and as he grew into his adult years he maintained his Jewish heritage.   Paul was born in Tarsus, which is located in Asia Minor not Israel.   Many of the Jews who lived outside of Israel in the Diaspora became Hellenized Jews, which means that they became assimilated into Greco-Roman culture.   Paul did not do that.   He remained true to the ancestral traditions, spoke Hebrew, and went to Jerusalem to study under the highly esteemed rabbi Gamaliel.   Paul was so committed to walking in his Jewish heritage that he could confidently assert: "all Jews know my manner of life from my youth up, which from the beginning was spent among my *own* nation and at Jerusalem" (Acts 26:4).   Few people could match Paul's devotion to his Jewish heritage, so for these reasons Paul considered himself to be a Hebrew of Hebrews.

Trophy #5: Paul Was a Pharisee

This was a sect in Judaism that prided themselves in studying the law and being the guardians of the ancestral traditions.   When Paul says "as to the law," he is talking about not only the word of God but also the oral traditions that accompanied it and provided commentary on the same.   To be a Pharisee one must be extremely devoted to strict observance of the law, which Paul testified to by calling himself a "Pharisee, a son of Pharisees" (Acts 23:6), and "I lived as a Pharisee according to the strictest sect of our religion" (Acts 26:5).   Paul asserted that he was advancing beyond his contemporaries because he was extremely zealous for the ancestral traditions (Gal 1:14).   No doubt Paul took pride in being a Pharisee, which was a sect of Judaism that may not have had large numbers of adherents, but they were very influential in their culture, being held in high regard by the people.   If the Judaizers thought they were devoted to the Torah and oral traditions, Paul's level of devotion far exceeded theirs.

Trophy #6: As to Zeal, a Persecutor of the Church

Paul wasn't just zealous he was fanatically zealous. The danger of fanatics is that they often go to extremes. In their love for God and passionate devotion to him, fanatics often end up hating everything that stands in opposition to them. Paul's zeal was way off course and misguided such that he hated Christ and his church, persecuting them to the death. He testified to how he persecuted the church beyond measure and tried to destroy it (Gal 1:13). He was in full agreement with the stoning of Stephen (Acts 8:1) and seems to be the instigator of the mass persecution that broke out in Jerusalem on the same day of Stephen's death (Acts 8:1-3). He was on a search and destroy mission to rid the planet of believer's in Christ (Acts 26:9-11). Paul's level of zeal went way beyond that of his opponents, in spite of the fact that it was wrong and misguided. The Judaizers, in their zeal, just tried to convert Gentile Christians, but Paul took it a step-or-two further and persecuted Jews who became Christians to the death.

Trophy #7: As to the Righteousness Which is in the Law, Found Blameless.

To what degree did Paul observe the law and the oral traditions? He kept the law in all its minutest details such that he considered himself righteous and blameless. His conformity to the outward code of keeping the law was impressive, to say the least. He kept the Sabbath regulations, dietary codes, laws about ritual cleanness, and everything else scrupulously. Righteousness refers to his behavior in keeping the law, not imputed righteousness, or being in a right standing with God through Christ. Paul is talking about his own ability to keep the law and he knew he was good at it. This is not to suggest that Paul walked in sinless perfection, he's saying that he lived an exemplary life as a Jew similar to Zacharias and Elizabeth (Luke 1:6). Few Jews could come even remotely close to matching Paul in his strict Torah observance, especially the Judaizers that were opposing him.

Paul has just listed his spiritual trophies, which are things that he was, no doubt, proud of as a Pharisaic Jew. In his life before he became a Christian these are the trophies he acquired, some by way of birth, others by way of hard work, but any Jew would be proud of these accomplishments. He later came to regret his persecution of the church and realized that his zeal was misguided, but his zeal for God far exceeded that of the Judaizers. After stating his impressive list of spiritual trophies he will now make a 180-degree reversal and renounces every one of them.

But whatever things were gain to me, those things I have counted as loss for the sake of Christ. ⁸More than that, I count all things to be loss in view of the surpassing value of knowing Christ Jesus my Lord, for whom I have suffered the loss of all things, and count them but rubbish so that I may gain Christ, ⁹and may be found in Him, not having a righteousness of my own derived from *the* Law, but that which is through faith in Christ, the righteousness which *comes* from God on the basis of faith, ¹⁰that I may know Him and the power of His resurrection and the fellowship of His sufferings, being conformed to His death; ¹¹in order that I may attain to the resurrection from the dead. (Philippians 3:7-11)

Paul is speaking metaphorically as an accountant. He makes a ledger and has a profit and loss column. The seven trophies that were gain or profit to him as a Pharisee, that he took great pride in, he now sees as loss. In other words, the trophies that Paul valued so much he now sees as spiritual liabilities, or deficits that put him in the red with God. The reason for his reversal is that he came to see that his trophies did nothing to impress God, or help him secure a right standing with him. All his accomplishments blinded him from his need to acknowledge his own sinfulness, and depend on God for forgiveness. Paul could very well be alluding to Isa 64:6, where it says, "all our righteous deeds are like filthy rags." Paul came to see that his personal righteousness, or self-righteousness derived from keeping the law was of no value to God, in fact, his righteous works were repulsive to the Lord.

Reflecting on his former life in Judaism Paul "counts all things to be loss" when compared to "the surpassing value of knowing Christ Jesus my Lord" (v. 8). All Paul's personal achievements have been moved to the spiritual deficit column and pale in comparison to having a personal relationship with Christ. Knowing Christ is experiential knowledge not head knowledge, like the type one would acquire from reading a textbook. Paul gets intensely personal by calling Jesus "my Lord." Being a Christian is all about having a relationship with Jesus, and knowing him on an intimate level. Paul highly valued knowing Jesus such that he "counts all things to be loss" that he once valued in his former manner of life, because they did nothing to put him in God's favor.

Paul is so adamant about renouncing those things he once took pride in that he considers all his spiritual trophies to be "rubbish so that I may gain Christ." The Greek word translated rubbish is *skubalon*, which also carries the meaning of waste, refuse, manure, or dung. Paul's choice of this word to describe how he feels about his former accomplishments reveals the depth of his reversal. He renounces all the things that he once took great pride in, and he now considers them to be a pile of dung. It's as if Paul is taking all his spiritual trophies that he acquired as a Pharisee and is throwing them in the manure pile. He has come to see that they are totally worthless before God and actually served as spiritual liabilities. His focus on his own ability to keep the law and be righteous in himself, he now understands left him spiritually bankrupt before God.

He realized he had to make this reversal in his thinking "in order that I may gain Christ." This indicates that Paul realized that to gain Christ there must be a reversal regarding the direction of his spiritual life. He couldn't depend on his ability to keep the law for his salvation, he had to renounce that spiritual path and place his trust in Christ. Becoming a Christian requires a total departure from all things that stand in the way, or compete with one's devotion to Christ. Paul came to see that his former manner of life stood as a polar opposite to his life in Christ—they were totally incompatible with each other. Paul made the right choice and only acceptable choice to God; he completely renounced his former spiritual path, threw his spiritual trophies in the manure pile, and completely devoted himself to Christ.

By placing his faith in Christ for his salvation Paul now has a groundbreaking understanding of righteousness:

and may be found in Him, not having a righteousness of my own derived from *the* Law, but that which is through faith in Christ, the

righteousness which *comes* from God on the basis of faith. (Philippians 3:9)

Paul has seen that his concept of righteousness derived from being a good person by keeping the law was deeply flawed, and would never earn God's favor. True righteousness comes from placing one's faith in Jesus and being justified by faith (Rom 1:16-17; 3:20-28; 5:1). He now realizes that "by the works of the law no one will be justified" (Rom 3:20; Gal 2:16). When the sinner places his faith in Christ God declares him righteous, which means he is in a right standing with his Maker, and Christ's righteousness is imputed to the new believer (Rom 4:22-25).

Our sins were placed on Jesus, or imputed to him as he hung on the cross. God punished Jesus for all the sins each of us have ever committed, as if he were guilty. Then God imputes or places the righteousness of Jesus on the believer, so we are perfectly righteous in God's eyes. We are not just forgiven—we are given Jesus' righteousness. This is the bedrock of the gospel.

John MacArthur makes an insightful comment:

> On the cross, God judged Jesus as if He had personally committed every sin ever committed by every person who ever truly believed. When a sinner embraces Jesus as Lord and trusts only in His sacrifice for sin, God treats that sinner as if he lived Christ's sinless life (cf. Isa 53:2; 2 Cor 5:21; 1 Peter 2:24). (MacArthur, p. 238):

Paul's concept of righteousness is completely different since he's known Christ. He lists other benefits of knowing Christ:

that I may know Him and the power of His resurrection and the fellowship of His sufferings, being conformed to His death; [11]in order that I may attain to the resurrection from the dead. (Philippians 3:10-11)

Paul's life-long pursuit was to deepen his knowledge of Christ and know him in a more profound way. Additionally, Paul wanted to know the power of Christ's resurrection. The believer is raised to newness of life in union with Jesus (Rom 6:4). There is resurrection power given to believers through his Spirit which enables her to live the Christian life that pleases God by overcoming temptations, serving him, witnessing for Christ, and being more like the Lord Jesus.

Another way in which Paul wants to know Christ is in "the fellowship of His sufferings, being conformed to His death." The new believer is conformed to Jesus' death when he places his trust in Christ. He has been liberated from the power of sin (Rom 6:6-7), but the believer continues to carry the death of Jesus in their own experience as they suffer hostile reactions from the world, spiritual disappointments, rejection, and so forth. Knowing Jesus involves knowing his sufferings. The gospel spreads through the suffering of God's people. It was through suffering on the cross that Jesus atoned for sin and offered a way by which people can be saved. Believers are called to be in fellowship with Christ's suffering throughout their life.

The last benefit of knowing Christ, and perhaps the greatest of all benefits is the resurrection of the body. The future resurrection of the body will certainly happen—it isn't just a remote possibility (1 Cor 15; 1 Thess 4:13-18). Paul has no doubt in his mind that he will participate in the resurrection of the body and be in the glorified state. He isn't expressing doubt about being resurrected; he is being humble and modest.

Conclusion

Paul has used the phrase "the surpassing value of knowing Christ Jesus my Lord" (v. 8). Looking at all the benefits of knowing Christ that Paul mentions, we can see why he threw all his Pharisaic trophies in the manure pile. This is what enabled Paul to step out of the Pharisaic box of legalism so that he could effectively travel in the Gentile world and interact with them? His recognition of Pharisaic Judaism as a failed system is what made him stand firm against the Judaizers' false teaching? This is why he never budged an inch in his statement: "by the works of the law no one will be justified."

The Philippians passage under consideration reveals how Paul came to see the spiritual bankruptcy and worthlessness of his former manner of life as a Pharisaic Jew, strictly observing the Torah and traditions to gain his salvation. It was that understanding that enabled him to make such a radical break in his pursuit of attaining his own righteousness, and trust in Christ to make him righteous. He came to understand that Pharisaic Judaism was a failed system that left its adherents spiritually bankrupt.

He was so deeply convicted of these truths that he never slipped back into the old way of doing things. His break from Pharisaic Judaism was total and complete. That's how he was able to step out of that mold and travel about the Gentile world sharing the Jesus story. His transformation was nothing short of amazing.

Talk about a legalist, Paul was one of the best. Few people alive today could come close to Paul's Legalistic behavior. One of the benefits of studying Paul's life is to see how he came to view his personal efforts to be righteous as worthless. Each person should consider his or her efforts to be approved by God through trying to be a good person as an attempt in futility. It is only by placing one's trust in Jesus that God will consider the person righteous. It is all God's grace to be saved, it is all God's grace to be declared righteous in his sight, and it is all God's grace to continue on in one's sanctification.

Chapter 35 ~ The Paradigm Shift

Anywhere Christians gather there will be varying degrees of legalistic behavior. In the church you attend there are probably some believers who are extreme, moderate, and slightly legalistic people. Your pastor may be more of a legalist than some of his colleagues in ministry. To find a believer in Christ that has no legalistic tendencies is a rare catch! Why is this so?

From the moment of our birth we are conditioned to believe good behavior, and good performances are rewarded with love. In sports it is always the best player who gets praised by his coaches, fans, and the media. Players who don't perform well get yelled at by their coaches, booed by their fans, and the media shows them no mercy.

In the classroom the student who gets the best grades wins the accolades and kudos from his teachers. Those who don't do well academically don't get the praises of their teachers, and may not be able to participate in some extracurricular activities, if their grades aren't up to standard. When I was in eighth grade I had an English teacher who assigned seats based on academic performance. The one with the worse grades sat in the seat right in front of the door, and the one who sat in the row of chairs farthest away from the door in the back had the highest grades. If you were the one sitting in the first chair you would be embarrassed and humiliated because you don't perform well, and that teacher would have no problem letting you know about it.

When you take your report card home and show it to your parents they are very happy with you if you did well receiving high grades. They don't hesitate to tell you and their friends how proud of you they are because of your high GPA. If you are an honor student you really get the kudos. However, if you didn't do very well, they may react by punishing you with loss of privileges, scold you, and express their dissatisfaction with you, etc. Some parents put their children on the incentive program and offer them cash rewards for high grades. The message is clear: perform well and you will be rewarded and loved.

It's always the prettiest girls that seem to get the attention. Our culture has painted a portrait of beauty that is virtually unattainable for the majority of women. If you have beautiful hair, a great complexion, and less than 10% body fat you are considered beautiful, but how many women can actually look like that? You have to have good genes, workout everyday, be a makeup artist, and watch your diet scrupulously. The message sent to women is look good and you get the accolades of people and the attention of the boys. If you can't manufacture "that look" you're out of luck.

I could go on with many more examples, but I think the point has been made. If you do well, and perform well you earn the praises, accolades, and rewards from other people. We are conditioned from birth to think like this, because ours is a performance-based society.

This type of mindset can carry over to one's relationship with God, not just for initial salvation, but also in one's journey of sanctification. People often conclude: if I perform well, keep all the rules, and strive to be a good person then God will forgive all my sins and grant me access to heaven. In this way of thinking God's forgiveness and eternal life is to be earned, merited, worked for, and gained through sheer effort. However, this is the essence of legalism—God approves of me because I keep the rules and work hard doing so.

God's Grace and Unremitting Love in Salvation

The above thought process goes against the grain of God's grace. God offers everyone forgiveness of sins and eternal life by grace. God's grace is his unmerited favor, his free gift, that can't be earned. You don't work for God's grace you just receive it. This stands in stark contrast to our performance-based culture, which conveys the message *perform* and you will be rewarded and loved. In God's economy it is *believe* and you will be *saved*. The issue comes down to *performance* verses *faith*. One enters a relationship with God, by placing their faith in Jesus Christ (John 14:6), and repenting of their sins (Acts 17:30; 26:20). Good works have no part in being reconciled to God because the performance-based paradigm will not enable one to earn God's favor (Eph 2:8-9).

God's Grace and Unremitting Love in Sanctification

After someone becomes a believer in Christ they begin their journey of sanctification, where they mature and grow in the faith. The tendency may still exist to operate under the performance mode. In this scenario one believes that the reception of God's love, even all his blessings, is contingent on one's sheer effort. In other words, if he spends two nights per week serving at church, God will love him more than if he served just one night during the week. If he gives 15% of his income to the church rather than 10%, God will love him all the more. In this mindset the more sacrifices he makes for God, the more he will receive God's love and blessings. This person is operating under the performance-based mode, which employs the false assumption, that God's love and blessings have to be earned.

People who employ this view of God rarely feel secure in the fact that God extends his unremitting love to them just as they are, regardless of how hard they work in serving him, or how many sacrifices they make. They have difficulty grasping that God's love for them is a constant in their life. God's love is unrelenting, inexhaustible, and enduring. God loves the believer because the benefits of Christ's sacrifice have been applied to him the moment he placed his faith in Jesus.

A New Paradigm

When someone becomes a believer in Christ it is necessary to undergo a paradigm shift. In 1962 Thomas S. Kuhn wrote "The Structure of Scientific Revolutions," and defined a paradigm as the set of assumptions, or the vision of reality, through which each of us perceives the world. A *paradigm shift* occurs when one's set of assumptions regarding reality and the way we perceive the world changes. For example, for a long time the earth was thought to be flat, such that if a ship sailed in the ocean as far as it could go it would

340

drop of the earth. When it was discovered that the earth was circular, that was a paradigm shift, which radically altered the way we viewed ourselves in relationship to the planet.

Another example of a paradigm shift is when it was discovered that the sun was in the center of the solar system and all the planets revolved around the sun, not the earth. That radically altered the way mankind viewed himself. When someone becomes a believer in Christ they begin to operate under a new paradigm. They need to make a paradigm shift from the performance-based model to the faith-based model. This is an entirely new way of thinking, viewing reality, and, of course, interacting with God. God loves us because he loves us. His love for Christians is a constant. He has accepted us through faith in Christ, forgiven us, adopted us into his family, imputed Jesus' righteousness to us, and is our heavenly Father. He loves all believers equally, because the benefits of Christ's sacrifice have been equally applied to all who place their faith in Jesus. His love for us isn't based on our performance—he gives his love graciously to all who place their faith in Jesus.

He doesn't love us more if we work harder and serve three nights per week at church instead of two. He loves us just as we are. If believers don't go through the paradigm shift I've suggested, they will tend to be stuck in legalism their entire life. Their ability to understand and experience the depth of God's love will be impaired because they are operating under the performance-based paradigm of our culture, rather than the faith-based paradigm of God.

It has been my experience that all believers, including myself, struggle with making this paradigm shift in varying degrees. There are few believers that are free from all legalistic tendencies, walking completely in God's grace and unremitting love. Many believers may not even be aware of legalistic tendencies that exist in their life. The apostle Paul may have come very close to completely making the paradigm shift, but few, if any, ever achieve it. Most believers live somewhere in between the performance-based paradigm and the faith-based paradigm, which means they live in tension. They will be conflicted because they have insights into God's faith-based paradigm, but still operate in varying degrees under the performance-based paradigm they were raised in. The result of this is the believer isn't free; he's conflicted and is living under two paradigms that pull him in opposite directions.

If one stays in the performance-based paradigm they will be in a degree of bondage—striving to earn God's love through good deeds, being a good person, and running on the treadmill of trying in vain to earn God's favor. Loss of joy will result, the Christian life can become burdensome, and the reception of God's unremitting love can be impaired. Sadly, many believers live in that space.

After thirty years in pastoral ministry I've come to see that this is a big issue for many church-going people. As I've been writing this book I've had many discussions with older believers who tell me they still struggle with legalistic tendencies because of their upbringing in a legalistic church, a legalistic family, or being surrounded by legalistic friends. In other words, they still haven't broken out of the performance-based paradigm altogether. After being a believer for decades they still struggle with stepping completely into the faith-based paradigm, and experiencing freedom that Jesus wants them to have.

As Christians go through their journey of sanctification, and grow in their faith, one of the desired outcomes should be to deepen their understanding of God's unremitting love and make progress in experiencing the paradigm shift, so they can be free. The progress that each believer makes in this will vary and probably be a life-long process.

Why is the Paradigm Shift Hard to Make?

The belief that we have to work to earn God's love, for our salvation and sanctification, is rooted in the sinful nature of man (Gal 2:16). It is the product of sinful humanity to operate under the old performance-based paradigm of seeking to be righteous by being a good person and keeping the rules (Gal 2:16-20). Legalism is the religion of sinful humanity, which is why every believer in Christ has to keep his guard up and beware of legalistic behavior that he might display.

Satan is also a promoter of the performance-based paradigm for he is the father of lies, and this paradigm is a false doctrine that is to be avoided (John 8:44; 1 Tim 4:1). The sinful component of man, the Devil, and our culture all promote the performance-based paradigm. It is based on a false understanding of God's character, the way of salvation, and the way God interacts with humans. People who live in this paradigm need to deepen their understanding of God's grace and unremitting love by digging deeper into God's word, which will assist them in making the shift to the faith-based paradigm. One of the consequences of the sinful nature expressing itself is the tendency to slip into the legalistic mindset, and operate under the performance-based paradigm, that Christ wants to free you from. Note the contrast between the two paradigms below for salvation:

The Performance-based Paradigm
God accepts us through good deeds
God considers us righteous by obeying his commands
Salvation is earned
God loves me because of my good works

The Faith-based Paradigm
God accepts us through faith in Christ
God considers us righteous through faith in Christ
Salvation is of grace—freely given
God loves me because of my faith in Christ

The above contrast of the two paradigms reveals that they are polar opposites. Scripture is clear that we live in a spiritual battleground (Rom 7:13-23; Gal 5:16-26). Every believer needs to be cautious of legalistic behavior that may appear in his life, for it is part of our sinful nature.

Every day believers should practice the discipline of renewing their mind with Scripture (Rom 12:1-2; Col 3:9-10), take up their cross (Luke 9:23), put off the old self and put on the new (Eph 4:22-24), be filled with the Spirit (Eph 5:18), and through the Spirit's power not let sin reign in their mortal bodies (Rom 6:12-13). The sinful nature is still a powerful force in the life of a believer, and one of the characteristics of church-going religious people is that legalistic tendencies may appear. I believe this is one of the most prevalent sins of religious people that they need to be freed from.

Conclusion

This chapter has set forth the idea that believers need to undergo a paradigm shift from a *performance-based* to a *faith-based* paradigm, which will result in them being able to experience freedom to receive God's love and not feel they have to strive to be acceptable to God, whether it is for salvation or in their journey of sanctification. The performance-based paradigm is difficult to break out of because people are conditioned from childhood to believe that love is received by being good, performing well, and keeping the rules. This paradigm is also a false doctrine that stands at odds with the teaching of Scripture, and is promoted by the demonic realm. In fact, the biggest advocate of the performance-based paradigm may very well be Satan, because this belief will keep people out of heaven. The person who is duped into thinking that he will go to heaven on the basis of his personal goodness, rather than faith in Christ is in for a big disappointment.

Those who are born again believers in Christ may be plagued by legalism in their journey to becoming a mature believer because of demonic influences and temptations. Satan wants to keep us out of the faith-based paradigm. The world, the sinful nature, and the demonic realm will work against the believer from stepping into the freedom that the faith-based paradigm offers.

Chapter 36 ~ The Fruit of Obedience

If God loves me unremittingly, and his love is a constant in my life, then what role do good works play in my walk with the Lord? Since God loves me continuously does that mean I'm off the hook and have no obligation to be obedient to his commands? Of course not! As I suggested in the previous chapter, God doesn't love us all the more because we serve two nights per week at church instead of one. Every disciple has the same *position* before God: Christ's righteousness belongs to him, and God loves him just as he is.

One of the greatest remedies for getting out of the jail of legalism is to understand that God loves you with an unrelenting love, not because of anything good about you, but because the benefits of Christ's sacrifice have been applied to you. God values you, has adopted you into his family and is your heavenly Father. For that reason God loves you and every other believer as a Father loves his sons and daughters. Christians should be anchored deep in the ocean of God's love, forgiveness, mercy, and grace.

Our *position,* mentioned above, must be separated from our *practice*, meaning the way we live our lives for God's glory, which will vary from individual-to-individual. Those who are living a God-honoring life will be pleasing the Lord. Those believers who aren't living in a way that honors God are still loved by him, but God may not be pleased with them.

What Does it Mean to Live a God Honoring Life?

It is critical to make the distinction between God's enduring love given to every believer, and the Lord being pleased with the way the believer is living. The Lord may not be pleased with the way some of his people are living, but he still loves them. Any earthly parent loves his children, but may not always be pleased with their behavior.

What do I mean by those who aren't pleasing their heavenly Father? I'm referring to one who is deliberately rebellious, who chooses to deliberately pursue a lifestyle that is in opposition to God's word, and who grieves the Spirit. Believers are commanded to live as children of light and not to participate in the deeds of darkness (Eph 5:1-12). Therefore, when I refer to the Christian who isn't pleasing the Lord I'm talking about one who is willfully rebellious—which, of course, can happen in varying degrees in different parts of our lives.

Often times we hear the expression so-and-so is a *disobedient Christian*. We all struggle with sin and will have moments of failure and disobedience every day. To a degree we are all disobedient believers, even the best of us, which is why I prefer to use the phrase "God honoring life." We are going through a process of becoming more like Christ, so we will struggle with resisting temptations to sin and have setbacks. The sinful nature is still a powerful force in the life of believers, so we don't live in sinless perfection. God understands that! He has compassion for us, is willing to help us overcome temptations (1 Cor 10:13), and is willing to give us grace to help us in times of need (Heb 4:16). He understands that we are in process and have moments of disobedience. Those who live God-honoring lives will still sin and have disobedience in their lives, but they are moving in the right direction, and maturing in their walk with Christ.

The Experience of God's Love

Those who are living in a way that pleases the Lord will also have an *experience* of God's love that exceeds those who are not living God-honoring lives. A disciple's daily *experience* of God's love is conditional on the overall quality of his walk with the Lord. The *fact* of God's love as my heavenly Father adopting me into his family never changes. Regardless of my level of obedience, or lack thereof, God's love is a constant in my life. However, if I'm living in a state of rebellion against God, my experience of his love in my daily life will be impaired, because God isn't pleased with my lifestyle. I'm not living in a way that brings glory and honor to him.

Thus it is important to distinguish between *positional* love, which never changes, and the *experience* of God's love in our daily walk. God's love remains with every believer, but the rebellious believer will not experience God's love in a way that he could if he was living in a way that pleased the Lord. Rebellion against God can result in loss of blessing, peace, and joy in one's daily experience, and may bring God's discipline to bear in his life. It is like a parent who is upset with his children and brings discipline on them, but he hasn't stopped loving them.

The Experience of God's Love

If you're a believer God loves you whether you believe it or not—it is a fact. Can a believer experience God's love in his heart? Of course he can! In the previous section I've said that a lifestyle that doesn't please the Lord can impair the experience of God's love, and other blessings, in our daily life. The following passages reveal that obedience to God's word, on the other hand, enhances the reception of God's love in the believer's life.

> Just as the Father has loved Me, I have also loved you; abide in My love. [10]If you keep My commandments, you will abide in My love; just as I have kept My Father's commandments and abide in His love. [11]These things I have spoken to you so that My joy may be in you, and *that* your joy may be made full. (John 15:9-11)

> By this we know that we have come to know Him, if we keep His commandments. [4]The one who says, "I have come to know Him," and does not keep His commandments, is a liar, and the truth is not in him; [5]but whoever keeps His word, in him the love of God has truly been perfected. (1 John 3:3-5)

> The one who keeps His commandments abides in Him, and He in him. We know by this that He abides in us, by the Spirit whom He has given us. (1 John 3:24)

Beloved, if God so loved us, we also ought to love one another. [12]No one has seen God at any time; if we love one another, God abides in us, and His love is perfected in us. (1 John 4:11-12)

We have come to know and have believed the love which God has for us. God is love, and the one who abides in love abides in God, and God abides in him. [17]By this, love is perfected with us, so that we may have confidence in the day of judgment; because as He is, so also are we in this world. [18]There is no fear in love; but perfect love casts out fear, because fear involves punishment, and the one who fears is not perfected in love. (1 John 4:16-18)

Keep yourselves in the love of God, waiting anxiously for the mercy of our Lord Jesus Christ to eternal life. (Jude 21)

Christians can experience God's love glowing in their hearts on a daily basis. Obedience to his commands unlocks the door to his love such that it can be experienced. One who keeps the commands will experience a deeper level of fellowship and intimacy with God than one who doesn't. God's love isn't just an intellectual concept to be studied; it is a reality to be experienced every day.

The Obligation to Obey

Scripture tells Christians to obey the Lord—it is an obligation. A vast amount of Scripture depicts the way a believer should live, for the Bible is filled with moral imperatives to be obeyed. Some may wrongly conclude this is legalism! The Bible contains huge numbers of rules to be obeyed, so we have to conform to the code, which causes some people to conclude that we are under law not grace.

After one becomes a believer a transformed lifestyle should naturally follow his conversion experience, such that good works become normative. The fruit or evidence of one's relationship with Christ will

348

be a transformed lifestyle that consists of obedience—good works (Eph 2:10; 1 John 2:4; 3:10).

Christ is the Lord and Master of every believer. Paul considered himself the slave of Christ (Rom 1:1; Gal 1:10; Phil 1:1; Titus 1:1) and the Lord's prisoner (Eph 4:1). Slavery was common in the First Century, with over half the people living in the Roman Empire in that condition. Many believers were slaves (Eph 6:5-7) who attended church with their master, while others may have served someone who wasn't a believer.

In today's world slavery is a pejorative term with very negative connotations. In Bible days it was considered an honor to be the slave of Christ. It was never considered an oppressive relationship to have Christ as your Master.

The Christian is to give the Lord Jesus his allegiance and obedience—that's what is expected. The Lord Jesus made this point in Luke 17:7-10:

> "Which of you, having a slave plowing or tending sheep, will say to him when he has come in from the field, 'Come immediately and sit down to eat'? [8]But will he not say to him, 'Prepare something for me to eat, and *properly* clothe yourself and serve me while I eat and drink; and afterward you may eat and drink'? [9]He does not thank the slave because he did the things which were commanded, does he? [10]So you too, when you do all the things which are commanded you, say, 'We are unworthy slaves; we have done *only* that which we ought to have done.'"

The Lord Jesus brings out in this teaching the obligation that rests upon all his people. There are things that believers in Christ are expected to do and responsible for. This is the type of obedience that Christians should render to their Master. To think that Christians don't have any expectations to obey the Lord, out of a sense of duty, is a woefully distorted view of the Christian life.

Joyful Obedience

The expected obedience depicted in the above passage isn't to be viewed as laborious, burdensome, and taxing to the point of exhaustion. The Christian obeys the Lord and will experience a blessed joy in the process (Ps 1). Pleasing the Lord should be the heartfelt desire of every believer (Rom 12:1-2; Eph 5:8-10). We want to live in a way that honors the Lord as his representatives (2 Cor 5:17-21). To claim that God's commands are like a crushing weight on one's shoulders doesn't line up with what the Bible says. The apostle John said:

> By this we know that we love the children of God, when we love God and observe His commandments. [3]For this is the love of God, that we keep His commandments; and His commandments are not burdensome. (1 John 5:2-3)

John refutes the notion that obedience to God's word is a weight that causes people to collapse. God may call us to do some difficult things at times, but his commands are not a burden that weighs God's people down.

Reading Psalm 119 reveals that the word of God is: a delight (v. 77), a source of comfort (v. 52), a source of liberty (v. 32), is good (v. 39), is trustworthy (v. 42), is to be loved (v. 47), and is a source of hope (v. 43), and more. The commands of God are viewed in a positive light and only bring benefits to the one who obeys them. His word should occupy an authoritative place in the life of a Christian, thus his commands are to be obeyed.

Obedience isn't legalism! Obedience is the fruit of a transformed life. When one becomes a disciple of Christ one of the characteristics that should naturally appear in his life is obedience to God's word. The believer obeys out of a sense of love, thankfulness, and gratitude for all that the Lord has done for him. There is a deep-seated desire in the heart of every believer to please the Lord and honor him by the way they live. The Christian doesn't obey God's word begrudgingly, resentfully, fearfully out of guilt, or to earn God's love. Trying to earn

God's love doesn't make sense because God already loves the believer. Trying to please the Lord by living a godly lifestyle and experience God's love is an entirely different matter.

God's Discipline

God is our heavenly Father and will discipline his sons and daughters just as our earthly fathers do, except his discipline is perfect (Heb 12:4-11). He never makes parenting mistakes, as our earthly parents do. His disciplinary measures are always for corrective purposes to produce more righteousness, enable us to share in his holiness, and draw us closer to him. In fact, one of the characteristics of true believers is that they will receive God's discipline in their life; it is the proof that they are God's children, and that the heavenly Father loves them. The author of Hebrews views God's disciplinary activity as something that should be a source of encouragement to believers because it is proof of God's love for them. God disciplines the believer in love always to make the disciple a better and more fruitful person.

If a believer is living in a way that isn't pleasing to the Lord he may experience God's hand of discipline in his life, always done in love to make improvements in his character. In the same way that our parents disciplined us to give guidance and correction, our heavenly Father does the same, but without any errors. When we discipline our children because of misbehavior, we may not be pleased with them, but we don't stop loving them. The same is true of our heavenly Father. He may not be pleased with us at times, but his love for us is a constant.

Conclusion

When Christians consider how much God loves them it is life transforming (Eph 3:17-19). Every believer can rest in the knowledge that God—the Father—loves him or her unremittingly and relentlessly. That is the greatest incentive for believers to do all things for the glory of God. Out of our appreciation for all God has done for us we willingly want to please him by honoring him through our lifestyle. Pleasing the heavenly Father is a great source of joy; it is not a burden and it isn't being legalistic. As the believer grows in his understanding of how much God loves him or her it becomes easier to want to please him by being obedient.

Chapter 37 ~ Breaking Free

So Christ has truly set us free. Now make sure that you stay free, and don't get tied up again in slavery to the law. (Galatians 5:1, NLT)

As I write the final chapter of this book I have to go back to why I wrote the book in the first place. The above verse says it all. There are a great many people who love the Lord, but are living in a state of spiritual oppression because they are in the prison of legalism. Perhaps, you attend a church that has a very legalistic culture, or has a legalistic pastor. Maybe you're part of a very legalistic church-going family, or many of your friends are legalistic and have a negative influence over you. If that's the case you're not walking in the liberty that Christ offers you. You may be so used to being in an oppressive church situation that it has become normal for you. Understand that you are in a very bad situation.

When you go to see your doctor for your annual checkup and he informs you that you have some serious health issues that will require some lifestyle changes, most people will take it to heart and follow their doctor's instructions. For example, if your doctor tells you that you have high blood pressure, you have to drop 20 pounds, start exercising, and eat better foods or you could take years off your life, most people would take it seriously and put forth the effort to change their lifestyle.

If you are in a legalistic church you need to make some lifestyle changes. You're in a situation where you are being damaged spiritually and emotionally. In other words, you are in a very unhealthy situation that will only cause more heartache and pain. It is time to be proactive and look out for yourself and also consider the harm that is being done to the spiritual welfare of your family, not just yourself.

Christ has set us free from the law, and any religious system that consists of rules, regulations, and codes that are man-made, but not all believers walk in that freedom. Jesus wants you to walk out of the prison cell of legalism and stay free. For some people that means you may be facing some difficult decisions ahead to find your freedom. If you are in a church where you hear condemning sermons every Sunday that sap the life out of you, and notice many of the things this book has identified as red flags it may be time to be proactive. I would suggest the following course of action.

Let Scripture Be Your Guide

Study the Scriptures, and let the truth of God's word be your guide. You should weigh everything that is taught in your church against the teaching of Scripture. Be a student of God's word. If you are in a church where there is false teaching you are under no obligation to stay there. Read some other books on the topic of legalism to gain further insights about your situation.

You are a steward of your spiritual life and must take appropriate action for your own spiritual health and that of your family.

You Should be Praying

As you're studying God's word be praying that God will lead you by providing you with the insights you need to gain clarity about your situation. God promises that if we need wisdom we can ask him and he will give it to us (Jam 1:5). Don't do anything before praying about it and getting a sense for what the Lord wants you to do.

Talk to Other Believers

It is wise to discuss your situation with other believers and get their input. If you know some wise and godly people you may want to talk with them about what is being taught in your church. Before making any major decisions it is always wise to get godly counsel. Proverbs 15:22 says: "Plans fail for lack of counsel, but with many advisers they succeed." Listen to what they tell you about the church that they are attending and compare that with your church. They may be part of a healthy fellowship where the teaching is sound and legalism isn't prevalent as it is in your church.

You May Want to Talk to Your Leaders

If after studying the Scripture you conclude that the teaching is not in line with the Bible, you may want to discuss your findings with the church leaders—the pastor or the elders. If you do this and they heap words of condemnation and guilt on you because you disagree with their teaching that tells you a lot right there. If you do tell them you disagree with their teaching and why, they probably won't change their views. They are most likely locked in a prison cell of legalism themselves, and may be very unhealthy people both spiritually and emotionally. Don't expect them to just change over night or be receptive to whatever you tell them. In fact, you should expect them to reject what you have to say.

Leaving Isn't Easy

If trying to reason with your church leaders establishes no common ground, and you feel that you have satisfied your need to be a responsible and free follower of Christ, it may be time to consider leaving your church. It is important to not just pull the plug without bringing things to a point of closure. This will make your transition to a new situation much easier. You don't want to leave with things unsaid, or undone, so bring your situation to complete closure, as best you can.

It may be very difficult to leave your church because you may have been attending that fellowship for many years, and your whole network of friends is in that church. Your spiritual life and social life all revolve around your church. You may have grown up in that church and know nothing else but that situation. If you leave the church your life will be disrupted, and it may mean the loss of some friendships and people that you won't see any more. You have to be willing to go through this in order to find your freedom. It is worth it to leave so that you can be free. You have to count the cost of going through the pain of leaving, but you also have to count the cost of staying in an abusive situation. Christ wants you to walk in the liberty that he died to give you so it's worth it to leave and get a fresh start.

Looking For a New Church

Leaving a church may be difficult, but it can also be hard to find a new church where you feel comfortable. If you have come out of a spiritually traumatic situation don't hesitate to go talk to the pastor and inform him of your circumstances. Find out what his take is on legalism and make sure that he is a grace-oriented pastor. You may know some people who can recommend a church to you and maybe even attend with them. Jesus wants you to be free! Better days are ahead for you. Be hopeful and as positive as you can during this time.

Don't Give Up on Jesus

Don't become a church dropout. Men may disappoint us but don't give up on Jesus—he isn't the problem! He wants you to be free, so you have to trust that he will lead you to the right situation where you can prosper spiritually. Jesus is for you, not against you. Don't become a believer that watches one of the high profile preachers on TV every Sunday morning and isolate yourself from the body of Christ. That is only going from one unhealthy situation to another. The author of Hebrews reminds us to not give up being in fellowship with other believers (Heb 10:24-25).

Find Freedom and Stay Free

The passage cited at the beginning of this chapter (Gal 5:1) commands us to be free and to keep our freedom. If you step out of your present situation to become part of a healthy church and discover the joy and freedom of being a Christian, don't let anybody take your freedom away from you by trying to impose some man-made rules on you (Col 3:16-23). Find freedom and keep it. You may struggle with your newfound freedom and have a tendency to want to go back. It will

356

take you some time to make adjustments, for even the apostle Peter went back into legalism on one occasion.

Having known many people that came out of legalistic backgrounds, I have seen them struggle with feelings of guilt because they aren't complying with the old laws imposed on them. It has taken some of these folks years to break out of the mold and they still struggle with it. Resist the temptation to go backwards into the prison of legalistic behavior. Stay free! Surround yourself with people who are filled with grace and understanding of your situation.

Final Thoughts

Maybe you're in a healthy church situation that has a focus on grace and isn't at all oppressive. Perhaps, after reading this book you've learned some things about yourself. You may have discovered some attitudes and practices that you've maintained over the years that you can be freed from. Hopefully, after going through this book and noting all the Scriptures cited herein, you are moving into a place of greater freedom in the Lord. I hope that you can discover a more fruitful and enjoyable relationship with Christ, by living in the freedom that he died to give us. Don't go back into the jail cell of legalism—stay free!

Reference List

Barclay, William. *Daily Study Bible.* Studylight.org.

Bock, Darrell L. *Luke.* Baker Exegetical Commentary on the New Testament. Grand Rapids: Baker Academic, 1996.

_____ *Acts.* Baker Exegetical Commentary on the New Testament. Grand Rapids: Baker Academic, 2007.

Bruce, F. F. *The Book of Acts.* The New International Commentary on the New Testament. Grand Rapids: Eerdmans, 1984.

Carson, D. A. *Matthew.* The Expositor's Bible Commentary. Grand Rapids: Zondervan, 1984.

_____ *The Gospel According to John,* Grand Rapids: Eerdmans, 1991.

Erickson, Millard J. *Christian Theology.* Grand Rapids: Baker Book House, 1985.

France, R. T. *The Gospel of Matthew.* The New International Commentary on the New Testament. Grand Rapids: Eerdmans, 2007.

Fee, Gordon D. *The First Epistle to the Corinthians.* The New International Commentary on the New Testament. Grand Rapids: Eerdmans, 1987.

Fung, Ronald Y. K., *The Epistle to the Galatians.* The New International Commentary on the New Testament. Grand Rapids: Eerdmans, 1988.

Grudem, Wayne. *Systematic theology: An Introduction to Biblical Doctrine.* Grand Rapids: Zondervan, 1994.

Hansen, Walter G. *Galatians.* The IVP New Testament Commentary Series. Downers Grove: InterVarsity Press, 1994.

Hendricksen, William. *The Gospel of Matthew.* New Testament Commentary. Grand Rapids: Baker, 1973

_____ *The Gospel of Mark.* New Testament Commentary. Grand Rapids: Baker,

Keener, Craig S. *The Gospel of Matthew: A Social-Rhetorical Commentary.* Grand Rapids: Eerdmans, 2009.

Kernaghan, Ronald J. *Mark.* The IVP New Testament Commentary Series. Grand Rapids: Downers Grove, 2007.

Kistler, Don. *Law & Liberty: A Biblical Look at Legalism.* Orlando: The Northamptom Press. 2013.

Larkin, William J. Jr. *Acts.* The IVP New Testament Commentary Series. Grand Rapids: Downers Grove, 1995.

MacArthur, John. *Matthew.* The MacArthur New Testament Commentary. Chicago: Moody, 1985.

_____ *Acts.* The MacArthur New Testament Commentary. Chicago: Moody, 1996.

_____ *Romans.* The MacArthur New Testament Commentary. Chicago: Moody, 1994.

_____ *Galatians.* The MacArthur New Testament Commentary. Chicago: Moody, 1987.

McKnight, Scot. *The Sermon on the mount.* The Story of God Bible Commentary. Grand Rapids: Zondervan, 2013.

_____ *Galatians.* The NIV Application Commentary. Grand Rapids: Zondervan, 1995.

Michaels, Ramsey J. *The Gospel of John.* The New International Commentary on the New Testament. Grand Rapids: Eerdmans, 2010.

Moo, Douglas J. *Galatians.* Baker Exegetical Commentary on the New Testament. Grand Rapids: Baker Academic, 2013

_____ *The Epistle to the Romans.* The New International Commentary on the New Testament. Grand Rapids: Eerdmans, 1996.

Nolland, John. *The Gospel of Matthew: A Commentary on the Greek Text.* New International Greek Testament Commentary. Grand Rapids: Eerdmans, 2005.

Osborne, Grant. *Matthew.* Exegetical Commentary on the New Testament. Grand Rapids: Zondervan, 2010.

_____ *Romans.* The IVP New Testament Commentary Series. Downers Grove: InterVarsity Press, 2004.

_____ *Matthew.* Life Application Bible Commentary. Wheaton: Tyndale, 1996.

Schreiner, Thomas R. *Galatians.* Exegetical Commentary on the New Testament. Grand Rapids: Zondervan, 2010.

_____ *Romans.* Baker Exegetical Commentary on the New Testament. Grand Rapids: Baker Academic, 1998.

Stein, Robert H. *Mark.* Baker Exegetical Commentary on the New Testament. Grand Rapids: Baker Academic, 2008.

Turner, David L. *Matthew.* Baker Exegetical Commentary on the New Testament. Grand Rapids: Baker Academic, 2008.

_____ *The Gospel of Matthew.* Cornerstone Biblical Commentary. Carol Stream: Tyndale, 2006.

Whitacre, Rodney A. *John.* The IVP New Testament Commentary Series. Grand Rapids: Downers Grove, 1999.

Wilkins, Michael J. *Matthew*. NIV Application Commentary. Grand Rapids: Zondervan, 2004.

Witherington, Ben III. *The Gospel of Mark: A Socio-Rhetorical Commentary*. Grand Rapids: Eerdmans, 2001.

_____ *Paul's Letter to the Romans: A Socio-Rhetorical Commentary.* Grand Rapids: Eerdmans, 2004.

_____ *Conflict & Community in Corinth: A Socio-Rhetorical Commentary on 1 and 2 Corinthians.* Grand Rapids: Eerdmans, 1995.

Made in the USA
Middletown, DE
03 October 2021